The Revolution of Moral Consciousness

The Revolution of Moral Consciousness

Nietzsche in Russian Literature,
1890–1914

Edith W. Clowes

Northern Illinois University Press
DeKalb, Illinois 1988

© 1988 by Northern Illinois University Press
Northern Illinois University Press, DeKalb, Illinois, 60115

First printing in paperback, 2018
ISBN 978-0-87580-797-3
All rights reserved
Cover design by Yuni Dorr
Book design by Anné Schedler

24 23 22 21 20 19 18   1 2 3 4 5

Permissions

R. J. Hollingdale, trans., *Nietzsche: Thus Spoke Zarathustra*. Copyright © 1961, 1969 by R. J. Hollingdale. Excerpts reprinted with permission of Penguin Books, Ltd.

Bernice Glatzer Rosenthal, ed., *Nietzsche in Russia*. Copyright © 1986 by Princeton University Press. Excerpts reprinted with permission of Princeton University Press.

Nicholas Luker, ed., *Fifty Years On: Gorky and His Time*. Copyright © 1987 by Astra Press. Excerpts reprinted with permission of Astra Press.

Library of Congress Cataloging-in-Publication Data

Clowes, Edith W.
  The revolution of moral consciousness : Nietzsche in Russian literature, 1890-1914 I Edith W. Clowes.
      p.   cm.
  Bibliography: p.
  Includes index.
  ISBN 0-87580-139-0 : $27.50
  1. Russian literature-19th century-History and criticism.
  2. Russian literature-20th century-History and criticism.
      3. Nietzsche, Friedrich Wilhelm, 1844-1900-Influence. I. Title.
  PG3015.5.N46C46   88-534

to my mother, my father, and Craig

Contents

	Acknowledgments	ix
	Note on Transliteration	xi
1	The Problem of Nietzsche's Influence on Russian Literature	1
2	The Precursors	15
3	Nietzsche's Early Reception	43
4	From Populist to Popular Art	83
5	The Mystical Symbolists	115
6	The Revolutionary Romantics	175
7	Conclusion	225
	Key to Abbreviations	231
	Notes	235
	Selected Bibliography	255
	Index	269

Acknowledgments

My interest in Nietzsche's philosophy and the response to it in Russian letters has developed over several years. Thanks are due to the institutions and people that supported my work along the way. The International Research and Exchanges Board supported a year of dissertation research in Moscow and Leningrad in 1978–1979. I wish to thank my Russian friends and colleagues, particularly my adviser at Moscow State University, Lidia Andreevna Kolobaeva, for their interest and curiosity about Nietzsche's role in prerevolutionary Russian culture and for their generosity with their time and resources. Archivists and librarians at the Lenin Library and the Gorky Archive at the Institute of World Literature in Moscow and at the Saltykov-Shchedrin Library and the Library of the Academy of Sciences, both in Leningrad, were generally very kind and helpful in letting me use materials.

I am grateful to my thesis adviser at Yale University, Robert Louis Jackson, who kindly but firmly urged me in my dissertation work to look into the specifically "Russian" nature of Nietzsche's reception: the journalistic debates, the process of creating a Russian image of Nietzsche, and finally the popular cult of Nietzsche in the first decade of the twentieth century. Thanks are due to Marianna Tax Choldin who shared important information about the reaction of the censorship committee to Nietzsche and to Betty Yetta Forman who was always willing to spend hours mulling over the details of Gorky's tangled response to Nietzschean thought.

I wish to express my gratitude to the editors who have kindly permitted me to use previously published material. Part of chapter 3 dealing with censorship appeared in my "Friedrich Nietzsche and Russian Censorship," *Germano-Slavica*, 3 (1983). Thanks are due to Penguin Books for permission to quote excerpts from *Thus Spoke Zarathustra* in my discussion of censorship. I am grateful to Princeton University Press for permission to use in chapter 4 material from my chapter, "Literary Reception as Vulgarization: Nietzsche's Idea of the Superman in Neo-Realist Fiction," *Nietzsche in Russia*, edited by Bernice Glatzer Rosenthal. J. M. Terry of Astra Press (Nottingham, England) has kindly allowed me to take material for chapter 6 from my chapter, "Gorky, Nietzsche, and God-Building," *Fifty Years On: Gorky and His Time*, edited by Nicholas Luker.

The people who generously gave their time to read versions of the present work deserve special acknowledgment. John Burt Foster, Jr., gave me the benefit of a comparativist's perspective on the encounter between Nietzschean thought and the Russian tradition. George Louis Kline made numerous, valuable comments on both philosophical and philological aspects of my work. My warmest thanks go to Bernice Glatzer Rosenthal whose recent research on turn-of-the-century Russian culture has done a great deal to stir the interest that this field currently enjoys.

I would like to thank the people whose steady help was important in the process of finishing research and preparing the manuscript. The library staff who run the Summer Slavic Research Laboratory at the University of Illinois in Champaign-Urbana have been patient and friendly over many years, making the Slavic Room a congenial place to do research. Kathy Garner of the Interlibrary Loan Office at Purdue University helped me to obtain a number of indispensible resources. Carol Gog at Purdue's Department of Foreign Languages and Literatures worked long and carefully to type and revise the manuscript on the word processor.

Special thanks are due to Mary Lincoln, the director of Northern Illinois University Press, for her interest and encouragement of this project and to Susan Bean and Susan Thornton for their careful editing and production of the book.

Note on Transliteration

The system of transliteration used throughout is Thomas Shaw's System II. To make the text easier to read, however, I have made a few modifications. Although Russian titles of written works are transliterated according to System II, names of people and cities are changed in the following way. Names that end in *ii*, have been shortened to *y*, as in Gorky, Merezhkovsky, Nizhny Novgorod. Some other vowel combinations have been shortened, so that, for example, Anastasiia becomes Anastasia. Diacritical marks have been dropped. For the sake of correct pronunciation, I have chosen to spell the last name Solov'ev as Solovyov.

The Revolution of Moral Consciousness

The oft-mentioned world crisis of culture is also a crisis of morals, a revolution of moral consciousness.

As a differentiated sphere of cultural life, morality has ceased to inspire; it is losing its vitality, and it is degenerating. It is perceived as a hindrance to the creative energy of existence [tvorchestvo bytiia]. A moderate morality, a morality of security, a morality which delays the coming of the end . . . must sooner or later itself come to an end and be overwhelmed by the creative intensity of the human spirit. Nietzsche's significance for this crisis . . . is immense. His creative spirit yearned to go beyond the secure middle of canonical morality. . . . Nietzsche was a great unmasker of the moderate-common spirit of humanism. . . .
　　　　　　　—N. Berdiaev, "Creativity and Morality,"
　　　　　　　The Meaning of the Creative Act: An Essay in the Justification of Man, 1916

1

The Problem of Nietzsche's Influence on Russian Literature

THE GOAL of this study is to examine the role played by Friedrich Nietzsche's philosophy in the rich ferment of Russian literary life at the turn of the twentieth century. In this renaissance period, flowering in the arts, philosophy, and religious thought was motivated by a profound crisis of faith. Intellectuals disillusioned with ineffectual ideologies of the late Populist period searched for new overarching visions and justifications. To many observers Nietzsche's provocative philosophy epitomized the revolt against convention. Critics of all different schools—the Marxist, V. Lvov-Rogachevsky; the historian of Russian modernism, S. Vengerov; and the religious thinker, N. Berdiaev—all colored the period in Nietzschean terms as a time of "transvaluation of values" (*pereotsenka tsennostei*).[1] To them, this rubric meant a turn away from the "utilitarian," "liberal" worldview long held by the intelligentsia. If social duty was the highest virtue of an earlier generation, now intellectuals strove toward the goals of self-discovery and self-realization.

In this shift of attitude "morality," as Berdiaev notes, was perceived as a "hindrance to the creative energy of existence." Berdiaev pinpoints Nietzsche's thought as the intellectual force that made this opposition clear. The sacrifice of moral values for aesthetic pleasure has become a cliché used to define turn-of-the-century culture.[2] This means that the precise significance of moral and aesthetic valuations and their relationship to each other in this era has been lost behind the historiographical preconception that they were necessarily opposed. Thus, we still lack a clear profile of the mentality of the age and the actual codes of valuation that motivated cultural change.

The argument of the present work is that the shift in moral consciousness at the turn of the century was much more complex and important for the general shape of twentieth-century Russian cultural history than is usually assumed. Writers typically were searching for a creative but still *moral* solution to the perceived failure of conventional values. What *was* sacrificed was the canonical morality of the preceding Populist age. The new generation gained for itself a distinct sensibility, its own mode of discourse, and indeed, its own mythic view. It is the final purpose of my discussion here to show how this process of cultural coming-of-age was refracted in the response to one important mentor, Friedrich Nietzsche.

Soviet critics, if they discuss the topic at all, usually claim that Nietzsche's reception was little more than a passing if intense fashion.[3] Their argument for this position is that reading Nietzsche had small significance for the mature worldviews of most so-called Nietzschean writers. Their objections raise a number of issues concerning the nature of influence study. Traditionally the influential text is viewed as what Lionel Trilling called a "baton that is handed from runner to runner in a relay race."[4] Thus, in Nietzsche's case, it is assumed that there is one "Nietzsche," that is, one way of understanding Nietzsche's thought. It is implied that influence is proved by some degree of imitation: each reader grasps, or should grasp, the text in the "right" way. Trilling's image of runners in a relay race suggests yet another problem: what is the relationship between the influence process and broad cultural-historical change?

My study builds on rather different assumptions about influence. I agree with Harold Bloom, who writes in *The Anxiety of Influence* that influence is least of all the imitation of received images, styles, and ideas.[5] The influence relationship may be most productively characterized as a "transaction" between text and reader in a specific cultural context.[6] It is a dialogue in which the vision of author(s) and reader(s) is transformed: the "strong" reader develops his own literary voice, and the influencing text is resurrected in the reader's process of self-discovery.

The present discussion rests on a view of the reader as the more active transformative force. One chapter is devoted to influential texts and contexts and four to the deformations carried out by the readers who overcame imitation and evolved their own characteristic styles and worldviews. This "prejudice" rejects the literary critical convention that the strong text is the source of influence; that is, it imposes on the reader its own themes, motifs, and ideas. Even the prominent Russian Formalist Viktor Zhirmunsky held to a rigid view of the influencing text's "ideal existence" (ideal'noe bytie).[7] This "ideal" text, he claimed in *Byron and Pushkin* (1924), exerts an influence and as such is the proper subject of literary criticism. Understood this way, influence study loses its dynamism as a mode of writing literary history because it is to be assumed that all sufficiently informed readers will come to essentially the same interpretation of the text. More recent critics, including those as different as Hans Robert Jauss and Harold Bloom, argue that the influencing text permits readings from a large variety of approaches. Jauss and Bloom both claim that every epoch, indeed, each individual makes a different reading of the text. Meaning is achieved through a complex interaction between text and reader. Bloom, the more psychologically oriented of the two, denies the existence of the text as an a priori source of meaning. As soon as we speak of influence, in Bloom's view, we are compelled to admit "that there are *no* texts, but only relationships *between* texts."[8]

Jauss, who views the text as common ground for social-cultural dialogue, finds an approach to the text that is most useful for this study. He foresees many possible readers and many approaches to the text, but admits of a phenomenon that can be called the "text" that exerts a kind of force. He defines the specific ways in which the author guides and orients readers within the text.[9] Established in the text, Jauss says, is a "horizon of expectations," a set of values and experiences that the author anticipates in his reader. These expectations are meant to appeal to the actual reader, who has his own socially and psychologically conditioned "horizon of expectation." After winning his interest and involvement, the narrator manipulates and indeed tries to shock the reader in order to change his expectations. The reader then interprets the signs in terms of his own "system of references," his experience, beliefs, and values. Jauss's view of the text will certainly be more useful than the others in the case of Nietzsche's Russian reception. Bloom cannot account for the active role played by the text in historical discourse carried on across national, social, and cultural boundaries. Zhirmunsky seems to lessen the literary-cultural value of all but highly informed readings of texts. Although he may be right that readings should strive toward and could ideally converge on an interpretation that is perfectly informed and "fair" to the aesthetic, moral, and philosophical structures within the text, this approach cannot explain cultural change. Historically multiple readings are likely and are ultimately the source of innovation. In literary history the interaction between reader and text is more important and vital than the view sub specie aeternitatis of a perfect text.

In chapter 2 Nietzsche's thought is examined in terms of the horizon of expectation established within the Nietzschean text. Although discussion is oriented to the subject of moral consciousness, which most attracted Russian readers, it is not guided by their interpretations and appropriations. These are the focus of later chapters. Rather I am concerned here to point out the markers in the text that suggest an authorial sensibility. My goal is not to establish some absolute, authoritative version of the text but to suggest the ways in which the Nietzschean text anticipates, attracts, and orients its reader. What emerges is a "literary" reading of Nietzsche's philosophy that concentrates on the persona within the text and the means by which he invites the reader to understand his critique of conventional morality. Finally I ask how Nietzsche leads the reader to different expectations of himself and his existence. The second part of the chapter deals with the Russian cultural context: literary predecessors and their tradition of metaphysical rebellion. Most important here is Dostoevsky. The two most significant precursors, Dostoevsky and Nietzsche, would interact in the literary imagination of the turn of the century in ways essential to the creative process of the age.

The rest of this study is devoted to readers and their appropriations of the Nietzschean text. Chapter 3 deals with the critical reception of Nietzsche, the transmission of his work to Russia, and the popular cult of Nietzsche that sprang up in the 1890s and 1900s. The popular reception would set the stage for more creatively significant responses. This aspect of influence study has received relatively little attention from theorists. Since the Formalists, critics have tended to concentrate on individual instances of reader response and have shied away from the ugly distortions that an idea undergoes when it interacts with a whole sociocultural milieu. Such problems are typically left to intellectual or social historians. However, to understand Nietzsche's impact on "high" Russian literary culture, we must immerse ourselves in the broader cultural dialogue. Writers and critics studied here were engaged in a lively debate with the press and best-selling novelists about the real meaning of Nietzsche's philosophy. Moreover, the fact that such a difficult philosophy found such a large following outside the narrow circles of the intelligentsia is of tremendous importance for what it suggests about popular moral sensibility.

We encounter a theoretical vacuum when we undertake to examine how such an esoteric philosophy could have influenced values among the broad readership. Jauss addresses this question, but he isolates the author and reader too fully from culture-specific habits of reading and interpretation to explain the process of social influence. For example, one characteristic of Russian reading in the nineteenth century is the naive tendency to relate literary experience directly to social practice.[10] The general pattern of reception in Russian belles lettres shows the intention to enact what has been read. Ideas were typically brought out of their abstract state into the interpersonal sphere of emotions, interactions, deeds. There they were strongly and compellingly deformed to fit the moral, aesthetic, and political searchings of their fictional bearers. Social experimentation in belles lettres was easily applied to social actuality. Examples are provided by Tsar Aleksandr II's legendary reading of Turgenev's *Sportsman's Sketches* (1852) or Lenin's lifelong devotion to Chernyshevsky's *What Is to Be Done?* (1863). Perhaps Lermontov's hero in *Hero of Our Time* (1840), Grigory Pechorin, best put the special Russian perception of this interrelationship when he exclaimed, "Ideas are organic creations . . . their birth gives them form, and this form is action."[11] Thus, the Russian equation between art and social action leads naturally to an interpretation of Nietzsche as a social philosopher whose ideas were meant to be enacted in the public arena.

Other problems arise when the work is relatively inaccessible and the reader uninformed or only informed in the narrow framework of a particular culture. If the author is a philosopher and the reader a semicultivated, semieducated person, no link is likely to be made. Neither is there likely to be a reception if artificial barriers are placed between author and reader. For example, in Russia censorship worked decisively to bar ideas and information from all but the intelligentsia. In all these cases, the usual two-party relationship between text and reader breaks down. A mediator of some sort is required to facilitate the establishment of contact. Nietzsche became accessible to most Russian readers, including some critics and writers and much of the reading public, through a chain of intermediary texts that simplified and "translated" Nietzsche's ideas into Russian equivalents. Formally speaking, this mediator was a work of criticism or fiction that used current events or more often some national cultural tradition to clarify Nietzsche's thought to a broad audience. Alfred Kelly in *The Descent of Darwin* gives an example from German popular culture. Darwinian theories, he shows, were frequently presented to German readers of the late nineteenth century in terms of Idealist *Naturphilosophie*.[12] In his book *Nietzsche in England, 1890–1914*, David S. Thatcher analyzes the popular refraction of Nietzsche's philosophy of the superman through the prism of Darwin's theory of natural selection.[13] Similarly, many Russian writers and critics presented Nietzsche's philosophy to their broad readership in terms of the "nihilist" worldviews of Dostoevsky's and Turgenev's heroes.

Nietzsche's Russian reception was shaped by two styles of mediation: popularization and vulgarization. *Popularization* may be defined as a simplified but largely accurate explication of an abstract idea or theory. The intention of a popularizing work is to make the idea comprehensible to nonspecialist readers. The author's tone is sympathetic and balanced. He summarizes essential points, using examples familiar to a reader from a particular social and cultural background.

Fiction often serves a popularizing function in a society in which reading is a favored pastime. A character in a novel who reads a certain thinker and uses his ideas often makes those ideas accessible to the reader. For example, the German novelist Hermann Hesse helped to popularize Nietzsche's works in the years following World War I. Emil Sinclair, the hero of Hesse's novel *Demian* (1919), reads Nietzsche and is led to deny traditional Christian morality and rethink his own personal values. The novel appealed strongly to the generation that fought in World War I, and it gave Nietzsche's thought renewed popularity in the 1920s. Much earlier, in the 1890s and 1900s in Russia such broadly accessible writers as Petr Boborykin and Anastasia Verbitskaia helped their readers to a certain appreciation of Nietzsche's thought.

Iury Tynianov's concept of the "literary persona" (*literaturnaia lichnost'*) suggests another possible vehicle for popularization. In his article, "On Literary Evolution" ("O literaturnoi evoliutsii," 1927), Tynianov notes that readers form an impression of a popular author's character and life from the experiences and feelings of his heroes or poetic personae.[14] The author's literary persona, Tynianov cautions, has little relation to actual biographical fact. This image of a writer can exert its own influence on readers' thoughts and actions. Nietzsche clearly acquired a Russian literary persona based not only on Zarathustra but on comparisons with fictional characters such as Dostoevsky's underground man. In addition, Nietzsche's three most widely known followers, Gorky, Merezhkovsky, and Balmont, developed their own "Nietzschean" literary personae. Gorky and Balmont particularly stood apart from their works, exerting a secondary influence as focal points for a Russian cult of Nietzsche.

Vulgarization is more elusive than popularization because it often requires a value judgment of the reader. We will define *vulgarization* as a negative, distortive popularization. No thought is given by the vulgarizer to the author's intent. The idea is falsified when it is equated in a simplistic way to familiar situations. It is identified with superficially similar, but essentially different phenomena—whether events, stereotypes, or ideas—that bring about unjustified discrediting. A deliberate vulgarization is easy to identify: the author of the vulgarization makes it his goal to subvert the ideas he is presenting. A good example is Max Nordau's *Entartung* (*Degeneration*, 1891), a much-read treatment of "decadent" nineteenth-century European culture. Nordau consistently concretizes, personifies, and dramatizes abstract ideas, linking them to clearly abhorrent theories, situations, and character types. His vulgarization of Nietzsche's moral

8   *The Revolution of Moral Consciousness*

thought would have an abiding impact upon the philosopher's image in Russia.[15]

It should be noted that vulgarization is frequently inadvertent. For example, most readers of Nietzsche now recognize his sister's two-volume biography and her attempts to edit his works as blatant exercises in distortion.[16] However, Elisabeth Förster-Nietzsche and many of her contemporaries, including a large number of Russian readers, felt that she was giving an accurate, popularized presentation of her brother's life and ideas. And, indeed, her misinterpretations exerted an influence on German social and political life for over four decades. Such vulgarizations can be extremely destructive of the original idea because they become identified with it in the popular mind. Ultimately, the vulgarization is discredited and, along with it, the original idea. Only when the idea is rediscovered and reassessed is the vulgarization revealed as a "wrong" interpretation.

Typically literary critics treat popularization and vulgarization as unavoidable but contemptible side effects of the reception process. Insofar as both forms of mediation grossly misrepresent markers and guides within the text, this attitude is justified. However, as the popular author Anastasia Verbitskaia pointed out in her Nietzschean best-seller of 1909, *The Keys of Happiness* (*Kliuchi schast'ia*), "often inadvertently the artist destroys current moral standards with one outstanding book more completely than the philosophers or sociologists can: he speaks with the masses" (KS,I,101–102). It is through such popularizing texts that a philosopher such as Nietzsche could have an impact upon the thinking of a broad span of the educated public.

Popularizations have one other important use. The judgments and perceptions implicit in them are invaluable as revelations of self-image, of what Nietzsche in *Twilight of the Idols* called "the most precious realities of cultures and inner worlds" (TI, 55). Certainly, for understanding the moral and cultural consciousness of the quarter-century preceding the October Revolution, Nietzschean popularizations are of major interest. By examining the way this philosophy was interpreted and reshaped we are afforded an insight into the ways that educated and semieducated society perceived and evaluated itself and its future.

In chapters 4 through 6, I examine a broad spectrum of literary readings and rereadings that emerged in part through polemic with vulgar Nietzschean positions. While attempting to identify the characteristics of each individual response, I am also interested in apprehending in this diversity a framework of cultural unity. Did shared issues and concerns link these writers to a common cultural context? Do these texts conceal a common mythos that helps us to understand the age as a whole? Here I distinguish three major literary orientations that developed in the same period, took part in the same debates, and, although often from different standpoints and with different styles of discourse, share much the same deep-lying mentality.

Chapter 4 deals with "middle-" and "lowbrow" popular writers and their search for an ideology of personal fulfillment. These writers do much to "democratize" the idea of the superman. Among middlebrow writers I deal with Leonid Andreev (1871–1919), Aleksandr Kuprin (1870–1938), and V. Ropshin (Viktor Savinkov, 1879–1925). Lowbrow writers include Mikhail Artsybashev (1878–1927), Anastasia Verbitskaia (1861–1927), and Anatoly Kamensky (1877–). Because especially the lowbrow writers were much in demand among the broad readership, I examine the way their mythos of self-realization influenced public consciousness.

Chapter 5 treats the response to Nietzsche of "mystical" Symbolists. These were writers, critics, and poets who were preoccupied with what came to be known as "God-seeking" (*bogoiskatel'stvo*), that is, the search for spiritual renewal. They include primarily Dmitry Merezhkovsky (1865–1941), Viacheslav Ivanov (1866–1949), Aleksandr Blok (1880–1921), and Andrei Belyi (Boris Bugaev, 1880–1934). The central question posed in this chapter is how an anti-Christian, seemingly antireligious philosophy interacted in the atmosphere of broad religious myth building and how it could have been a positive force in the Symbolists' reconsideration of Christian belief. My approach to these Symbolists is somewhat unusual in the sense that I see them as participating in a broad cultural dialogue that includes much more than the small, elite groups to which they belonged. Typically these writers are held apart from overall literary development at the turn of the century and are perceived as being closer to Western European neoromantic trends.[17] However, their response to Nietzsche and Nietzschean trends in popular culture shows their taking from and participating in middlebrow culture in unexpected and very productive ways.

Chapter 6 focuses on the "revolutionary romantics" and their appropriations of Nietzsche's philosophy.[18] They are the radical writer Maksim Gorky (Aleksei Peshkov, 1868–1936) and two Marxist literary critics, Andreevich (Evgeny Andreevich Solovyov, 1867–1905) and Anatoly Lunacharsky (1875–1933). This chapter treats the social myth known as "God building" (*bogostroitel'stvo*) as an important encounter with Nietzschean thinking. Here I am concerned to show how such an antisocial philosophy as Nietzsche's could mingle with the social utopianism inherent in revolutionary romantic writing and indeed inform a new myth of social transformation. This group, like the Symbolists, will be examined partly in the light of its relationship to popular literary culture.

The claim that Nietzsche had no abiding influence on turn-of-the-century literature is easily answered if we allow that influence is much more than mere imitation. Certainly Nietzsche's worldview did not become an openly acknowledged, freely imitated model as Hegel's, Schelling's, or Schopenhauer's had in Russian intellectual circles earlier in the nineteenth century. However, it must be asked whether any "strong" writer in the modern era admits the pervasive domination of a precursor. The Formalists as well as later critics see in the strong reader an adversarial attitude to the influencing text. The reader commonly underplays and even denies the impact of a text upon him. In his early article, "Dostoevsky and Gogol" (1921), Tynianov analyzes Dostoevsky's attempt to discredit his predecessor Gogol by parodying his style.[19] Zhirmunsky focuses upon Pushkin's struggle with Byron's influence, tracing it from his early adulation of Byron to his unique transformation of Byronic forms and his rejection of the socioliterary fashion of "Byronism." Bloom shows how English Romantics intentionally "misread" an influential text in order to avoid admission of literary influence. These poets, Bloom argues, gradually subverted strong influences, remaking influential personages, ideas, and poetic forms in their own image. The denial of influence is then complete. Among Nietzsche's leading Russian adherents, we will find several important examples of such creative adversity. Merezhkovsky and Gorky, as well as later "strong" readers such as Ivanov, Belyi, and the best-selling writer Artsybashev, assimilated a great deal from Nietzsche, but for a variety of reasons seriously reduced or denied their debt to him. A similar pattern becomes evident on a national scale: having appropriated a great deal from Nietzsche, all participants in the cultural nexus—readers, writers, critics—almost universally reject him. Ultimately, as John Burt Foster points out in *Heirs to Dionysus* (1981), such denial, whatever its motivation, is a natural and necessary part of the process of innovation. By distancing himself from his mentor, the writer is no longer the epigone but asserts his own literary personality.[20]

An interesting and fruitful crystallization of the adversary relationship between author and reader is Bloom's idea of the "psychology of belatedness."[21] Central to his theory is the observed syndrome in English and American Romantic poetry of resistance to and open denial of influential predecessors who lived in some "idyllic" time. These poets, Bloom says, scorned the idea of imitating anyone and were fearful of living in the shadow of great forebears. Bloom's psychotemporal thinking suggests a vital point about writers in the Russian prerevolutionary period. If modern American and British poets lived with the anxiety of imitation, then Russian prerevolutionary writers shared with their Russian nineteenth-century precursors a feeling of "future anxiety." They saw themselves as the last survivors of a decadent time and the precursors to a total regeneration of humanity. Merezhkovsky foresaw the coming epoch of the Third Testament. Popular writers such as Andreev and Verbitskaia urged their readers to strive for personal transfiguration. Gorky and Lunacharsky looked forward to a utopian age in which people would live in harmony and dignity and realize their full creative potential.

These writers feel a sense of inadequacy before the perceived demands of the future. Writers as divergent as the Symbolist Belyi, the popular novelist Artsybashev, and the socially engaged Gorky all yearn for a new human nature and all fear that they as men of the present lack sufficient power to generate this transfiguration. The future anxiety spurs an increasingly revolutionary mentality that welcomes the idea of total departure from the present. Literary debate on all levels focuses on the issue of how the radical transformation of human consciousness is to happen. Is art a powerful enough medium to carry out change or is some greater, more potent force needed? Is change to be brought about organically by individual creative will or through an external order imposed from without?

The mentality of future anxiety has decided implications for the influence relationship. It may be seen as a strategy that helps the younger writer to cope with the overbearing presence of a precursor. Before the great unknown of the future, everyone is an equal. Nietzsche himself used this strategy when, claiming that "the time for me has not come yet," he appealed to readers of the future as the only people who could really appreciate and understand him (EH, 259). Gorky reiterated the same thought in 1907: "The act of mastering [predecessors] enriches a person and awakens in [him] . . . the desire to compete in creative activity [*tvorchestvo*] with past generations and to make models which are worthy of serving the future."[22] The precursor thus becomes a partner in polemic and a competitor for the most powerful conceptualization of future life.

The literary outcome of this syndrome is the production of future-oriented metanarratives or "myths" of social and spiritual transfiguration. To see these patterns as myth is to work toward a resolution of the problem implied in the title of this study: why is specifically *moral* consciousness central to literary creation? Myth, to use Mircea Eliade's definition, implies codification of values, and first among them, moral value. It is a narrative of a past sacred time when a supernatural power penetrated nature to establish a "right" state of things. This event also justifies a right mode of behavior and, thus, a right way of evaluating human actions.[23] Thus, the turn-of-the-century revolt against conventional moral stricture was the most visible symptom of a quest for new overarching frameworks of signification, for new existential purpose, and finally, in this sense, for new myth.

It is important to point out the differences between these modern myths and their traditional counterparts. In Eliade's view, whereas traditional myths are a means of canonizing a value system, modern myths are meant to break down canon and celebrate change. However, it should be mentioned that these myths do point to a future time when another value system will be established. Another difference between traditional and modern myth making is the "sacred" time when the transformation will happen. Whereas in conventional narratives it is usually the deep past, in these modern ones the sacred time is the future, more often than not, the near future as it is encompassed in the narrative itself or within the characters' framework of expectations. A final essential difference is the way in which the interpenetration of human and other-than-human forces is conceptualized. The supernatural powers of traditional myth are supplanted in these modern narratives by earthly, subconscious forces within the human psyche (but beyond human control) to which the self must open itself in order to achieve transfiguration.

Nietzsche's thought appealed to the urge to literary myth making across Europe. Cults grew up around his literary-philosophical persona. Yet the popular cult and the mature literary myths that eventually emerged in Russia are revealing of a mentality that, although it partakes in European literary history, is specifically Russian. How writers imagined their future, their society, and their art gives us insight into the moral consciousness of a particular culture that brought itself to expect and even welcome cataclysm.

Ultimately, nobody can get more out of things, including books, than he already knows. For what one lacks access to from experience one will have no ear. Now let us imagine an extreme case: that a book speaks of nothing but events that lie altogether beyond the possibility of any frequent or even rare experience—that it is the first language for a new series of experiences. In that case, simply nothing will be heard, but there will be the acoustic illusion that where nothing is heard, nothing is there.

This is, in the end, my average experience and, if you will, the originality of my experience. Whoever thought he had understood something of me, had made up something out of me, had made up something out of me after his own image—not uncommonly an antithesis to me; for example an "idealist"—and whoever had understood nothing of me, denied that I need be considered at all.
—*Ecce Homo*, "Why I Write Such Good Books," I

[In Nietzsche] we see a most noble and daring thinker, at another glance a dreamer, an idealist, who sets his demands from the vantage point of an extremely lofty concept of individualism.
—Nikolai Mikhailovsky, "Once Again on Nietzsche," 1894

The original sin of Nietzsche's philosophy is its replacement of religious passion with scientific [passion], its lack of mystical distance, of that fathomless atmosphere in which matter is transfigured and acquires a symbolic-ideal quality.
—Nikolai Minsky, "Friedrich Nietzsche," 1900

the view that puts Nietzsche's superman of Ivan's [Karamazov's] man-god "beyond good and evil" and makes "everything permitted" is not the only point of contact between the two: each reiterates a principle of egotism, a rejection of altruism. . . . The self-serving grandeur of the superman, the [concepts of] master and slave morality,—these are the inevitable "fruits of the heart's desolation". . . . Nietzsche's and Ivan Karamazov's spiritual drama are one and the same—
—Sergei Bulgakov, "Ivan Karamazov as a Philosophical Type," 1902

2

The Precursors

Nietzsche's Philosophy of Morals

Friedrich Nietzsche's anxiety at being taken for an idealist seems needless and even incongruous in the light of early Russian responses to his thought. Despite the perception of the Populist thinker Mikhailovsky that Nietzsche was a "dreamer" and a "idealist," Russian readers (and indeed Mikhailovsky himself) recognized the materialist assumptions upon which he founded his philosophy. Approvingly or disapprovingly, they saw him as a moral thinker of a special sort, one who fit less into the German tradition of philosophical Idealism than into their own social and literary tradition of moral revolt. One popularizer compared Nietzsche to the "most noble and talented" social thinker, Aleksandr Herzen (VP, 119). Another likened him to Dostoevsky's underground man who loves the paradoxes of moral belief and behavior (NKM, 463). Readers immediately recognized the criticisms of conventional morality that they had rehearsed in novels of Turgenev and Dostoevsky. However, Nietzsche's strongest adherents would be won by his efforts to go beyond mere moral criticism: by his yearning for existential renewal and vital mythic vision. They admired the struggle in his personal life as well as in his writing to transcend the spiritual decline of his age. In this sense Nietzsche promised much as a model. It is to

Nietzsche's search beyond nihilism that we direct the following discussion.

Nietzsche's concern with moral consciousness springs from his earliest work, *The Birth of Tragedy*, and it accompanies him through his active career. His early specialization as a classicist let him go beyond the borders of German culture with its specific valuative codes and survey it from a fresh perspective. *The Birth of Tragedy* shows his subtle sense for differences in valuative attitude. For example, his comparison of two mythic narratives, the Prometheus story and the Biblical myth of the Fall, highlight the process through which myth codifies moral consciousness (BT, 70–71). His middle career, centering on *Human-All-Too-Human*, was devoted to observing his own culture in an anthropological-psychological vein. The late philosophical works, after *The Gay Science*, will concern us most because of their strong attraction for Russian readers. Here Nietzsche launches an intense attack on the moral consciousness informing nineteenth-century culture. He singles out Christian morality and philosophical Idealism for his most passionate vituperation. The ultimate purpose of these forays is to find a resolution to the moral bankruptcy of his own time.

Since the subject of morality (understood now as restrictive code) is treated in Nietzsche's work with extreme harshness and irreverence, it is surprising when Nietzsche calls himself the first philosopher to approach morality as a philosophical "problem." However, the purpose of his hostility is partly to distinguish himself from the conventional moralists of the past and to shock his reader into a new awareness of the process of moral valuation. He remarks in *Beyond Good and Evil* that other philosopher-moralists have really avoided the nature of morality as a subject for philosophical scrutiny. It has always been accepted as a "given." The result is that the greatest moral philosophers, even Kant, furnish a "scholarly variation of the common *faith* in the prevalent morality" (BGE, 98). Nietzsche implies that he alone has the "subtlest fingers and senses" needed to describe a "*typology* of morals" (BGE, 97). His last works are devoted to studying moral value by moving "outside" all moral systems as such and penetrating the kinds of psychology that inform moral judgment (GS, 342). Thus, he arrives at his own typology.

Nietzsche's moral inquiry is prompted by the view that the idealists' "more real" world no longer exists. His provocative words, "God is dead," mean that the idea "God" has lost its function as a justification of human existence. European civilization faces the broadening "specter of unbelief" (BGE, 219): metaphysical nihilism. Gradually over the past century, Nietzsche argues, the most penetrating minds have intuited but tried to ignore that there is no metaphysical cause or purpose for earthly life. In the face of shattered expectations, earthly existence appears as a lie, a deception, and people as "grotesque caricatures," to use Schopenhauer's phrase.[1] The overt collapse of the whole idealist system of values—its modes of justification and judgment and its standards of the good, the true, the beautiful—is imminent, Nietzsche hopes as soon as 1890 (EH, 289)!

Despite his protestations against Christianity, Nietzsche possesses a strongly religious sensibility. He misses a view of the world, a myth, that incorporates and legitimizes in some way the destructive, "evil" aspects of human nature and gives a goal to human existence (GM, 68). His response in his last works is aggressive and cathartic: he wants to be done with the painful decline and failure so he topples the major mythic edifice that is already half-ruined: the Christian cosmology (Z, 226). He angrily unmasks the "evils" long given place and meaning by Christianity. He attacks the Christian "other world" as a dangerous, deathly fiction. He dwells overly long on the cruelty, even sadism inherent in Christian ritual (BGE, 67). His tone becomes most heated when he discusses the mendacity and maliciousness of the "priest-type," the earthly representative of the Christian God and traditionally the ideal sort of human being.

Christian myth and idealist thinking, Nietzsche's twin philosophical dislikes, both build on a similar kind of mythic event. Both strive for "salvation," which is understood traditionally as transcendence of earthly existence. These goals are achieved through the contact of a human self with an otherworldly, "more real," superhuman force. Around this event is built a morality of self-denial. Nietzsche departs from tradition by suggesting that vital transfiguration can only come about through knowledge and acceptance of earthly existence as the only possible existence. He transfers the central, life-giving mythic event from the outer sphere to the inner. The greater-than-human

18 The Revolution of Moral Consciousness

force resides not beyond, but within the human psyche. New life and new consciousness can be realized only by uncuffing the daimon within.

Nietzsche's "psychological" approach to the subject of moral nature is conditioned to a large degree by his acknowledged precursors, Schopenhauer, Stendhal, and Dostoevsky. With Schopenhauer, he sees the psyche as the motivating element in the formation of worldview. Nietzsche, however, surpasses his teacher. Schopenhauer holds to the standard ethical virtues of self-denial and love of one's neighbor as "moral facts." Nietzsche undermines and sweeps away these values with the assertion that there are no "moral facts," but only "interpretation of certain phenomena, more precisely *mis*interpretation" (TI, 55). Thus wanting to understand how and why we judge, he explores the only possible a priori to moral evaluation: the human subconscious. From this "underground" perspective, all conventional "virtues" and "vices" are called into question.

The problem of morality is for Nietzsche a uniquely human, psychological, "unnatural" problem. Thus, he defines nature as "valuelessness" and pictures it in terms of the most hostile landscapes in which nothing grows and there are few contours. Throughout the later work Nietzsche "quotes" a common romantic image: the sea with its broad, flat horizons and lack of distinguishing features. He sees the confrontation with spiritual nihilism in terms of a boat at the mercy of the elements (GS, 180–181). Throughout *Thus Spoke Zarathustra*, he also uses the desert as an image of cosmic meaninglessness. Both of these settings help Nietzsche to make the point that all values are artificial, a human fabrication. Nature is "nothing": it provides no inherent moral meaning.

The contoured, vertical landscape of high, snow-covered mountains is used in Nietzsche's work to suggest the existential isolation and harshness with which each person lives. Only the strongest, most self-reliant spirit can withstand this environment and uncover the valuative center within himself. It is in the mountains that Zarathustra meditates on human existence, confronts the fictionality of all human value, and tests and retests his love for existence.

Since it is the inner world of the human psyche that for Nietzsche has the energy to produce meaning, it is here that we must turn to confront the moral nihilism of the age. Nietzsche employs exotic, often shocking and incendiary imagery in order to bring alive the strange, uncharted world of the subconscious. He is a master at what Viktor Shklovsky called "making strange" and, indeed, had his own term for this process: "reversing perspective" (EH, 223). His idiosyncratic choice of words is well known. He acknowledged the acidity of his style in a letter of 1887 to the Danish critic Georg Brandes: "For me a great many words have acquired an incrustation of foreign salts and taste differently on my tongue and on those of my readers. On the scale of my experiences and circumstances the predominance is given to the rarer, remoter, more attenuated tones as against the normal, medial ones."[2] Nietzsche sees himself "at war" with Christianity and its ethereal "other world." Thus, he consciously and consistently makes use of destructive imagery: grotesque or sarcastic images of disease, distortion, ugliness; harsh economic and political imagery of exploitation, violence, rape, war. His tone is at times offensively arrogant, and his attitude to his subject unremittingly deprecatory.

When he treats subconscious, "premoral" processes, Nietzsche uses alienating metaphors that cure the reader of facile moralizing. For example, he uses temporal images of long epochs and slow evolutions to suggest the development from an amoral, unself-conscious state to one of moral consciousness. Nietzsche draws the comparison himself: "all *protracted* things are hard to see, to see whole" (GM, 34).

When he describes the underworld of the submoral psyche, Nietzsche gives a sense of its strangeness by allowing the reader only limited use of his senses. In the "subterranean," "dark workshop" where "ideals are made" (GM, 46), the reader sees nothing but a "false iridescent light." The reader hears voices but cannot see shapes: "There is a soft, wary, malignant muttering and whispering coming from all the corners" (GM, 46). Through this kind of disorientation Nietzsche challenges and prepares the reader for the strangeness of his new interpretation.

It is important to note that all Nietzsche's "strange-making" imagery is this-worldly: none of it is fantastic or expressive of a transcendent reality. It is metaphorical, however, but the terms of the metaphor have changed. If for idealists and romantics the image correlates with an "other" reality, now it points to a this-worldly if subliminal level of being. Through this imagery he implies the connectedness of opposites: past with present, high with low, inner with outer, bad with good. In this idea of being as a continuum will be found the greatest difference between Nietzsche and his Idealist forebears, particularly Plato, Kant, and Schopenhauer. Idealists, in his view, insist on the isolation of opposites into separate spheres: heaven and earth, reason and instinct, being and seeming (TI, 40–41). Belief in one necessitates the discrediting of the other, and ultimately the collapse of the whole fabrication. Nietzsche will propose a different ordering process: instead of discrediting and denial the subordination and sublimation of one in the other.

The central goal of Nietzsche's later work is to comprehend the nature of moral consciousness, which he views as humanity's "highest development"; to trace its evolution to the "sick," declining mentality of his own time; and to anticipate its resurgence as a vital force. He devotes *The Genealogy of Morals* to its analysis. Possibly following Dostoevsky (whose *Notes from the Underground*, part II, he had just read), he takes us into a dark underground with its unpleasant subliminal voices.[3] As Dostoevsky implies in his work, so Nietzsche argues that moral sense and metaphysical need spring from the ugliest and worst sentiments: self-contempt, gloating, cruelty, resentment. Here Nietzsche shows the development of moral consciousness and its most potent and beautiful products—memory, self-awareness, self-discipline, responsibility, sense of justice—as the gradual "history" of harnessing and sublimating the darkest, most destructive urges.

One aspect of Nietzsche's quest for the origins of moral consciousness that causes difficulty in interpretation is his tendency to concretize and personify psychological phenomena. His archetypes—the "blond beast," the "master," the "slave," the "free spirit," the "priest," the "philosopher"—are recognizable as psychological orientations, and not as social or political archetypes, when they are seen against the background of his style. The "blond beast," then, represents a preconscious form of being. This type enjoys physical liberty: his movements, his instinctive drives are unhampered. He is simple, literal-minded, innocently cruel, naive, yet "healthy" and noble. He resolves conflicts rapidly, then forgets them. He does not torture himself or others by dwelling on past events. The blond beast may be seen as a prototype of the more complex and "noble" master psychology. The "master" type shares the same naiveté and shortness of memory, sense of health and self-confidence, and ability to act. However, in the context of developed human civilization the master is better "trained," more responsible, more self-conscious than the blond beast. It should be said that Nietzsche is generally less interested in these psychological phenomena than he is in the difficult, troubled, but ultimately productive "slave" psychology. It will be only in contrast and in combination with the slave type that he discusses the master.

Much of *Genealogy of Morals* is devoted to tracking the heritage of moral feelings of conscience and guilt, and the self-consciousness, insight, and reflectiveness that accompany moral consciousness. He finds that guilt, in its original meaning of owing, is basic to the operation of society, but notes that as such it contains no concept of moral conscience. Primitive guilt involves, instead, a simple system of training people to be responsible, to live up to "promises," to pay their debts in social, political, and economic life. The notion of public, physical punishment as the equivalent of redeeming a debt indicates to Nietzsche an underlying master psychology: the continuing outward-directedness of cruel urges and the enjoyment of physical suffering suggest a simple, unhampered, "healthy" mentality. Here is a primitive concept of justice and law (GM, 83). The effect on each person, as Nietzsche sees it, is to "tame" him, to make him cautious, refined, and responsible. Although Nietzsche certainly does not question the need for this kind of ethical training, he quickly moves on to the mythopoetic, "metaphysical" aspects of moral nature. This kind of social relationship does not affect the life of the psyche and the essence of deeper moral consciousness.

The origin of moral consciousness, in Nietzsche's view, is analogous to a different kind of power relationship. If the idea of social contract and repayment of debts is workable justice among equals, an entirely different idea of justice as revenge emerges in

22 The Revolution of Moral Consciousness

a relationship of unequals. In his discussion of this development Nietzsche uses images of weak against strong, slave against master, conquered against conqueror, priest against warrior. The desire for revenge arises from a sense that the state of things on earth is inherently and immutably unjust. A naturally impotent, weak person is forced to live under conditions that are wholly unfavorable to him: he is made to see himself as weak, bad, contemptible. The resulting feeling of hostility to the external world, Nietzsche argues, is the basis for a negative self-consciousness. Because retribution cannot be active and quick, desire for revenge is satisfied through "reactive" means. The man of resentment, the "priest," remembers his pain. He reflects, plots, and rehearses. His long brooding becomes productive when he learns how to think symbolically, to control himself, to manipulate values, to falsify (GM, 38). Finally he wins his revenge through a reversal of conventional "master" values—strength, self-confidence, nobility, happiness, health. The man of resentment reinterprets them as "evil." His own resentfulness is renamed as love; his weakness, kindness and gentleness; his vengefulness, justice. The feeling of resentment, it appears, is the "dark workshop" where otherworldly ideals are made. Nothing is any more what it seems on the surface. The world is perceived as divided, and its unseen aspects appear "truer" than its visible ones.

The most vexed, yet deepest and most fruitful aspect of moral consciousness, in Nietzsche's view, is the phenomenon of "bad conscience." Bad conscience arises from a sense of total weakness and misery, from being irredeemably in debt. This feeling is created through the intense inhibition of all one's urges and drives by some insurmountable existential necessity. Nietzsche compares the conditions that produce bad conscience to the shift of sea animals to the land or the imposition of a "state" structure on a loosely knit, roving people (GM, 84). They also invite comparison with the experience of Dostoevsky's underground man, knocking his head against the stone wall of the "laws" of nature. In both cases, one is forced to face "truths" about life that cannot change, that offer no hope, and that force one to believe one is weak, ugly, and wrong. There is no person to blame. Revenge is pointless. The effect of such imprisonment is to sublimate aggressive, violent impulses; to turn them inward upon oneself; to tear oneself apart, analyze, and punish. The long-term result, Nietzsche says, is greater sensitivity, insight, and ability to impose form on existence. Now a person looks for explanations and causes outside his immediate condition. This search, according to Nietzsche, is the birth of the creative imagination (GM, 85). In the face of total despair, Nietzsche says, the notion of the "soul" and the "instinct for freedom" were invented to explain and justify human suffering (GM, 84, 87). Similarly, in the famous censored chapter of *Notes from the Underground*, Dostoevsky's underground man starts to "invent" Christ.

One of Nietzsche's most original insights is that the two mentalities of priestly resentment and artistic-philosophical bad conscience lead to very different kinds of society and culture. It is in this idea that the Symbolists Dmitry Merezhkovsky and Viacheslav Ivanov would see a way out of the dilemma of nihilism. The psychology of resentment, in Nietzsche's view, has a repressive social and cultural influence.

> Supposing that ... the *meaning of all culture* is the reduction of the beast of prey "man" to a tame and civilized animal, a *domestic animal*, then one would undoubtedly have to regard all those instincts of reaction and *ressentiment* through whose aid the noble races and their ideals were finally confounded and overthrown as the actual *instruments of culture* .... (GM, 42)

Nietzsche hates a moral sensibility that merely "tames" and controls, repressing rather than shaping elemental life energy, and giving no full range to human possibilities. The moral training inherent in it involves "lobotomy": the denial of a central part of human nature. The human self is divided, and threatening, uncontrollable, but ultimately potent irrational drives are dissociated from perceived "ideal" human nature. Contemporary German culture, in Nietzsche's view, is the futile result of this total repression of "evil" urges. To make human nature "safe" is to kill it in the subtlest way. Here are the roots of that quiet, empty nihilism that Nietzsche fears most.

Nietzsche sees the basis for genuine self-transfiguration in the history of bad conscience. Although bad conscience, in his view, is a kind of sickness, it is not poisonous as resentment is.

24   The Revolution of Moral Consciousness

Rather he calls it an "illness as pregnancy is an illness": it promises a future; it is a form of creation (GM, 88). Nietzsche sees in the process of psychological sublimation inherent in this phenomenon a real basis for human regeneration. Bad conscience, for Nietzsche, is a means of self-overcoming, building beyond oneself, imposing form upon existence. He describes the psychic effect of bad conscience:

> This secret self-ravishment, this artists' cruelty, this delight in imposing a form upon oneself as a hard, recalcitrant, suffering material and in burning a will, a critique, a contradiction, a contempt, a No into it, this uncanny, dreadfully joyous labor of a soul voluntarily at odds with itself that makes itself suffer out of joy in making suffer—eventually this entire *active* "bad conscience" . . . as the womb of all ideal and imaginative phenomena, also brought to light an abundance of strange new beauty and affirmation, and perhaps beauty itself.—After all, what would be "beautiful" if the contradiction had not first become conscious of itself, if the ugly had not first said to itself: "I am ugly"? (GM, 87–88)

This statement is possibly Nietzsche's strongest affirmation of the "evil," cruel psychic urges in human nature. He captures the process through which self-contempt, harshness, cruelty, ugliness, when they are sublimated, turned inward, and made conscious, work to create their opposite. It is here that Nietzsche shows best how he is to be distinguished from his opponent, the resentful priest.[4] The priest represses and condemns all evil urges, that is, the human "animal," as such, separating it from the good, the "ideal." Each exists in its own world. Nietzsche affirms the evil in its sublimated form as potentially productive energy. He insists on the function of the ugliest aspects of human nature in the conceptualization of our highest goals.

An important aspect of Nietzsche's late work, and the one that Russian readers would take up, is his attempt to answer his own moral-religious need. Having diagnosed the moral illness of his time, he is now faced with finding a way to moral health. Nietzsche's thinking here has been aptly called "progressive-regressive": his vision of the future draws heavily on myths from the distant pre-Christian, pre-Socratic past.[5] He attempts to resolve his moral rebellion by resurrecting the ancient myth of Dionysus. That this dark, paradoxical myth is given greater weight than the rationalist Apollonian one shows Nietzsche's concern with satisfying the emotional need long answered in the Christian cosmology. While holding up an anti-Christian guise, he arrives at a rereading of his religious heritage.

Briefly, the myth of Dionysus celebrates "life" as a cyclical, burgeoning, destructive-creative, suffering-ecstatic force. The god's character is divided without separating the opposite members of the pair into a hierarchical order or separate spheres. Dionysus is bisexual, embracing and affirming all nature. The god is both earthly and divine, visible and invisible, full of youthful energy and death-bearing. Rebellion alternates with resignation to self-sacrifice in this character. As a leader, Dionysus is at different stages heroic or tyrannical.

In his final work, Nietzsche builds his own Dionysian myth on the concepts of *amor fati,* "eternal return," and "will to power." The highest formulation of self-affirmation and life-affirmation, for Nietzsche, is the idea of "eternal return." This concept involves an attitude of affirmation of everything—all the contradictions, the dilemmas, the despair, death as well as life—to the degree that one actually desires its repetition. It is built on the same psychic process of "bad conscience." Through cold clarity of vision ("an Asiatic and supra-Asiatic eye," BGE, 68), through acknowledgment even of the worst, darkest, and most nihilistic of world perceptions, a person may discover the opposite in himself: "the most high-spirited, alive and world-affirming human being who has not only come to terms and learned to get along with whatever was and is, but who wants to have *what was and is* repeated into all eternity" (BGE, 68). In the idea of eternal return is the essence of Nietzsche's revaluation of values: he has channeled the ugliness, the suffering of earthly life; he has sublimated the "evil" energy of the "ancient animal self" and given it a legitimate place in existence.

Nietzsche senses the highest justification of existence in the most creative, combative, truthful personalities. These people embrace unconditionally the idea of "eternal return." There have been only a few of them in German history: Nietzsche mentions Goethe, Kant, Heine, and Schopenhauer. The ability to "experiment," to test oneself, to force oneself to face the worst, to accept "great suffering," to balance and confront the master and slave within oneself—all are signs of what Nietzsche calls "higher nature." The ultimate justification, however, lies in the future: the appearance of the superman. This concept has been interpreted in many different ways. It can be seen as Nietzsche's highest realization of the liberating, productive aspect of Dionysus.[6] The superman represents the release of deep creative energy in the psyche through a process of personal self-discovery and self-overcoming.

Nietzsche's formulation of new myth prompts the question that Walter Kaufmann asked: to what degree did the German philosopher actually carry out the revaluation of values he promised?[7] His constant preoccupation with nihilism and the harmfulness of Christian doctrine shows that he does not fulfill the requirement of transcending that pair of opposites, relegating them to the past, and creating new values (BGE, 136). Nietzsche's position seems analogous to that of John the Baptist. He lays the groundwork; he prepares human perception and expectation for future revaluation. However, although he does not create the "new" values that so many readers of Nietzsche have seen in his work, he does redefine the highest Christian values: love, truth, asceticism (self-discipline, self-restraint).

In *Thus Spoke Zarathustra* and *Beyond Good and Evil*, Nietzsche offers his own definition of love in contrast to the Christian concepts of pity and neighborly love. Pity, in his view, should be felt by the "healthy," strong, and noble for the weak: it is a feeling of condescending benevolence (BGE, 205–208). Christian altruism, however, reverses the equation. The resentful and weak condescend to the strong and to each other from the imagined heights of spiritual superiority. This kind of pity, Nietzsche argues, is merely disguised resentment aimed at supporting what is worst and weakest—making those closest to one more aware of their own misery. Real love is a rarely experienced emotion, possible only among equals, people who, at least implicitly, are also worthy opponents of each other. Nietzsche stresses as more important than love of one's neighbor the idea of self-love. For him, self-love combines clear vision, self-knowledge, and "amor fati," the acceptance of the "guiding idea" that emerges from the gradual subliminal ordering of one's dominant "capacities" (EH, 254).

Nietzsche values clear-eyed acknowledgment of life as it is. This existential truth stands for him in opposition to the idealist and Christian views of the world. Nietzsche supports a Schopenhauerian "naturalist" view of the world: there is no reality other than the physiopsychological reality of feelings, perceptions, interpretations, judgments.[8] Here are contained all polarities formerly segregated into two realms. Nietzsche departs from Schopenhauer in that he rejects any other "truer" or "more real" but undemonstrable reality, for example, the idea of the thing-in-itself or the Will. He does, however, see an overriding principle of cohering energy that is intelligible in all earthly effort: the "will to power" (BGE, 48). It is important to stress that this principle is not dualist in that it has no otherworldly, unknowable component that is somehow better than its earthly manifestation. The physical and psychological presence of the will to power is the only reality it has. It should be said that Nietzsche clearly values certain manifestations of will to power over others. The crude, physical expressions of this idea are not even given consideration: Nietzsche is concerned only with the higher, cultural forms it takes. In addition, its creative, fulfilling, and life-affirming manifestations are valued over the self-negating, deathly, priestlike, nihilistic ones.

Perhaps most important in Nietzsche's revaluation is his idea of asceticism. Here he distinguishes "philosophical asceticism" from the priestly "ascetic ideal." The ascetic ideal posits earthly life as a "wrong road," a "bridge to that other mode of existence" (GM, 117). The ascetic priest wants to vindicate his own insufficiency by destroying life itself. Thus, the love he preaches is belied by vengefulness. Through the idea of philosophical asceticism Nietzsche prizes integrity of character (TI, 96) and a self-loving, world-affirming attitude. In these two types of asceticism we see the same opposition as in the concepts of resentment and bad conscience: the priest represses and denies instinctive drive, and the philosopher sublimates and channels it. A good example of such sublimation is found in Nietzsche's discussion in *Genealogy*, part III, of sexual drive transformed as aesthetic sense in the ascetic philosopher's consciousness. Here he is referring specifically to his predecessor, Schopenhauer:

> the sweetness and plenitude peculiar to the esthetic state might be derived precisely from the ingredient of "sensuality" . . . so that sensuality is not overcome by the appearance of the esthetic condition . . . but only transfigured and [it] no longer enters the consciousness as sexual excitement. (GM, 111)

Although Nietzsche does everything possible to discredit his opponent, the ascetic priest, he by no means denies the search for higher meaning that gave the priest his power. He abhors the priest's "mendacity." However, the self-consciousness, sensitivity, refinement, and depth of memory resulting from this painful, long inner training are among the very highest achievements of humanity. Now Nietzsche wishes to lay claim to them for his own purposes. Just as the Christian priest repressed and discredited the "ancient animal self" of preconscious humankind, so Nietzsche uses the same slippery tools to judge the priest as malicious, lying, hateful, impotent, and ultimately sick and destructive. He introduces a new kind of moral consciousness in which total divisions of animal and spiritual, natural and moral, earthly and heavenly, evil and good, master and slave are abolished. He insists on the continuum between the two. He proposes a new "health" based on a psyche that contains these contradictions, that is a "genuine battle ground of these opposed values" (GM, 52). Nonetheless, Nietzsche shows his still strong relation to the otherworldly, upward-looking priest when at the end of section II he invokes a new kind of Messiah, the superman, the "*redeeming* man of great love and contempt, the creative spirit whose compelling strength will not let him rest in any aloofness or any beyond" (GM, 96). Although this "messiah" is earthly, not otherworldly, he does not yet exist. Like the Christian Messiah, the superman is to come in the future. Moreover, the idea of redeeming or "paying for" the actions of others is still alive in this type. Just as the Christ of the priest pays for the sins of the "ancient animal self," so this new human ideal will pay for the wrongs of repression and denial of the earth. Instead of the priests' life-repressing "ascetic ideal," Nietzsche's redeemer will be the life-affirming philosophical ascetic. This new mythic archetype will take human consciousness beyond both Christianity and its decadent form, nihilism, and will formulate a different mode of moral sensibility.

It can, however, be argued that Nietzsche did indeed revalue the Christian moral values of his day. He replaced metaphysics with a "metapsychology," that is, a psychological rationale for moral consciousness. He uncovered the psychological attitudes underlying moral consciousness. He refused to call the "ancient animal self" of human nature "evil" in the sense that it should be destroyed. He created for it a legitimate function and purpose in psychic life. Most importantly, he brought to light the tension between dominative, proscriptive and nurturing, sublimative kinds of moral psychology.

Nietzsche's philosophy conveyed a sensibility that would be powerfully attractive to Russian readers. His mix of literary allusion with abstract thought, his personification of ideas as archetypes, his emotional, intense, and strongly polemical mood—all resonated with the nineteenth-century Russian "literature of ideas." His own strong sense of future anxiety, moreover, intensified the messianism apparent in Russian intellectual life. The moral quest of his late works, their confrontation with existing ontological fictions and value systems would sound very familiar yet fresh to Russian readers. They would first interpret the new philosophy according to long-held expectations that the written word provide a model for social behavior. But in part through their experience with Nietzschean philosophy, some readers would discover a fresh way to read and, indeed, to evaluate their own literary heritage. Perhaps most importantly, Nietzsche's search for vital myth appealed to readers first as a model and later as an opponent in their own quest to go beyond moral nihilism and cultural stagnation.

Preconditions to Reading Nietzsche

The sensibility that linked Nietzsche to his Russian readers is best characterized as a romantic impulse to moral and metaphysical rebellion overlaid with a rationalist, positivist code of values. Russian readers immediately saw the similarities between Nietzsche's philosophical voice and the voices of fictional characters found in their own midnineteenth-century novel of ideas. Nietzsche's literary-philosophical persona—that combination of biographical fact and literary legend—appeared to fit closely with the prevalent Russian fictional archetype of the moral rebel: in his style, the direction of his thought, and, most importantly, the mentality that informed his revolt. Indeed, Nietzsche's critique of conventional values was repeatedly compared to the Russian tradition of moral rebellion, so much so that the question ought to be raised as to whether Nietzsche exerted a genuine influence at all.[9] At times his ideas seemed merely to disguise a reappropriation of similar Russian ones. Nonetheless, more discerning readers differentiated one from the other, and even those who did not see the difference confused their precursors in interesting and revealing ways. In order to discuss this interrelationship later, it will be useful now to distinguish the Russian history and myth of moral rebellion from Nietzsche's idea.

The Russian fictional archetype of the moral rebel emerged from cultural soil thick with social and political malaise. The Decembrist revolt of 1825 had been thoroughly crushed but had left in its wake a legend whose heroes were noble, free spirits in search of political reform and social justice. Later, during the last decade of the reign of Tsar Nikolai I (1825–1855), the theoretical framework for social and political change was added. In the 1840s intellectual circles cropped up in major university centers, particularly in Moscow and St. Petersburg. Here French socialist theories mixed in a heady ferment with German Idealist and post-Idealist philosophy. At the risk of giving a skewed picture of the times, it is important to single out the thinkers from this period who would provide a cultural subtext for Nietzsche's reception a half-century later. Foremost among these was a relatively minor thinker, the post-Hegelian Max Stirner (Johann Kaspar Schmidt, 1806–1856). Stirner's book, *The Ego and His Own* (*Der Einzige und sein Eigentum*, 1845), had been read in Russia in the 1840s and 1850s with some enthusiasm. His philosophy of anarchistic egotism asserted the primacy of individual will. He advocated social anarchism because he believed that only in complete social and intellectual freedom could each person realize his full individuality. Thus, Stirner encouraged social restiveness, resistance to the state, the "war of each against all." In the 1840s, to Belinsky and his circle, Stirner's thought raised inviting questions about the possibility of a "good" egoism.[10] These issues were further embellished by Turgenevian "superfluous men," social and moral outsiders such as Rudin (1856) and the "Hamlet" of Shchegrovsky District (1852) who worried about personal uniqueness and originality. In the 1890s this Stirnerian heritage would sensitize Nietzsche's readers to an anarchistic thread in Nietzschean thought.[11]

In the aftermath of the revolutions that shook Europe in 1848 most of the small intellectual circles were destroyed as subversive and their members punished. The lack of a real outlet in society for their ideas gave rise to a generation of Turgenevian "superfluous men" who had thought their way to social reform but were frustrated in the practice of it. However, the spirit of reform had not died, and when it reemerged, it was far more radical and uncompromising. After the halfway efforts of the Great Reforms of 1861 that liberated the serfs, conditions became ripe for political rebellion. A new generation of more radical thinkers arose among student groups in the late 1850s. Intellectual debate now was vigorous and sharply polarized. Important for this ferment were French radical thought and English scientific positivism. German Idealism had been cast aside as too vague and ethereal. An important precursor in the formation of Nietzsche's Russian image in the 1890s was the Darwinism of the 1860s and 1870s. Advances in biology, particularly Darwin's *Origin of Species* and Spencer's writings, provided a point of departure for Russian radical materialist thought. The nihilist Dmitry Pisarev and his literary alter ego Bazarov in *Fathers and Sons* (1862) both perceived social reality in hyperrational terms, as being knowable only through scientific theory. Pisarev compared ideal human society to a beehive, and Bazarov equated people with frogs. In the 1890s particularly, Nietzsche's detractors would accuse him of such crude materialism, of denying the spiritual aspects of human nature in favor of the animal.[12]

In the heated, combative atmosphere of the 1860s emerged many of Russia's greatest novels. Here social unrest was linked to roots of moral and metaphysical discontent. In the nihilist personalities that emerged in these novels can be seen a most profound expression of the Russian tradition of moral rebellion. It is to these characters that we must turn if we are to perceive the ambience in which Nietzsche's thought was read and the distinctive quality of Nietzsche's thought within that ambience.

Strong parallels between Nietzsche's rebellious persona and the Russian archetype of the nihilist certainly exist. Both may be characterized as "higher natures." All share a well-developed sense of moral honesty, a disdain for life as it is, and a strong desire to find some worthy life goal, or what Nietzsche called a "ruling idea" (Z, 89). Each challenges conventional valuative codes and exposes them as false. Both in Nietzsche's inquiry into moral consciousness and in the Russian tradition, moral skepticism is sparked by a deep disgust at the "human-all-too-human," that is, the gullibility and predictability of unselfconscious human nature. As it is, human nature appears vain and stupid, a cruel joke. What is worse, people seem incapable of perfection. Both Nietzsche and the Russian archetype probe a fateful split between "heart"—passion, need, instinct, intuition—and "mind"—control, clear vision, rationality. Russian protagonists give in to disdain for what seems weak and vulnerable, the heart, and must as a result rely only on the arrogance of mind. For example, Pechorin in Lermontov's *Hero of Our Time* (1840) demonstrates to himself and those around him the contemptible predictability of human nature when he calculatedly wins and then spurns Princess Mary's affection. In *Fathers and Sons*, Bazarov reduces feeling to a biologically calculable quantity. Dostoevsky's underground man (1864) goes to the other extreme in his effort to avoid seeming predictable and manipulable: he insists that his perverse enjoyment of suffering keeps him from being a mere "piano key." Still, like the others, he abuses the heart in his affair with Liza. By contrast, Nietzsche will try to surpass the tradition of nihilism from which he springs: he wants to bridge the gap between heart and mind by giving the irrational in human nature its due and by positing a productive relationship between rational and irrational.

The fictional nihilists and Nietzsche's philosophical persona share a kind of moral ambiguity: there is a breach in their character between higher moral sensitivity and very immoral behavior. Although their actions seem often cold and nasty, they are prompted by a passion for truth, by some penetrating consciousness of the "unjust" nature of things, and by too noble expectations of life. As outsiders, they see the inconsistency of conventional values and the self-delusion of traditionally good people. All of them—Pechorin, Bazarov, Prince Andrei in *War and Peace* (1863–77), Ivan Karamazov (1880)—have a spark of nobility: they are ruthlessly honest with themselves and the people closest to them. Their more profound vision seems to mitigate their cruel behavior and to promise some possible road to social and spiritual fulfillment.

Whereas Nietzsche suggests that these "free spirits" have the highest sort of human consciousness, which will eventually transform itself into a more productive, life-affirming sense of selfhood, in the Russian tradition they are shown to be hostile to a fundamental, instinctive feeling for life itself. Contempt for other people's feelings and a certain squeamishness about his own feelings lead the hero to deny real needs in himself: the need to trust, to feel, to believe in something and the need simply to live. The result is a strange form of asceticism combined with a cold, destructive form of hyperrationalism that undermines the ability to cope in this world. For example, Pechorin is driven farther and farther from human society into exotic, wild realms of the Caucasus and beyond. Prince Andrei is driven to war and to his fatal wound, appropriately enough, in the "animal" part of his body, his gut. Bazarov cuts his finger while treating peasants for typhus and dies from the infection. This "accident," like Prince Andrei's wound, may be seen as an inadvertent denial of the body, the animal self. The underground man mutters to himself in his dark isolation, apart from society. Raskolnikov considers suicide, Stavrogin and Kirilov commit suicide, and Ivan Karamazov contracts brain fever.

To compensate for the failure of existing valuative codes, both Nietzsche and the Russian rebels conceive their own archetypes of the "new man." All these archetypes idealize the faculties that the nihilists themselves rely on: ego, intellect, and will. They express a fervent wish for the radical transformation of human nature and human society into something noble, beautiful, and inviolable. Bazarov is the only one to see himself as the actual embodiment of the new man: he possesses boundless energy, knowledge, and passion. Although he has no positive plan for society, he anticipates a future very different from the present. Other conceptualizations are modeled on historical or religious archetypes. For example, Prince Andrei believes in Napoleon as the ideal of the perfect man: he is a glorious military leader, a social reformer, and a rational, just ruler. Raskolnikov in *Crime and Punishment* (1866) also looks to a Napoleon-like leader who enjoys special moral privilege in the interests of molding a new society.

Other nihilists conceive of mystical archetypes to answer their need for truth and justice. For example, Kirilov in Dostoevsky's *The Devils* dreams of a Christ-like martyr, the man-god, who will be cured of metaphysical malaise by overcoming the fear of death and divine judgment. Kirilov's moral orientation shares a great deal with Nietzsche's. Both reread Christian myth. Kirilov and Zarathustra are latter-day ascetic Christ figures. Nietzsche's superman is remarkably close to Kirilov's idea of the man-god in that it promises a transfigured, liberated human consciousness in the future. Both see present humanity as a "bridge" to a more fulfilling existence. Zarathustra's image of humanity as a "bridge between ape and superman" is well known. Kirilov is an engineer and has come to the province purportedly to build a bridge. The "bridge" he means to build is, of course, a spiritual one: he means to use himself to build a way to universal happiness. Finally, both Kirilov and Nietzsche try to supplant the traditional inhibitive morality with a productive one. Both reject absolutist, otherworldly laws and codes. The man-god, like the superman, revalues moral values by judging not his own actions but himself. Kirilov believes that the person who truly feels himself to be good will necessarily do good, while Nietzsche argues that deep self-love is a necessary component of a "value-creating" mentality (BGE, 205).

There are, however, some essential differences between the two archetypes. The superman differs from Kirilov's ideal in that it overcomes the alienated self-will on which Kirilov's man-god is founded. Future transfiguration is achieved through self-knowledge, through facing the abyss and still affirming life, not through the ultimate form of denial, suicide. The superman posits a deep connection with the subconscious forces of life in the "Body," which in a sublimated state give the self energy to strive, to be creative, and finally to celebrate existence itself (Z, 62–63).

All these moral archetypes suffer from the same ambiguity as their makers do: all represent the real sacrifice of conventional standards for the realization of higher goals. Moral renewal is imagined at the expense of traditional sanctions governing behavior. Nietzsche reenforces this tendency by arguing that basic laws, such as the Ten Commandments, are themselves destructive of the very well-springs of life energy. Thus, he proposes consciousness "beyond good and evil" in the sense that the free spirit must transgress existing laws in order to recover deep-creative forces and shape vital myth. However, in contrast to Russian precursors, he values human feeling (Z, 44; A, 148). Despite his stand against the virtue of compassion, Zarathustra cannot purge himself of it. Moreover, he values "love" as a rare and very strong motivating force. Thus, Nietzsche, unlike the Russian rebels, revitalizes long-standing virtues by doing combat with them and revaluing them.

In the Russian tradition, moral rebellion and the resulting nihilism are typically treated as a kind of noble, heroic sickness.[13] In the deepest sense they are destructive and self-destructive. These heroes become more wedded to their own myths of salvation than to life itself. They measure the actual unfavorably against the ideal and thus conceive a murderous contempt for earthly existence. Here Nietzsche goes beyond his predecessors because he insists at once on the value of the nihilist experience and on the fullness of life. Nietzsche sees this sort of illness as the "pregnancy" that culminates in the birth of life-affirming consciousness. In the nihilist revolt is enacted the passion of the dying, mad, tyrannical Dionysus, who will eventually be reborn. In contrast, nineteenth-century Russian writers found the most compelling "solutions" to the terrible split of mind and heart in myths of reconciliation and self-denial. Such valuative frameworks that Nietzsche would later revile for their spiritual "tiredness" were for these writers the source of true salvation.

Two myths that emerged as solutions to moral rebellion were those of the long-suffering Russian people and the self-sacrificing, earthly Christ. Both had deep roots in medieval Russian Christianity but were revived in the Slavophile ideas of *obshchina*, the ideal of social communality, and *sobornost'*, the idea of collective faith.[14] One myth idolizes the masses of the peasantry. As Donald Fanger points out, this image of the peasant gains its power not as a conceptualization of individuality but as an icon of the masses.[15] Indeed, it is an answer to the misguided individuality of the superfluous men. This type, moreover, has a "feminine" moral profile that stands in contrast to the "masculine" willfulness and egoism of the nihilists: it is all-forgiving and long-suffering as well as wise and nurturing. Protagonists such as the patient cripple Lukeria in Turgenev's "Living Relic" (1852); the kind, young peasant Gerasim in Tolstoi's "Death of Ivan Ilich" (1886); the loving Marei in Dostoevsky's "The Peasant Marei" (1876); and even Makar, the simple, suffering peasant in Korolenko's "Makar's Dream" (1885) possess the serenity and fearlessness before fate that moral rebels covet. It is important to note that all these figures, except Marei, are death-oriented: the great event that they must face is their own or some other character's demise. They do it with tranquil joy.

The myth of the earthly, living Christ arises in conscious contrast to the rather abstracted idea of Christ established by the Church. This image of Christ is "feminized," as the peasant type is. It is no wonder that among the first such figures are women such as Sonia Marmeladova in *Crime and Punishment* and Princess Maria in *War and Peace*. Like peasant types, these women exhibit a serenity, acceptance of suffering, and willingness to sacrifice. To the moral rebels the Christ figures are more accessible than iconlike peasant characters. They appear to offer a realizable resolution to nihilism. Socially these characters are on the same level as the hero, and sometimes, as in the cases of Princess Maria or Alyosha Karamazov, are related by blood. Psychologically they are more complex than peasant characters and capable of growth and change. They, more than the peasant icon, can understand and incorporate the experience of moral rebellion into the search for living faith. In these characters we sometimes find a joy in existence and a love of fate similar to the spirit of Nietzsche's ideas of eternal return and *amor fati*. However, there is never the Nietzschean yearning to create something new from themselves. These myths show the way to salvation from existence. Only Dostoevsky in *Brothers Karamazov* would approach a concept of self-realization in existence.

One other figure stands somewhat to the side of the Russian nihilist experience but nevertheless should be mentioned as an important "literary persona" in the Russian mythologization of Christ. This is the philosopher Vladimir Solovyov. The mystical Symbolist poets Ivanov, Belyi, and Blok identified the person of Solovyov with the myth of a living Christ. Belyi remembered him as a tall, thin graying figure with an almost saintly aura about him.[16] In Nietzschean terms, Solovyov was a philosopher-ascetic who eclipsed his Russian predecessors and developed a sublimative, life-affirming moral consciousness. His idea of "Godmanhood" amplified Dostoevsky's idea of Christ, stressing active, personal experience and growth. He supported and embellished the Slavophile concept of *sobornost'*, or religious and social collectivity, which for him meant a union of individuals striving for Godmanhood. This concept of *sobornost'* would become an important model of the mystical Symbolists.

Despite dissimilar cultural backgrounds, Nietzsche and his Russian predecessors share an important characteristic: a common fundamental taste, or moral sensibility. Both have an extreme and critical perspective on nineteenth-century rationalism and liberalism. Despite his desperate battle with canonical Christianity, Nietzsche, like the Russian novelists, appropriates elements of Christian myth: like Christ, Zarathustra is a wandering teacher and prophet. He speaks in allegories and borrows Biblical images. However, Nietzsche differs in significant ways from his Russian counterparts in moral rebellion. He arrives at the impulse to embrace what Russian nihilist characters try to suppress: the irrational in human nature. He wants not just to accept it but to grow from it: to channel inward drive and to sublimate it as creative energy. Nietzsche, like his fictional Russian precursors, certainly seeks the transformation of human nature. However, he sees the way to that goal through a process of self-acknowledgment and self-scrutiny. He uses the "knowable" basis given in human nature and consistently points out the danger of idealist thinking. That is, he warns against the denial of sensuous reality in favor of a tenuous fabrication.

The Russian tradition of moral rebellion would act in Nietzsche's reception as a horizon of expectation in a complex interaction between the Nietzschean text and its turn-of-the-century Russian reader. In some cases, his thought would be indiscriminately and directly identified with that of another writer, most commonly, Dostoevsky. This process can be seen in Nietzsche's popularization and vulgarization and his reception with best-selling writers such as Andreev and Kuprin. In other cases, such as Merezhkovsky's reevaluation of moral rebellion in Russian literature, the reading of Nietzsche helped to stimulate a very productive rereading of the Russian tradition.

The general positions of the Russian tradition—and not the counterinfluence of any one author—were the ultimate factor in determining readers' "horizons of expectation" and the extent to which Nietzsche's philosophy would be effective in changing them. The view of the superman as just another version of the ruinous superfluous men helped to condition the ultimate rejection of Nietzsche's "doctrine" and the reappropriation of Russian "solutions," that is, the theosophical and collectivist myths that would be reformulated in the works of both Symbolists and revolutionary romantics. Nietzsche's most enduring impact will be seen here in the way in which authors reclaimed the older myths. His celebration of the "earth" in human nature would not be lost: it would be sublimated in Andreevich's, Lunacharsky's, and Gorky's image of the self-creative people and in the image of the tragic Dionysian Christ of the Symbolists.

Taken in the European context, the Russian reception of Nietzsche was remarkable for its earliness and for the intensity of its debate. The question naturally arises: why were readers so eager to read Nietzsche by around 1890? Certainly Russian literature had grown through the two-decade experience of moral rebellion, but in the next decade of the 1880s nihilist archetypes had been outlived and more quietist, "populist" resolutions to social and moral issues found. Although Nietzsche would seem a close relation to previous intellectual fashions, this proximity might be sooner a reason to put him aside as already familiar, tested, and perhaps misguided or even "wrong." Indeed, such is the early reading that Nietzsche would receive from many older intellectuals, for example, the philosopher N. Ia. Grot, the literary editor F. I. Bulgakov, and the popular novelist P. D. Boborykin.[17] It is possible, nonetheless, to point to certain tensions and tendencies in this period that made fresh modes of thought appealing and permitted a more sympathetic reading of Nietzsche.

The literary culture emerging in the 1890s has already been adequately described in a large array of histories. However, it will be useful to delineate the features that made this time so receptive to novelty. One is the failure of Populism to provide spiritual fulfillment or social results. A famine in 1891 and 1892 made very plain the terrible misery of peasant life. It could hardly be held up as a model for a social utopia. Another factor is the emergence of a new generation of writers, and still more importantly writers from a different social stratum. The literary culture of earlier decades had been created by an uneasy mix of educated gentry and alienated sons of the Orthodox clergy. Now the children and grandchildren of former serfs, whose prospects for education and advancement improved after the Great Reforms of 1861, would blend with the children of urban professionals to build a culture with rather different goals and values. Some of the age's most prominent writers and literary entrepreneurs were the descendants of serfs: the poet and critic Briusov; the organizer of a major literary-philosophical salon Margarita

Morozova; the writers Chekhov, Gorky, and Sologub. Many others came from families of professionals and petty civil servants: for example, Andreev was the son of a land surveyor, and Belyi the son of a famous mathematician. These writers, as they came into their own, saw populist attitudes from a different perspective. Maksim Gorky, who emerged from a brutal petit-bourgeois milieu, remembered being irritated by the condescension of student activists in Kazan, where he was eking out a bare living (PSS, XVI, 33). To them, he was no more than a token "son of the people," a kind of mascot for their social dreams. Merezhkovsky conveyed in early poetry a sense of futility at the prospect of shouldering the moral weight of mass suffering. These people were very open to intellectual currents that would free them from the ethical and aesthetic strictures of their elders.

Urban and future-oriented in its outlook, the new culture seemed to oppose everything that Populism had represented. Older intellectuals, Tolstoi and the Populists alike, fostered a rural social ideal. They idolized the peasant as the best type of human being, and they wanted to retain an agrarian form of society. The traditional, the primitive, and the "natural" were their models. By contrast, many younger writers who were one or two generations removed from their peasant roots were interested in further distancing themselves from that world. Others, the children of civil servants and urban professionals, had few emotional ties to country life and did not believe in the Populist rural idyll. These writers saw the city and its cultural community as the center of life. For them, "artifice" was more important than "nature." While the older generation was concerned with refining and modifying existing social forms, the attention of the young was turned toward the untried possibilities of the future. If they looked to the past, whether the medieval Germany of Wagner's operas, or the ancient Athens or Italian Renaissance of Jakob Burkhardt, or, indeed, the eighteenth-century Russia of Peter the Great, it was always with an eye to its promise for the future. It is no wonder that future-oriented philosophies of Karl Marx and Friedrich Nietzsche and the apocalyptic Christianity of Vladimir Solovyov's last works found an enthusiastic audience.

The decade of the 1890s is usually viewed as a "transitional" one: that is, certain trends were declining while others were gathering momentum. For the purposes of this study it is more useful to view this period as an integral part of the cultural and social developments that led to the revolutions of 1905 and 1917, ending their forward movement in 1928 and declining in the Stalinist years. Now the politically repressive and culturally stagnant 1880s were giving way to a bright, searching mood.

In these years there were still no new alliances and only the first flickerings of movement in a fresh direction. The people who would become the most influential literary entrepreneurs, organizers, and theorists—Merezhkovsky, Briusov, Gorky, Gippius—were only starting to formulate aesthetic views that would replace the civic art of earlier decades. Literary historians typically divide literary development as symbolist or realist. However, both trends shared certain romantic characteristics, particularly a yearning for a superhuman sense of selfhood, for semidivine insight, for a heightened reality: both shared a strong mythopoetic tendency. Before 1900, and even after, there was considerable dialogue between Symbolists such as Merezhkovsky or Balmont and so-called realists such as Gorky or Lunacharsky. Gorky contributed to the Symbolist journal, *Severnyi vestnik* (*Northern Messenger*). Early Marxist critics such as Posse and Andreevich (Evgeny Solovyov) valued irrationalist thinkers such as Stirner, Schopenhauer, and Nietzsche at least as much as they did positivist and materialist philosophers. After the turn of the century the borders between the two strands of literary development remained more open in Moscow, Briusov's domain, than they were in St. Petersburg, where Merezhkovsky and Gippius held sway. For example, Briusov, Balmont, and other Moscow Symbolists would openly admire and even work with Gorky throughout this period.

Despite the irreconcilable differences that would arise between them, these people who emerged as the literary trendsetters, organizers, and leaders of the new age shared some fundamental aesthetic traits. None of them stood out as a great artist, as, for example, the younger poets Belyi or Blok would. All of them, however, were remarkable personalities driven by a desire to extend art and the creative process beyond their usual borders. What Andrei Belyi said of Merezhkovsky might apply to all of them: "for all the immensity of his gift, [he] nowhere completely realizes it: he is not a truly great artist, not a truly penetrating critic, not a real theologian, not a historian, not a philosopher. But he is more than just an artist, than just a critic."[18] All these artistic leaders of the 1890s were both looking for deeper, hidden truths through the medium of art and seeking the creative principles of life itself. It would be this passion coupled with a genuine ability to inspire, organize, and recognize talent in other people that made them the movers of the coming age.

Turn-of-the-century culture has often been characterized by a shift form "ethical" to "aesthetic" values, and this shift has been attributed in large part to Nietzsche. This opinion oversimplifies the actual terms of the "revolution of moral consciousness." It opposes two categories of value and suggests a casual, amoral attitude. Indeed, Nietzsche's adherents strongly sensed the bankruptcy of populist myths and along with them the ethical norms of social duty, self-sacrifice, love of the peasant and "natural man," of communal harmony. They strove for a different vision of the world that would reveal fresher, more promising vistas and a more potent ethic. In this sense they were aesthetically inclined without being aestheticist: they first rebelled against traditional inhibitive ethics and looked to subliminal creative drives in human nature as the source from which new cultural, social, indeed, spiritual purpose would spring. The complex relationship between creative drive and moral consciousness was a major issue in this period. By thorough examination of specific resolutions that each writer found we can arrive at a better understanding of the period as a whole.

One morning . . . [Zarathustra] awoke before dawn, deliberated long upon his bed, and at length spoke to his heart:

Why was I so frightened in my dream that I awoke? Did not a child carrying a mirror come to me?

"O Zarathustra," the child said to me, "look at yourself in the mirror!"

But when I looked into the mirror I cried out and my heart was shaken: for I did not see myself, I saw the sneer and grimace of the devil.

Truly, I understand the dream's omen and warning all too well: my *doctrine* is in danger, weeds want to be called wheat!

My enemies have grown powerful and have distorted the meaning of my doctrine, so that my dearest ones are ashamed of the gifts I gave them.

My friends are lost to me; the hour has come to seek my lost ones!

—*Thus Spoke Zarathustra*, II, "The Child with the Mirror"

it is clear that there are many profound thoughts in Nietzsche's doctrine; but it is odd: this writer reflects the truth of things in his mind as in a crooked mirror.

—N. Ia. Grot, "The Moral Ideals of Our Time," 1893

3

Nietzsche's Early Reception

Censors, Detractors, and Popularizers

Shortly before he became insane in 1889, Nietzsche started to worry that his philosophy had found no comprehending readers. He wrote to the Danish critic Georg Brandes and asked for the addresses of some foreign intellectuals who might like to read his books.[1] His own countrymen, the Germans, Nietzsche lamented, would never understand his ideas, but the French and Russians might. Brandes confirmed that Nietzsche was little known, especially in Russia, where his books had been completely banned. He gladly suggested several people, among them a leading St. Petersburg intellectual, Princess Anna Dmitrievna Tenisheva. Nietzsche sent Tenisheva a copy of his latest work, *The Case of Wagner*. For an unknown reason, he did not put his own name on the package, but instead signed himself as "The Antichrist." Tenisheva, Brandes reports, was offended by this "joke," wondering "what kind of strange friend [Brandes] had recommended to her."[2] She did, however, read the work. She translated it and even published a small, heavily censored portion in 1894 in the Moscow journal, *Artist*.[3]

Tenisheva was not the only person to be confused about Nietzsche. In 1891, Nietzsche's very first Russian popularizer, Aleksandr Reingoldt, mistakenly reported that Nietzsche's first work was *Thoughts Out of Season*, and his last was *Beyond*

Good and Evil.[4] The Populist critic Nikolai Mikhailovsky further illustrated the ignorance about Nietzsche among the Russian reading public. In a Russian translation of a history of recent developments in German philosophy, Nietzsche's name had been spelled alternately as *Niche* and *Nitche* (NKM, 444). This oversight suggested to Mikhailovsky that the translator had no idea of who Nietzsche was.

The young writer Andreev described this early period of Nietzsche's reception in his tale "The Story of Sergei Petrovich" ("Rasskaz o Sergee Petroviche," 1900): "In that recent time of which we are speaking, only a few people in Russia knew about Nietzsche: neither the newspapers nor the journals printed a single word about him. . . . [Sergei Petrovich] neither knew nor thought about who Nietzsche was, whether he was young or old, alive or dead" (SP, 244). These examples all point to the same fact: Nietzsche's work came to Russian readers as a complete surprise. Nobody had ever heard of him or knew anything about him. In the early 1890s it seemed that there was no receptive audience in Russia for the German philosopher. However, this was in large part an artificial situation created by the censorship. Censors would do much in the early years to determine the relationship between author and reader, at first proscribing access, then limiting and shaping critical discussion. Even well after 1898 when the ban was lifted, its early influence was reflected in lingering misconceptions.

Nietzsche was one of several European philosophers whose works had been either totally banned in Russia or at least badly distorted by excisions. Russian censors had traditionally been wary of Western philosophy, and only with the greatest circumspection did they permit the publication of individual works. Only seemingly harmless works of philosophers such as Schelling and Schopenhauer were printed. Books that appeared to challenge the political or ecclesiastical status quo were banned. Prominent in this category were works by the atheist Ludwig Feuerbach and the skeptical theologians David Strauss and Ernest Renan.[5]

After the assassination of Tsar Aleksandr II in 1881, censorship of political, religious, and philosophical works became especially strict. Archconservative officials, epitomized by the lay head of the Church Synod Konstantin Pobedonostsev, dominated academic and ecclesiastical institutions. Censors proscribed any books that questioned the magnificence of the Russian state, doubted the absolute nature of God, or criticized the institution of the Church. It was late in this decade, surprisingly enough, that Nietzsche's work reached Russian intellectuals. It is not surprising, of course, that Nietzsche's books were prohibited. The German philosopher was a most provocative critic of social and ecclesiastical institutions, political and religious leaders, Christian morality and secular ideologies. The censors were quick to grasp that Nietzsche was an "enemy" of conventional moral values and institutionalized religion. And just as quickly they made the fateful mistake that others subsequently made and that was to assure Nietzsche at least some measure of notoriety: they assumed that his inquiry into moral consciousness was actually a new moral doctrine ready to be practiced. Censors described Nietzsche in their notes variously as a "bold free thinker" and an "extreme materialist who denies free will."[6] Either way, the new "doctrine" was clearly meant to subvert tradition and thus was dangerous in the extreme.

Almost all of Nietzsche's books were banned for about a quarter-century, from 1872 to 1898. During the last few years of the reign of Tsar Aleksandr III (1881–1894), a mere handful of translations appeared in print, among them Reingoldt's aphorisms from *Human-All-Too-Human*, Tenisheva's translation, and some badly mutilated letters to Brandes.[7] Censorship policy changed gradually after Nikolai II became tsar in 1894. In a recent study, Daniel Balmuth notes a mood of indecision among Nikolaevan censors.[8] These men were compelled to devise new strategies to deal with an expanding population of literate Russians and a bolder mood among writers and political activists. The result was sometimes unexpected leniency. Nietzsche's works benefited from this mood. Suddenly in 1898 there appeared an abridged and rather poor translation of *Thus Spoke Zarathustra* by Iuly Antonovsky. In following years almost all of Nietzsche's books were published. This deluge was remarkable for the large size and number of editions and the inaccuracy of translation. After 1906 control relaxed almost completely. Even so, no accurate and complete translation of Nietzsche's opus was produced. The only critical edition of Nietzsche was begun in 1909 by a variety of known philosophers and writers, among them, S. L. Frank, M. O. Gershenzon, Balmont, Briusov, Belyi, and Ivanov. Only four volumes, *The Birth of Tragedy* (1912), *Thoughts Out of Season* (1909), *Human-All-Too-Human* (1911), and *The Will to Power* (1910), were published before the project was abandoned. Thus, the censorship probably affected Nietzsche's popular reception in two tangible ways. By restricting publication of Nietzsche's work on grounds that it provided an antimoral ideology they set the context for positive interpretation along those lines. When the ban was loosened, the practice of hasty, poor-quality translation was probably supported by fears that censorial leniency would not last.

Nietzsche's earliest admirers chafed against the ban. The Marxist editor Vladimir Posse warned Gorky in 1898 that a translation of *Thus Spoke Zarathustra* could at best be published in excerpts.[9] Even in 1904, Dmitry Merezhkovsky, who was then editor of the Symbolist religious and literary journal, *Novyi put'* (*The New Way*), mentioned in a letter that Nietzsche's work was still a kind of test for the mood of the censor.[10]

It is difficult to give a complete delineation of censorial influence on Nietzsche's reception in Russia. There were odd chinks in the censorship's armor that allowed access to whole groups of readers. Even before the lifting of the ban in 1898, censorship did not keep Nietzsche's books out of Russia entirely. In 1888, Nietzsche himself sent a copy of *The Case of Wagner* through the mail. As early as 1893, one of Maksim Gorky's friends from Nizhny Novgorod, the student Nikolai Vasilev, acquired a copy of *Thus Spoke Zarathustra*, which he subsequently translated but could not publish.[11] The editor P. P. Pertsov reported in his memoirs that a few intellectuals in the provincial city of Kazan were talking about Nietzsche as early as 1890 and 1891.[12] Mikhailovsky remarked in 1894 that such provincial newspapers as *Minskii listok* (*The Minsk Flyer*) were taking notice of the "spread of Nietzsche's misunderstood ideas" (NKM, 444). Vladimir Posse wrote in his memoirs that he first read Nietzsche in 1895 in Kostroma with a group of other intellectuals.[13] It is true, the pre-1898 censorship could not prevent all contact with Nietzschean thought. However, it did limit readership to a relatively small number of people.

Nietzsche's work sometimes bypassed the censorship through the help of foreigners who visited St. Petersburg, bringing with them books and ideas. Georg Brandes traveled to the capital frequently. Nietzsche's former student Lou Andreas-Salomé spent the winter of 1895-1896 there. She met with the editors of the Symbolist journal *Severnyi vestnik*, Liubov Gurevich and Akim Volynsky, who subsequently published a part of her study, *Nietzsche in His Works* (*Nietzsche in seinen Werken*).[14] The proscriptive effect of censorship was also weakened through Russians' travel and study abroad. It is well known that the popular philosophies of Schelling and Hegel first entered Russia via Russian students enrolled in German universities.[15] Similarly, Nietzsche's thought was discovered by some Russians during sojourns abroad. Merezhkovsky and Lev Shestov read Nietzsche while in Europe.[16] As a student in Germany, the poet and theorist Viacheslav Ivanov found out about Nietzsche.[17] The censorship certainly had little control over these people. However, it bears repeating that censors of the 1890s were less worried about the influence of Nietzsche or any other European thinker on a few privileged intellectuals than on the increasing number of readers among the general public. The newly literate might be very susceptible to the power of the written word. As readers, they were certainly more naive and literalist in their interpretations than the intelligentsia.[18] Before 1898, the censors focused their effort on curtailing the mass production of Nietzsche's works and related critical material. And here they had their greatest influence: by banning most of Nietzsche's works and critical commentary and by permitting the publication of just a handful of aphorisms and articles, the censors helped to instill in the public mind a very distorted version of major Nietzschean concepts.

Censors corrupted Nietzschean texts throughout the prerevolutionary period. They deleted passages and distorted translation concerning delicate topics. Most susceptible to the blue pencil were Nietzsche's criticisms of priests, Christian dogma and ritual, and the authority of the state. Even before the ban lifted in 1898, a few critics quoted generously from Nietzsche's works, no doubt to share more of the original with the Russian audience. These quotations were sometimes distorted if they related to one of the taboo subjects. For example, two major critics, the young idealist philosopher Vasily Preobrazhensky (1864–1900) and the famous Populist Nikolai Mikhailovsky (1842–1904), both cited the same passages from *The Gay Science:*

> [T]he praise of virtues has always been far from "selfless," far from "unegoistic." Otherwise, one would have had to notice that virtues (like industriousness, obedience, chastity, *filial piety*, and justice) are usually harmful for those who possess them, being instincts that dominate them too violently and covetously and resist the efforts of reason to keep them in balance with their other instincts. (GS, 92, my italics)

The Russian word for "piety" is *nabozhnost'* or *blagochestie*. In Mikhailovsky's article (1894), *piety* was left untranslated; in Preobrazhensky's (1892) it was translated as "uvazhenie k avtoritetu i vlasti" or "respect for authority and power" (VP, 136). This distortion stands out as the work of the censor in two articles where other passages were accurately rendered. This omission shows a concern to erase references to religious modes of behavior.[19]

After 1898, deletion of whole passages and corruption of others were common practice. The most popular and seemingly accessible of Nietzsche's works was *Thus Spoke Zarathustra*. Thus, we will draw examples of both kinds of censorship from its pages. Even as late as 1913, well after the almost total abolition of the censorship in 1906, the censor made significant excisions in translations of *Thus Spoke Zarathustra*. The translator and editor of the 1913 edition, V. Izraztsov, announced in his introduction that "due to the decision of the (St. Petersburg) district court . . . concerning the case of the translation of *Thus Spoke Zarathustra*, the present edition omits the chapters: 'On Priests,' 'Out of Service,' 'The Festival of the Ass,' and the second part of the chapter, 'Awakening.'"[20] In these sections, Zarathustra speaks directly and openly about the maliciousness of priests and even the hypocrisy of God himself. Zarathustra also pokes fun at Christian ritual. In the most widely published and read translation, that of Iuly Antonovsky, large parts of other sections, for example, "Of the New Idol," "Of the Apostates," "Of Old and New Law Tables," were excluded.

Some omitted excerpts call into question the legitimacy of religious and political ideologies to which the Russian autocracy subscribed. For example, the censors cut the section of "Of the New Idol" in which Zarathustra questions the assertion that the modern state represents the spirit of its people. In the following quotation, italicized parts were deleted:

> The state is the coldest of all cold monsters. Coldly it lies, too; and this lie creeps from its mouth: "I, the state, am the people."
> *It is a lie! It was creators who created peoples and hung a faith and a love over them: thus they served life.*
> *It is destroyers who set snares to many and call it the state: they hang a sword and a hundred desires over them.*
> Where a people still exists, there the people do not understand the state and hate it as the evil eye and sin against custom and law.
> *I offer you this sign: every people speaks its own language of good and evil: its neighbor does not understand this language. It invented this language for itself in custom and law.*
> *But the state lies in all languages of good and evil; and whatever it says, it lies—and whatever it has, it has stolen.*
> *Everything about it is false; it bites with stolen teeth. Even its belly is false.*
> Confusion of the language of good and evil; I offer you this sign as the sign of the state. (Z, 75–76; Antonovsky, 1903, 64)

Nietzsche's assertion called into question the validity of one of three "pillars" of the Russian autocracy, its alliance with the *narod* or "people." Thus, this section was deleted. What remains is confusing and absurd.

Other sections that could reflect badly on the autocracy were omitted. For example, in "Conversations with the Kings," Zarathustra thinks up a ditty that blasphemes both political and religious institutions:

> Once on a time—'twas A.D. One, I think—
> Thus spoke the Sybil, drunken without drink:
> "How bad things go!
> Decay! Decay! Ne'er sank the world so low!
> Rome is now a harlot and a brothel too,
> Rome's Caesar's a beast, and God himself—a Jew!"
> (Z, 260; Antonovsky, 1903, 330)

The censors excluded this piece and surrounding portions.
The censor's pen struck out the passages where Nietzsche most clearly challenges Christian values, particularly the Ten Commandments, the sanctity of Christ and God. For example, Nietzsche brings to light the contradiction inherent in the commandments against stealing and killing:

> "You shall not steal! You shall not kill!"—such words were once called holy; in their presence people bowed their knees and their heads and removed their shoes.
> But I ask you: Where have there ever been better thieves and killers in the world than such holy words have been?
> Is there not in all life itself—stealing and killing? And when such words were called holy was not *truth* itself—killed?
> Or was it a sermon of death that called holy that which contradicted and opposed all life?—O my brothers, shatter, shatter the old law-tables! (Z, 219; Antonovsky, 1903, 271)

Nietzsche suggests here that the search for truth involves "stealing" and "killing," that is, on psychological and moral levels. However, it would be easy to read this passage as leniency toward crime. To avoid such unwelcome encouragement the censors demanded excision.

Less than complimentary remarks about Christ himself were removed from "The Ugliest Man." In the following quotation, deleted parts are italicized:

> Too long have they been allowed right, these little people: *thus at last they have been allowed power, too*—now they teach: "Only that is good which little people call good."
> And "truth" today is what the preacher said who himself sprang from them, that strange saint and advocate of the little people who testified of himself "I—am the truth."
> *This immodest man has long made the cock's comb of the little people rise up in pride—he who taught no small error when he taught "I—am the truth."*
> *Was an immodest man ever answered more politely?*
> But you, O Zarathustra, passed him by and said: "No! No! Thrice No!"
> You warned against his error, as the first to do so, you warned against pity—no one else, only you and those of your kind. (Z, 278; Antonovsky, 1903, 350)

The effect of these many deletions was to deprive *Thus Spoke Zarathustra* of a thought-provoking critique of traditional Christian dogma and contemporary political institutions. More general sentiments were left intact.

The effort of censors to guide readers away from Nietzsche's criticisms of Christianity was supported by distortions in translation. The most outstanding were references to God. The word *God* was replaced frequently by "the gods." Thus, the "death of God" became the "death of the gods," implying that the pagan gods had died (Antonovsky, 1903, 8, 65, 76). Through loose translation parallels between Zarathustra and Christ were eliminated. For example, Zarathustra's descent to human society, *Untergehen*, might be translated as *niskhozhdenie*. This choice, however, would call forth undesirable comparison. Thus, it was decided to compare Zarathustra's descent with the setting sun with the word *zakat* (Antonovskii, 6).

Censors distorted Russian readers' perceptions of Nietzsche in other ways. Before 1898, they prevented contact with the growing body of European interpretations of Nietzsche's thought. Even in the 1890s European opinions and evaluations varied widely. Some critics, such as Andreas-Salomé, saw in Nietzsche's work a deeply personal quest for a new god. Others, for example, Nietzsche's sister, Elizabeth Förster-Nietzsche, interpreted the same texts as a blueprint for a militant state ruled by a "master race."

Russian censors were aware of the powerful formative influence that criticism would exercise on readers who did not know Nietzsche's work directly. One essay was banned for its uncritical attitude to Nietzsche's "sophistry." Someone whose interest in Nietzsche was more than "purely academic," the censor wrote, might use such an interpretation as a "guide in the vital area [of moral values]."[21] Only two works of European criticism appeared in the early 1890s: Lou Andreas-Salomé's *Nietzsche in His Works*, of which only a very small portion appeared in 1896 in scattered issues of *Severnyi vestnik*, and Max Nordau's *Degeneration* (*Entartung*), which came out in three large, cheap editions in 1893, 1896, and 1901.

Degeneration, which contained a lengthy chapter on Nietzsche, was a most distortive and hostile misinterpretation of this philosophy. It was the only European criticism to reach the broad Russian reading public during the vital period when people were forming their first impressions. Nietzsche, Nordau wrote, was an "egomaniac" whose notions of master morality, free spirit, and superman idealized arrogance and megalomania. Nordau saw Nietzsche's concept of master morality embodied as a distinct primitive human type, a "beast of prey" who is sadistic by nature. This master type "calms his destructive urges and his thirst for blood by attacking weaker men."[22] The ideal of the master type, Nordau claimed, lay at the foundation of Nietzsche's other ideal types, the free spirit and the superman: all, in Nordau's view, were driven by a need for sadistic self-gratification. The free spirit "judges his impulses and actions by how they help him, not by how they help other people, the herd: he does what gives him pleasure even when, especially when, it torments and harms . . . others."[23] Sadistic hedonism, Nordau said, was at the center of Nietzsche's new morality. By allowing broad access only to Nordau's interpretation, the Russian censors did much to deform Nietzsche's image in the public mind.

In the case of Nietzsche's reception, there appears to have been a strong measure of cooperation with the censors by journal editors. This editorial practice did a great deal to distort early perceptions of Nietzsche. Throughout much of the last decade of the century journals and newspapers, the media of intellectual discourse in Russia, were largely controlled by social utilitarians, philosophical idealists, and editors of other philosophical orientations naturally hostile to Nietzsche's critique of moral values. During the 1860s, Dobroliubov, Chernyshevsky, Nekrasov—all radical social utilitarians—had assumed control over the leading "thick journals." In the 1880s most radical journals had been closed, and more moderate and, in some cases reactionary, editorial postures had been assumed. Until the turn of the century, when Marxists and Symbolists finally gained a foothold in publishing and editing, editors tended not to challenge the status quo. Mikhailovsky, a moderate Populist, headed *Russkoe bogatstvo* (*Russian Wealth*), one of the most active thick journals of the period. Other major journals, such as *Russkaia mysl'* (*Russian Thought*) and *Vestnik evropy* (*Herald of Europe*), were modestly reformist in their views.[24]

Other journals were more conservative. *Russkii vestnik* (*Rus-*

sian Herald) was among the most reactionary. Philosophical and literary journals tended to show moderate interest in new intellectual trends. Such was the case with Russia's only journal of philosophy, *Voprosy filosofii i psikhologii* (*Problems of Philosophy and Psychology*) and the popular literary journal *Vestnik inostrannoi literatury* (*Messenger of Foreign Literature*). The journal *Severnyi vestnik* were the only major exception.[25] Its two editors, Liubov Gurevich and Akim Volynsky, were eager to introduce fresh literary and philosophical points of view. Volynsky, who formulated the ideological position of the journal, was a philosophical idealist. He did not get along with most other editors, particularly those from the Populist establishment, and welcomed ideas that challenged prevalent opinion.

Editors helped the censors to limit the Russian discussion of Nietzsche's work and to curtail growing interest. A slight and misinformed first introduction to Nietzsche by A. Reingoldt had appeared in the newspaper *Novosti* in 1891. Late in 1892 the almost unknown young philosopher, Vasily Preobrazhensky (1864–1900), published a very sympathetic introduction to Nietzsche's thought, entitled "A Critique of the Morality of Altruism" ("Kritika morali al'truizma"), in *Voprosy filosofii i psikhologii*. The journal's editors tried to neutralize Preobrazhensky's positive evaluation. They wrote a lengthy prefatory footnote to set the desired tone of condemnation:

> The editors have decided to publish Preobrazhensky's discussion of the moral doctrine of Friedrich Nietzsche, the conclusions of which are shocking, in order to show Russian readers what strange and sick phenomena are being generated by a certain trend . . . in Western European culture. (VP, 115)

They continued:

> Blinded by hatred for religion, Christianity, and God himself, Friedrich Nietzsche cynically preaches total indulgence in the most horrifying moral decadence, criminality, and depravity, all for the purpose of . . . creating certain "geniuses" (in whose ranks Nietzsche puts himself), who are limited by no legal or moral restraint, and who blasphemously use the masses of humanity as a pedestal upon which to exalt themselves. (VP, 115–116)

The editors did not stop with this attack. In the very next issue, three well-known professors of philosophy at the University of Moscow, Lev Lopatin, Petr Astafev (who also worked as a censor), and the editor of *Voprosy*, Nikolai Grot, delivered rather hostile assessments of Nietzsche's work.[26] These articles were meant to offset Preobrazhensky's glowing account. Meanwhile, Nordau's book appeared in 1893. The next year, 1894, Mikhailovsky made his own attempt to give a clear introduction to Nietzsche. His three articles seemed balanced and fair, given the circumstances. During these years, a variety of other critics and editors added their own mostly disapproving opinions.

It is worthy of note that none of Nietzsche's early literary admirers, for example, Merezhkovsky or Gorky, contributed anything to this discussion. The translator Nani, for example, refused to write an introductory essay to his *Thus Spoke Zarathustra: Nine Excerpts* because he was afraid "to speak of Nietzsche in as confused, distortive, and dishonest a manner . . . as everything until now has been written."[27] Perhaps here is a sign of the greatest success of the censor: to force intellectuals to silence by hacking up their work and distorting its message. Such reticence is particularly remarkable when compared to the relative liveliness of admirers after 1898. For example, later translators of Nietzsche often included a large amount of commentary in forewords and footnotes.[28] Lev Shestov and Nikolai Berdiaev, who count as two of Russia's best and most prolific philosophers of this period, devoted a large amount of effort to the discussion of Nietzsche's thought. After 1900, literary critics of all kinds, for example, the radical Andreevich and the Symbolists Ivanov and Belyi, all published articles on Nietzsche.

The effects of the cooperation between censor and editor were a narrowness of critical approach and an overall negativity of tone. Almost every Russian interpretation of Nietzsche was refracted through the familiar nihilist views of Dostoevsky's and Turgenev's heroes but in a denigrating, vulgarizing way. Even the sympathetic Mikhailovsky saw in Nietzsche's work something of what he characterized as Dostoevsky's hysterical, neurotic, and cruel underground man. The philosophical idealist Nikolai Grot, in his article of 1893, saw Nietzsche as another Ivan Karamazov with a mind like a "crooked mirror," for whom "all is permitted."[29] The Kievan critic Ivan Bichalets compared the German thinker to Ivan Turgenev's hero, Bazarov.[30] Both, Bichalets claimed, viewed man as pure beast with no higher moral nature.

These critics generally supported the view of the censors: Nietzsche was a ruinous moral influence. Like the censors, they were enraged by what they viewed as Nietzsche's extreme materialism. The German philosopher appeared to them to deny not only God, but any higher human striving. Grot argued that he had confused all moral standards. Nietzsche, he wrote, believed that "the more evil there is, the more good." A person, according to Grot's interpretation, was "good" if he acted upon his darkest, most "evil" impulses. At base, Grot considered Nietzsche a kind of Social Darwinist whose "primitive," "pagan" ideals harbored a view of people as "beasts whose only purpose in life is the struggle for survival, power, and strength."[31] This new amorality could only appeal to the unscrupulous. The editor of the influential and popular *Vestnik inostrannoi literatury*, F. I. Bulgakov, similarly characterized Nietzsche as a dangerous "anarchist" and an "antimoralist" for whom "the words truth, morality, the good, right, etc., have no meaning."[32] The philosopher and critic V. Chuiko argued in his article that Nietzsche was a "negator" or "as Turgenev would say,—a nihilist," who aspired only to "egotistical enjoyment."[33]

It is clear that the intellectual establishment generally adhered to the view of Nietzsche implied by censorial ban and stated in the few remarks made by censors. Most critics castigated what they felt to be Nietzsche's dangerous moral views. Editors attempted to tailor more positive positions to the generally negative attitude.

Despite the hostile atmosphere there was considerable curiosity about Nietzsche. Already some people were seeing in his philosophy an antidote to the stultifying intellectual environment. Two sympathetic and illuminating popularizations, Preobrazhensky's and Mikhailovsky's, did find their way into print. It is important to ask why these two people would have been interested in Nietzsche. Preobrazhensky was a very minor figure in circles of Russian academic philosophy. He had contributed in the 1880s to the new turn from materialism to idealism with an article on Schopenhauer and Kant. With Nietzsche's thought he saw a chance to rethink Russian utilitarian ethics of social duty and the positivist mythos that identified psychology with biology, and to work out a fuller vision of human spiritual potential. In his article, Preobrazhensky defined several issues that would become central to the ideology of popular Nietzscheanism when it emerged in the 1900s. He justified and appeared to support Nietzsche's elitism and his critique of the morality of pity; he gave the word *evil* a broader meaning, and he created a vibrant representation of the strong, independent self. Preobrazhensky's article would become an important source for the popular archetype of the self-determining individual.

Preobrazhensky was the first Russian to clarify why Nietzsche considers such traditional virtues as pity and altruism to be fruitless: they lead to nothing higher than personal gratification. "By pitying another person," Preobrazhensky writes, "a person satisfies above all his own needs" (VP, 129). One can never understand the suffering of someone else; compassion for that person is really only a form of self-pity. Nietzsche, Preobrazhensky says, argues that a morality based on pity for one's neighbor is too weak to heal suffering or to uplift society. What is worse, that kind of morality has not encouraged but destroyed vital, creative instincts: "it has bent and weakened the will (of the individual)," Preobrazhensky writes; "it has dulled all of his strongest instincts and has tamed all the passions pulsating in him: it has destroyed what is magnificent and splendid and left only what is simple and worthless" (VP, 141).

Nietzsche's philosophy, according to Preobrazhensky, posits greater freedom for the self-motivated, creative person. As Preobrazhensky sees it, Nietzsche regards that type as the "be-all and end-all of humanity" (VP, 145). He has the inner power and productivity to improve society as a whole. What Nietzsche calls the "herd," the great masses of humanity, exist only to help realize the grand schemes of such a "creator."

From the point of view of contemporary moral values, Preobrazhensky says, the actions of the Nietzschean individual must be regarded as "evil." This individual's love of innovation would provoke the fear and hatred of the status quo. Preobrazhensky points out that Nietzsche values conventional notions of evil precisely because they aid the pursuit of change. Here Preobrazhensky quotes at length from *The Gay Science:*

The most powerful and abhorrent people have advanced the human race the furthest: they aroused sleeping passions . . . they instilled a spirit of contradiction, encouraging people to compare opinions and promoting what seemed new and threatening; they brandished their weapons, pushing back frontiers, and desecrating holy objects: they gave rise to new moral doctrines and new religions. (VP, 135)

Nietzsche's concept of evil does not suggest to Preobrazhensky, as it does to detractors, the pursuit of selfish pleasures or merely destructive urges. Rather, it refers to any value that is creative, powerful, and threatening to weak conventional "virtue." In this sense, the individual has to be "evil" in order to generate growth and change.

Preobrazhensky hastens to emphasize the great responsibility that Nietzsche's creator must take for his deeds: "only ideals freely created by a free humanity, *responsible to itself*, can provide real, meaningful values; true human dignity can arise only in the free and ennobling struggle toward this creatively conceived ideal, not through obsequious submission to someone else's positivist laws" (VP, 143–144, my italics). The strong individual must look within for a new impulse to creativity, and he must remain answerable to that impulse, whether or not it appears evil in the eyes of others. In addition to responsibility and dignity, Nietzsche's concern for personal integrity is given special emphasis: "It is a wonderful thing to create an integrated and finished personality, to give *style* and artistic unity to one's character. . . . It is a wonderful thing to become oneself and to find fulfillment in oneself: whoever is not fulfilled will continually try to avenge himself on others" (VP, 145, my italics). Integrity, Preobrazhensky shows, is very close to aesthetic concepts of unity and style. Such aesthetic considerations are as important as ethical ones in a productive, personally and socially fulfilling moral view.

The individual's struggle to find fruitful values, in Preobrazhensky's view, is the necessary preamble to the transformation of society. Nietzsche, he explains, foresaw in the world-historical future a time of strife, a "moral interregnum," when people would seem more evil but would actually be more honest and responsible to themselves. This would be followed by a new epoch of spiritual enrichment and creativity. Here is the first revival in this epoch of Bakunin's anarchic idea that the passion for destruction was a creative passion. Only now it was associated with Nietzsche.

Although Russian readers could find in Preobrazhensky's article powerful concepts of evil and self-determination, it is hard to see his article as a complete popularization. He did certainly make more concrete and systematic an inaccessible philosophy. However, he did not bring Nietzsche's thought into relief against Russian thinking of a similar order. At most, in the beginning of his article Preobrazhensky compared Nietzsche to Herzen for the fiery spiritedness of his writing and the loftiness of his ideals. Unfortunately, detractors would be more effective in setting Nietzsche in the Russian context—in a negative way.

Preobrazhensky did introduce the major issue of Nietzsche's ensuing reception: the role of aesthetic values in rethinking moral consciousness. Later detractors would suggest that an aestheticist attitude was replacing a real sense of conscience. Indeed, Preobrazhensky does appear to value aesthetic qualities highly. He praises creative impulses, heroism, personal style. By contrast, he uses Nietzsche to devalue the traditional virtues of pity and neighborly love. What most later readers missed was Preobrazhensky's attempt to marshal creative impulses for the purpose of realizing a different ethos of personal integrity, dignity, and social responsibility and to work out a moral consciousness that accepted the aesthetic as a justifiable element in an overall reunion of the good, the true, and the beautiful.

In 1892, only one person in a position to publicize an opinion supported Preobrazhensky's interpretations of Nietzsche's thought. This man was Nikolai Mikhailovsky. Of all the Populists, Mikhailovsky had been the most moderate. It is possible to explain his interest in Nietzsche through his long quest for a form of socialism that fostered the development of individual potential. He believed that socialism should lead to the greatest possible self-realization of each person. Early on he had been attracted to such anarchistic individualists as Max Stirner. Now in Nietzsche's thought he saw the lofty image of human selfhood that was sorely lacking in contemporary Russian thought. Mikhailovsky wrote three articles on the new philosophy. Nietzsche's work, he felt, deserved much more serious treatment than critics had given. Mikhailovsky was particularly worried about the dangerously misguided distortions that these critics brought to his central ideas. Nordau and Astafev, in particular, seemed wrong to call Nietzsche a practicing egotist or immoralist:

> We see an extremely noble and daring thinker, at another glance a dreamer, an idealist, basing his demands on an extraordinarily lofty concept of individualism. The individual self, in his view, is the measure of all things, and he requires for it such fullness of life, such aversion to all petty advantages and conditions which diminish its dignity, that there can be no talk of egotism in the vulgar sense or of any kind of "immoralism." (NKM, 478)

Mikhailovsky points out that critics such as Nordau and Astafev misinterpret Nietzsche in still another way: they turn what is meant as an inquiry into the nature of moral consciousness into a set of vulgar dicta. Nietzsche's statement that "there is no truth, all is permitted" does not give a person the freedom to behave as he chooses. Nietzsche, Mikhailovsky writes, wanted his readers to question and think about conventional values.

Mikhailovsky makes Nietzsche's moral views concrete and familiar by comparing them to those of three authors well known to Russian readers: Stirner, Dostoevsky, and Darwin. In Mikhailovsky's view, Nietzsche's critique of altruism and utilitarianism parallels Stirner's: both center on the idea that there are egotistic motivations, for example, hopes of self-fulfillment, in even the most selfless acts. Thus, both show, egotism in itself is nothing bad. Moreoever, Mikhailovsky implies, Nietzsche's "ideal" person is much like Stirner's: each philosopher admires the highest kind of egotist. Nietzsche's egotist is tough and independent, in much the same way that Stirner's is. As Mikhailovsky puts it, this archetype "scorns tranquility and wealth, he is active, hard, he seeks danger, he is belligerent [and] powerloving . . ."(NKM, 460–461).

A less enthusiastic tone takes over as Mikhailovsky turns to the Dostoevskian and Darwinian aspects of the new philosophy. For example, he finds in Nietzsche's writing the same "cruelty" he had condemned in Dostoevsky in his famous article, "A Cruel Talent" (1883). The German thinker and the man from the underground share the same view of human nature, Mikhailovsky says. The underground man claims that "man passionately loves suffering," and both Nietzsche in *Thus Spoke Zarathustra* and the underground man come to the same insight that cruelty and love of power are at the root of human nature. Mikhailovsky concludes with a remark that shows little more insight into this particular question than Nietzsche's detractors did: "There is no doubt that those gloomy depths of cruelty, limitless love of power, malice, into which Dostoevsky loved to look and which have become the basis for Nietzsche's theory, really exist and are a subject of great interest for the student of the human spirit, that is, the sick, unbalanced spirit; these are pathological cases" (NKM, 464). For all his love for ideal human selfhood, Mikhailovsky remained hostile to psychological probing and the antiutopian vision of human nature that resulted. Mikhailovsky in this particular point did not supersede Nietzsche's detractors, but stayed with the same type of distortive, literalist reading.

In Nietzsche's idea of the superman Mikhailovsky sees the Darwinian principles of natural selection and struggle for survival. The superman is presented here as a social concept. Nietzsche, writes Mikhailovsky, posits an elite, an "aristocracy" that "would contribute to the elaboration of the 'superman' at the cost of man, in other words, of an aristocracy at the cost of the masses" (NKM, 494). An aristocracy of the healthy and strong is to develop "from itself a new, still higher aristocracy" (NKM, 494). In this scenario Mikhailovsky sees Darwinian principles at work: the strong and fit are to survive, and indeed flourish, but only at the cost of the powerless, the physically weak and sick. He does admit, however, that Nietzsche's emphasis is different from that of other Darwinians. Nietzsche is not speaking primarily of physical survival, but of cultural strength and health. Mikhailovsky notes: "From the totality of [Nietzsche's] writings it is clear that he values highly not only physical health, but especially cultural energy" (NKM, 482). And he reiterates here that Nietzsche's talk about physical types, for example the "blond beast," is meant "to draw the concern of society away from the weak and sick and to direct it toward the strong and healthy in whose midst will be produced the superman" (NKM, 494).

It should be said that Mikhailovsky, who has been sympathetic toward Nietzsche throughout, sounds disappointed in the elitist idea of the superman. He feels that Nietzsche has "gotten off his original track" (NKM, 493). Here Mikhailovsky speculates:

> Judging from Nietzsche's original point of departure—the sanctity of the individual person—one would think that he would adhere in his own way to the general task of our century: to find a form of society which would ensure the fullest possible flourishing of the individual. Nietzsche's unique quality might have been expressed in the conclusion that such an ideal could not be achieved, but that nevertheless it remains an ideal and could be approached to a greater or lesser degree, and people should eternally strive for it (let us recall that he wants to "perish, striving for the great and impossible"). (NKM, 494)

Mikhailovsky feels that Nietzsche's scorn for the weak shows a certain "coarseness." He had thought at first glance that the German thinker propounded a form of social egalitarianism that encouraged everyone to develop himself. In this hope he was clearly disappointed.

Mikhailovsky was effective as a popularizer, particularly for radical intellectuals. Andreevich, writing in 1901, would praise his series of articles as the best Russian writing on Nietzsche so far. Like Preobrazhensky, he oriented his readership toward the search for some higher concept of "personality" (lichnost'). Both popularizers drew most attention to the idea of the superman, investing it with the aura of personal freedom and power that the younger generation would crave. To a greater extent than Preobrazhensky, the Populist critic framed this idea in the perspective of social interaction. He pictured the superman as something worse than Raskolnikov's Napoleon. This type of leader not only would be willing to sacrifice the many to achieve his aims: his ideal society divided elite and masses into fixed groups. Self-perfection was only for the very few. For a socialist of any stripe, this view was tantamount to condemnation of Nietzsche. Some later Marxists such as Andreevich would take Mikhailovsky's observation as proof that Nietzsche was not a social or political philosopher. However, this admission would not stop them from seeking some reconciliation between their social views and what was perceived as an uplifting personal philosophy.

The literary critic Nestor Kotliarevsky lamented in 1900 that "the teaching of the German thinker, around whom a whole body of criticism has arisen in the West, did not find in our country the many-sided and just presentation and appraisal which he deserved."[34] Indeed, Nietzsche's early critical reception in Russia was poor. However, around 1900, while Kotliarevsky bemoaned the response to Nietzsche's philosophy, the new generation was embracing it as its own. Soon after the old century died away, valuable critical essays by younger critics started to appear. And as the young Marxist critic Andreevich remarked, readers' interest was growing "not by the day, but by the hour."[35]

The market was flooded with European studies on Nietzsche. Ten years' worth of criticism appeared all at once. Some, for example, the famous "Essay on Aristocratic Radicalism" (Danish, 1891; Russian, 1901) by the Danish professor of literature Georg Brandes, were long overdue. Others, such as the widely acclaimed *La Philosophie de Nietzsche* (French, 1898; Russian, 1901) by the French professor of philosophy, Henri Lichtenberger, enjoyed a more immediate reading. During these years Russian editors printed translations of essays on Nietzsche by the philosopher Georg Simmel; Nietzsche's sister, Elisabeth Förster-Nietzsche, his "disciple," Peter Gast; the academic philosopher Ludwig Stein; and the famous critic Leo Berg.

The intellectual atmosphere in the first years of the new century was much less constrained than it had been in the 1880s and 1890s. Intellectuals experimented with all kinds of ideas without taking sides or deciding that one point of view was entirely incompatible with another. A broad span of philosophical positions were all read and discussed, compared and contrasted. As Andrei Belyi remarked in his memoirs, "we took Nietzsche, Solovyov, Spencer, and Kant under consideration, but neither Nietzsche, nor Solovyov, nor Spencer, nor Kant was our gospel, because our worldview was built under the militant motto: destroy gospels."[36]

Nietzsche's reception now was far more balanced and refined than the early one had been. Younger critics saw more deeply into Nietzsche's thought than their elders had done: the German philosopher, they argued, was inquiring into the nature of moral, cultural, and religious values, not proselytizing a new social "doctrine," ready to be put into practice. In his 1901 article,

"On Nietzsche" ("O Nitche"), Andreevich stated the new attitude well: "Nietzsche is not a solution but a foreboding, not an answer to questions but a statement of these questions, not a leader and prophet, rather a warning and threat."[37]

In this atmosphere of relative openness and tolerance, Nietzsche's thought enjoyed the serious consideration of intellectuals of many different orientations. The young antirationalist thinker Lev Shestov, who was developing an outlook that anticipated Western existentialism, valued Nietzsche for his bold, honest inquiry into moral consciousness. Nietzsche, Shestov wrote, addressed the nature of evil and suffering rather than ignoring it and being satisfied with simplistic moral systems, as other thinkers had.[38] Andreevich, who saw himself as an inheritor of the radical civic tradition of the 1860s, appreciated Nietzsche's distaste for "dogmatism and intellectual servility" and admired his high valuation of creative genius. Andreevich liked Nietzsche's consistent defense of the "freedom of human creativity and the faith in its power."[39]

It is important to note that these and other critics had at best an ambivalent attitude toward making Nietzsche's thought accessible to the broad reading public. Although they often took the popularized image of Nietzsche as a point of departure in their articles, they were not themselves popularizers. For example, at the beginning of his 1901 article, Andreevich praised Mikhailovsky's popularization. However, Andreevich himself wrote in a nonpopularizing vein, refusing to systematize or to restate Nietzsche's questions as easy answers. Lev Shestov and the radical historian Evgeny Tarle (1901), among others, lamented the continued "vulgarization" of Nietzsche's thought.[40] Shestov made the following plea against popularization: "one can only regret that journals and newspapers are so anxious to acquaint the general public with the [philosophical] profile of the new philosopher 'in a general way,' that is, in an accessible or, in other words, completely distorted form."[41] Shestov cautioned that Nietzsche was neither the hedonist nor the irresponsible "libre penseur" that the public believed him to be. He concluded that most readers were ill-equipped to appreciate the real intellectual experience of reading Nietzsche and implied that they should not try.

A positive, popular image did gradually take shape. Two

literary figures, the "decadent" poet Balmont and the fiery storyteller Gorky, became the focal points of the Nietzschean craze. Both were magnified by critics as poets calling to new life and to a new celebration of human powers.[42] A naive, youthful energy filled Balmont's poetry in *Burning Buildings* (*Goriashchie zdaniia*, 1901) and *Let Us Be Like the Sun* (*Budem kak Solntse*, 1903). The first collection of short stories with which Gorky burst onto the literary scene in 1898 bid readers to awaken from their torpor and to examine and challenge the society around them.

The connection with Nietzsche was made less by the writers themselves than by critics. Although both quoted and referred to Nietzschean thinking in early works and both took inspiration for their rebellion from him, they did it in ways that were hidden from the general reader.[43] It was critics of all stripes who gave Nietzsche's philosophy a clear and positive "Russian" profile by linking it to these two tremendously popular writers. Thus, Balmont's aestheticist egotism became a component of the popular image of Nietzsche. For example, in an attempt to illustrate Balmont's Nietzscheanism, the critic Evgeny Anichkov quoted the lines, "I am life, I am the sun, beauty,/I will enchant time with a fairy tale./In [moments of] passion I create stars,/I am all springtime when I love someone,/I am a bright god when I kiss."[44] Nietzsche in his popular image would become a bright singer celebrating personal creative powers. Through Balmont he pointed the way beyond the world-weariness of the 1880s and gave to readers a feeling of "sunniness," a "proud and bold optimism," an active, creative approach to life.[45]

The Russian image of the philosopher gained a quality of heady, anarchic freedom through Gorky's heroes. The critic Iury Aleksandrovich observed that Gorky had risen to fame on a wave of Nietzscheanism: "I remember how at that time [1898] Russian society quickened and trembled and intently caught the writer's every new word with a reverence bordering on prayer."[46] And now the equation of influence was reversed: the association with Nietzsche helped to make Gorky popular, and now Gorky's tramp-heroes helped further to solidify the popularized profile of the philosopher. The vagabonds who peopled Gorky's earliest tales became messengers bearing Nietzsche's philosophy to his Russian readership. Very popular characters, such as Konovalov who accepts responsibility for his fate, Chelkash who defies the powers that be, Varenka Olesova who celebrates physical power and beauty, were spokesmen who made Nietzsche comprehensible and appealing to the public.[47] Andreevich, for all his resistance to popularization, admired the way that Gorky brought Nietzsche closer to Russian life: "Nietzsche's superman is much nearer to us than one might first think. The superman knows no mortal terror and acts on the dictates of his own nature. He does not lie to himself, he is naive and bold. . . . Naive and bold as a child or a genius . . . Gorky's tramp is also something of a 'Nietzschean.'"[48]

Merezhkovsky and Gorky popularized and disseminated Nietzschean ideas through their personal association with other writers and through their publishing and editing activities. Both helped to publish other critics' articles on Nietzsche, and both tried without success to publish translations of Nietzschean texts. Each man had an impact on the writers around him. Belyi acknowledged Merezhkovsky as one of his literary mentors. Indeed, he remembered as a student working over his first literary experiments, the *Symphonies*, with Nietzsche and Merezhkovsky firmly in mind. In the post-1905 years Merezhkovsky harbored the fugitive terrorist V. Ropshin (V. Savinkov) in Paris and exerted an influence on Ropshin's Nietzschean novel, *The Pale Horse* (*Kon' blednyi*, 1912). Gorky, who had a wider following and encouraged many more writers, had a greater popularizing impact. Several authors who produced popular Nietzschean fiction did so while working in close contact with Gorky, and some published their work in his *Znanie* almanac. Their number includes some of the most successful popular novelists and storywriters of the day, Andreev, Kuprin, and Artsybashev. Many of these authors would inadvertently help to expand the Nietzschean cult of self-determination.

While popularizers profiled a new Nietzschean character type, it would be Nietzsche's opponents and vulgarizers who created the combative environment in which genuinely new ways of reading would emerge. Some, such as Solovyov and Tolstoi, would put forth serious moral objections to the new philosophy, while others, such as Boborykin, would give the new fashion a label, *Nitssheanstvo*, and define it in the easily understood terms of concrete stereotypes and plot situations. What follows is a look at the cult of Nietzsche from the outside, from the point of view of those dedicated to weeding out Nietzschean moral revolt before it became strongly embedded in cultural life.

Vulgar Nietzscheanism

Despite the openness, seriousness, and enthusiasm with which young intellectuals like Andreevich, Shestov, or Merezhkovsky approached Nietzsche's works, the sensitivity with which they read him did not extend far beyond their own circles. Even Balmont's and Gorky's images of tremendous Nietzschean vitality melded with a powerful, widespread vulgar image. The tidal wave of interest in Nietzsche after 1900 was made possible by a more lenient censorship that allowed all kinds of publication, good and bad, onto the market. A vulgar image of Nietzsche took root in part because of broad ignorance, overeager publication of suspect materials, and hasty, inaccurate translation. Nietzsche's books now appeared in multiple editions. Publishing houses, for example, Chicherin and Kliukin, started their own "collected works." Each competed with the others for the lively market in Nietzscheana. As one publicist observed: "Obviously the cheap popular publishers and booksellers interested in 'seizing the day' have more than just [young people] in mind when they print and display in their store windows various [books like] *Obscuring the Idols* [sic] and *Excerpts from a Book on the Antichrist* [sic] right next to other items like *What Does a Woman Want?*"[49]

The vulgarized view of Nietzsche took root with the zealous aid of older writers who were alarmed by the radical shift in mentality going on around them. They were determined to dampen the enthusiasm of the young and chose primarily to attack Nietzsche as the figure most inspiring this change. The moral authority of Tolstoi and the long-standing popularity of Boborykin would combine to establish a very unappealing image of Nietzsche that has lasted and indeed thrived well into the Soviet period. These and other writers and intellectuals dubbed as "Nietzscheanism" (*nitssheanstvo*) a desire for personal fulfillment popular among students, budding intellectuals, and young professionals. Nietzsche's thought, they argued, appealed to a desire to be unique; to have distinctive ideas, perceptions, experiences; in short, to be an "individual." Writing in 1900, Minsky, an older poet with mystic inclinations, warned against applying Nietzsche's brand of individualism to real life. Nietzsche's thought, he felt, was dangerous, "unbridled, born in slavery, and thirsting for liberation."[50] Since the 1890s, the great philosopher Vladimir Solovyov had carried on a polemic with Nietzsche both in the press and in his philosophical writings. His major work on moral value, *The Justification of the Good* (*Opravdanie dobra*, 1897), had been spurred by disagreement with Nietzsche's rejection of absolute moral systems. Here Solovyov tried to reconcile absolute moral value with an ethic that allowed some concept of freedom of choice and some possibility for self-realization. Now, in 1899 in an article entitled "The Idea of the Superman" ("Ideia sverkhcheloveka") he lamented Nietzsche's impact on Russian youth. He observed that the superman was among the most interesting ideas that had captivated the new generation of Russian readers. The others, he said, were Marx's "economic materialism" and Tolstoi's "abstract moralism." Like other detractors, Solovyov reduced Nietzsche's philosophy of morals to an attitude of arrogance and self-will:

> The vicious aspects of Nietzscheanism are striking. The scorn for weak and sick humanity, the pagan view of strength and beauty, the appointment to oneself *a priori* of an exceptional, superhuman significance—at first to oneself alone, then to oneself as a collective, a chosen minority of the "better," that is, the stronger, more gifted, powerful, lordly natures, to whom all is permitted because their will is the supreme law for other people,—here are the obvious errors of Nietzscheanism.[51]

Solovyov repeated the same objections that so many others had voiced: Nietzsche's elitism and egotism were abhorrent. Nonetheless, he was more tolerant than other detractors would be. The current infatuation, in his view, should be seen "as a comical ... but fundamentally necessary transitional step,—as a 'passing fancy of youth,' without which there can be no genuine maturity."[52] Nietzscheanism was a sign of intellectual coming-of-age of the new generation.

The Nietzschean cult found a vocal opponent in the last giant of the Populist era, the aging Tolstoi. The great novelist was sure that Nietzscheanism signaled the moral decline of Russian society. He was alarmed that a man whom he personally considered insane could turn the minds of the young. During December 1900, Tolstoi wrote in his diary:

> I was reading Nietzsche's *Zarathustra* and his sister's preface on how he wrote, and was fully convinced that he was completely crazy when he wrote, not in the metaphorical sense, but in the literal, most exact sense: [his writing is full of] disconnectedness, he jumps from one thought to another, he compares without saying to what, he begins a thought without concluding it, . . . he has an *idée fixe* that by repudiating the highest foundations for human life and thought, he is demonstrating his own superhuman genius. What kind of society is it that hails such an evil and crazy man as its mentor?[53]

Like many other detractors, Tolstoi saw in Nietzsche's philosophy dangerous moral confusion. In his view, Nietzsche represented everything the Russian intelligentsia traditionally interpreted as evil: egotism, aestheticism, sensuality. In "What Is Art?" ("Chto takoe iskusstvo?" 1897–1898), Tolstoi reviled the widespread taste for "empty" aestheticism, which he said was derived from Nietzsche's works and from the aesthetic theories of Wagner.[54] Still more serious, in Tolstoi's view, was the apathy toward moral issues that he saw around him in concrete, everyday life. Nietzsche's thought seemed to condone "bestial" behavior even in the higher spheres of Russian society. No one observed objective moral standards any more, but acted in any way that befit their selfish needs. Tolstoi believed that egotism, the view of the self as the arbiter of good and evil, lay at the heart of this vicious cult. He wrote in his article "To the Clergy" ("Dukhovenstvu," 1902):

> Those who deny religion involuntarily make mere self-love and fleshly lust the basis for human activity. A doctrine of egotism, evil, and hatred has emerged among these people, [a teaching] which was always at the root of materialist philosophy, . . . but which recently has been clearly and deliberately expressed in Nietzsche's doctrine and is spreading fast and fostering the coarsest and cruelest bestiality. . . .[55]

The popularity of Nietzsche's thought signaled to Tolstoi the imminent collapse of Russian morality. He saw the signs of the failure of moral values everywhere, in journalism, in the church, in belles lettres, and even in the work of the young writers dearest to him, Chekhov and Gorky. In a diary entry for January 16, 1900, Tolstoi remarked that Chekhov's famous short story "The Lady with a Small Dog" ("Dama s sobachkoi," 1899) was "all Nietzsche," focusing on "people who haven't worked out a clear worldview which distinguishes between good and evil. Before, people . . . searched; now they consider themselves beyond good and evil, so they stay on this side of it and almost became animals."[56] Tolstoi was uncomfortable with Gorky's work for similar reasons. In 1909, a year before his death, he wrote, "I read . . . about Gorky. And it is odd, I harbor ill feelings toward him which I am trying to combat. I justify them by saying that, like Nietzsche, he is a harmful writer: he has a great gift but absolutely no religious . . . convictions."[57] Tolstoi died, convinced that the world was becoming insane: the strongest proof was the widespread popularity of Nietzsche.

Solovyov's and Tolstoi's criticisms of Nietzsche take on a new dimension when we recognize that both Russians were polemicizing between themselves and with the German thinker to assert their own moral authority. Both Solovyov and Tolstoi enjoyed considerable influence as spiritual mentors. In the morally and politically oppressive decade of the 1880s, each had established himself as a strong moral voice against the government and its excesses. Solovyov had pled in 1881 for mercy for the assassins of Tsar Aleksandr II. After his rediscovery of Christian faith in 1880, Tolstoi had written a series of religious tracts that criticized the dogmas of the Orthodox Church. In the 1890s he was gathering around him a considerable following, and in 1901 he would be excommunicated from the Church. It is important to realize that Tolstoi's and Solovyov's attacks on Nietzsche took place in the context of their own competition for predominance. Being the younger and less well known of the two, Solovyov made more forays against Tolstoi than the older man did against him. Solovyov delivered his most vigorous attack on both of his rivals in his final work, *Three Conversations* (*Tri razgovora*, 1900). Here, in the form of a Socratic dialogue, he tore apart Tolstoi's idea of nonresistance to evil as being too weak to conquer real evil. In the final part of this work, "The Story of the Antichrist," he pictured Nietzsche's idea of the superman as a modern-day Grand Inquisitor who embodies all virtue but at base loves only himself. He seeks spiritual comfort and social welfare for all, but secretly yearns for total power for himself. To Solovyov, the superman is the epitome of earthly evil. However, despite their differences, Solovyov and Tolstoi had more in common with each other than either had with the German philosopher. Both Russian thinkers shared a long-standing Russian distaste for Western "egotism," that is, anything that put the self in the place of enduring social or metaphysical value. Both agreed implicitly that there had to be some higher, enduring moral principle external to human consciousness. Despite the strong impact of Nietzschean thinking, this desire for an extrahuman moral standard would persist in the thinking of individual followers of Solovyov and Tolstoi.[58] In this three-cornered polemic Nietzsche lost ground, and the vulgarization of his thought became further entrenched.

By far the most influential voice in shaping the broad perception of Russian Nietzscheanism was that of the best-selling novelist and playwright Boborykin. Boborykin had been part of the Populist generation of the 1870s. He had worked as a journalist in the liberal press. His dozens of novels and plays documented current social and intellectual trends and were widely read among the intelligentsia. Particularly successful were novels, such as *Vasilii Terkin* (1893), that pictured industrialization and the emergence of an entrepreneurial elite in the late 1880s and early 1890s. His vulgarizing treatment of Nietzsche grounded the new philosophy squarely in the context of emerging capitalism as a kind of antiideology of self-determination.

Boborykin's first Nietzschean vulgarization, entitled *The Pass (Pereval)*, appeared in 1893, just when people were barely starting to be aware of Nietzsche. It benefited considerably from the stir created in *Voprosy filosofii i psikhologii*. This novel, as well as Boborykin's later works, would be more effective than all the censors, editors, detractors, and even popularizers in implanting a tangible and identifiably Russian version of Nietzschean thought into readers' minds.

Boborykin remarked in 1900 that most of his readers had seen the hero of *The Pass* as a depiction of Preobrazhensky.[59] Boborykin's hero, Ivan Kostritsyn, is clearly and proudly "bourgeois": he works as a manager for the wealthy merchant Zakhary Kumachov and studies classical languages at the University of St. Petersburg. He fancies himself a philosopher and is known ironically as the "Socrates of the warehouse." He views his employer as the "new Man," who will give fresh direction to Russian life. Kostritsyn poses as his ideologue and spokesman.

Kostritsyn preaches a harsh kind of individualism to anyone who will listen. His Nietzschean credo is at once disdain for the weak and lowly and reverence for legendary heroes of the past. He admires periods of cultural revival and political grandeur and the heroes they engendered. He longs for "that which was created by a powerful and beautiful human race, Hellas, Rome, the Renaissance, the god-like knights, the mythic heroes, warriors, creators, who did not mourn and shed tears, but knew how to develop their 'I,' to dare and to shake people up, to show everyone what makes life on earth worth living" (P, 219–222).

The merchant Kumachov, Kostritsyn's new man, has all the symbolic trappings of a person with the adventuresome Renaissance spirit. It is a matter of pride to Kostritsyn that the man he works for lives in a lavish palace built in the Renaissance style and that he himself has received a classical education.[60] He sees in himself and his wealthy employer the forerunners of a new generation in Russia that will proclaim:

> we want to live, we do not want to strew ashes on our heads, we want to shake people up and to enjoy, not to snivel or surrender what we have created and won and made beautiful in order to feed the dirty, wild and malicious crowd! Never!! And that generation is already coming of age. . . . It was born thirty years ago. Only it was misunderstood and its credo was distorted. (P, 221)

Kostritsyn yearns for a heroic life. He hates the old populist ideals of self-effacement for the welfare of society and compassion for the weak and ugly. Although he dreams of becoming like the heroes of antiquity, his actual role models are protagonists from Russian literature. For example, Kostritsyn identifies with Turgenev's hero, Bazarov, who likewise scorns utilitarian values: "Don't you remember what Bazarov said about the peasant? The little peasant will live in bliss, but a 'thistle' will grow out of me? Eh? What is that if not a protest.... Turgenev's doctor is the smartest person in our literature. Only his author killed him, knowing that he wouldn't survive anyway. Ha-ha!" (P, 221). In contrast to the older generation, Kostritsyn revives Bazarov as a kind of superman and in doing so also makes Nietzsche's idea more comprehensible to the Russian readership.

The morality of altruism, in Kostritsyn's view, has dulled the nobler urges in man. Because the altruistic man strives to help those who are poorer and lower than he, he loses sight of the higher pursuits of the human spirit. Contemporary social mores, Kostritsyn asserts, have produced despicable results, something akin to Nietzsche's "last man": "Look at the good-hearted, clever, well-behaved little man of today. He stinks! It is sickening to look at him! I think it would be better to keep the slavery of ancient Hellas as the foundation for cultural life than to let people degenerate into driveling idiots who strive only for the great anesthesia of the spirit and flesh" (P, 221). Although Kostritsyn does succeed in discrediting the social utilitarian ethic, his morality of elevated egotism is challenged by another predominant set of values, philosophical idealism. An older intellectual and a relation of Kumachov's aristocratic wife, Prince Ilarion, asks Kostritsyn whether he personally supports Zarathustra's *netovshchina*, or moral nihilism. Kostritsyn argues that evil can be as useful for human betterment as good is. However, although he defends evil impulses as useful for the growth of the individual, he is not so sure about their value for social development.

Prince Ilarion offers a Hegelian worldview. He, like Kostritsyn, seeks an ennobling human vision. Yet he feels that to be truly great, a person must conceive of himself not as a creature who shapes himself and his own fate, but as an actor in a larger historic plan. A person, according to Ilarion, can grow beyond his narrow material being only if he understands the dialectical progression of history toward God and spiritual transcendence. "Being is opposed to nonbeing by means of becoming.... And, gentlemen, when this truth pervades your spirit, you will be saved from inconstancy of thought. You will achieve the full profundity of your human individuality" (P, 300). For the prince, there can be no individual greatness without participation in some higher goal in which all humanity is united.

Ilarion's philosophy reflects a broad mystic trend that emerged in the 1890s. Several people, among them the poet Minsky and Solovyov, disliked the gray materialism of contemporary thought. They felt that it neglected man's spiritual nature. In his path-breaking book, *In the Light of Conscience* (*Pri svete sovesti*, 1889), Minsky had tried to define a lofty and striving spirituality in human nature and to transcend mere material necessity. Solovyov argued in *The Justification of the Good* that, although human existence appears ever-changing, it is linked to higher, enduring concepts of the good. These values, he said, give the individual's life significance.

Like Solovyov, other philosophical idealists were often negatively inclined toward Nietzsche because they felt he was materialist in his outlook.[61] Minsky, for example, argued in 1900 that Nietzsche's philosophy was founded on Darwinian materialism: "The original sin of Nietzsche's philosophy is that it supplants religious passion with a natural-scientific one."[62] Nietzsche's philosophy, Minsky said, discredits the mystical, idealist perception of reality that gives man nobility and spiritual depth and separates him from the animals.

Although Prince Ilarion does not convert Kostritsyn to his particular philosophy, he does cast doubt on the vulgar Nietzschean morality. The young man abandons his individualist views when he falls in love with a former revolutionary, Lipa Uglova. He torments himself with the thought that by falling in love he has forfeited his individualist self-sufficiency, but solves this problem by devoting himself to the development of another person's talents: he tries to make Uglova into a great actress. Kostritsyn modifies his Nietzschean principles, resigning himself to a form of slave morality. He decides, finally, that love alone can ennoble and elevate.

Around 1900, Boborykin contributed two more stereotypes of the Russian Nietzschean. One was the antihero of a satire entitled *The Scum* (*Nakip'*, 1899) in which Boborykin again made fun of the new "aestheticist" culture and its capitalist patrons. The second was a novel, *The Cruel Ones* (*Zhestokie*, 1901), which showed concern for sexual license in contemporary urban society. Like *The Pass* these works are important because of their broad appeal. As one critic noticed, even their titles were important because they illuminated for their readers the essence of the latest issues.⁶³ Some even became "current buzzwords" (*khodiachee slovechko*). Most importantly for our discussion, Boborykin's work would have a strong intellectual as well as formal impact upon popular Nietzschean fiction.

Boborykin noted in 1900 that the butt of his satire, *The Scum*, was the "unbounded egotism" of young "decadent" literati.⁶⁴ Although it had very little aesthetic merit and angered serious writers, the play enjoyed considerable popular acclaim. The public, Mikhailovsky reported, was delighted by the travesty of esoteric, crowd-spurning "decadents."⁶⁵ The populist critic gloated over the angry protests of his old opponent, Akim Volynsky, who was now the editor of the Symbolist *Severnyi vestnik*.

Mikhailovsky characterized the hero of the play, the artist Anatoly Pereverzev, as a typical decadent and a Nietzschean. Pereverzev, he wrote, "considers himself a part of a natural aristocracy, the salt of the earth, the 'supermen,' who have the natural right . . . to govern . . . according to their own appetites."⁶⁶ Indeed, Pereverzev does consider himself to be, in his own words, "beyond good and evil." For him "all is permitted":

> Our ego is becoming ever more interesting. We bear within ourselves our own higher world. Only that world is worth anything. We have our own spiritual spectrum. To follow its ascent and its decline, to seek the most refined sensations, inaccessible to the crowd, and to scorn the crowd, swarming out there someplace: that alone is the meaning of life. (N, 5)

Pereverzev fervently believes that his own inner world is the only significant reality, yet Boborykin reveals this world as poor and pale. Pereverzev thinks himself a genius for dressing his fiancée, Olga, in all sorts of outlandish clothing. He congratulates himself on his originality when (in imitation of Oscar Wilde) he brings Olga a lily. The best that Pereverzev's creative imagination can offer is a plan for staging an experimental "danse macabre" in a new "Cabinet Macabre."

As always, Boborykin ties Nietzscheanism to the nascent Russian bourgeoisie. Nietzscheanism is their ideology, and Boborykin as the scion of a gentry family and product of the Populist era uses this vulgarization to its fullest potential to discredit the nouveaux riches. The minor character Nina Vorobina is a wealthy entrepreneur and a self-styled Nietzschean who patronizes Pereverzev's silly projects. She believes her money gives her the right to do exactly as she chooses. "Without the strength of capital," she remarks, "one cannot be—as it is put in Nietzsche's work—'beyond good and evil'" (N, 25). Vorobina feebly attempts to go "beyond good and evil" when she finances Pereverzev's production of the supposedly ingenious and risqué "danse macabre."

Other characters criticize this Nietzschean outlook and warn Olga not to marry Pereverzev. One, a certain Moiseev, proclaims that Pereverzev is part of the "band" of "those supermen," adding that, "it's all right to be supermen if only they would live in love and harmony and not as beasts" (N, 16). Olga eventually rejects Pereverzev's philosophy of egotism and elitism and embraces a more traditional Russian ethic of humility and kindness. She asserts that "one must know finally what is good and what evil, that something is beautiful not only because it is a symbol of something, but because it is noble and magnanimous" (N, 28). She finishes by reaffirming Boborykin's main point about the deplorable shift in mores: "all these words [noble, magnanimous] have been ostracized." Olga reaffirms the widespread impression that Nietzscheanism means the confusion of good and evil, the sacrifice of social values for aesthetic ones, and the indulgence in selfish pleasures.

Scum reflects cultural tensions of the late 1890s, tensions caused by dramatic changes in society, literary culture, and values. Olga, her Uncle Gorbunov, and Moiseev represent the genteel, socially conscious intelligentsia who had dominated cultural life until the 1890s. Through them Boborykin shows the plight of the landed classes who were gradually losing their estates and wealth through agrarian reforms. Pereverzev and Vorobina travesty the emerging modernist culture of tightly knit literary and artistic circles and French-inspired cabarets and literary magazines. Vorobina caricatures the urban, capitalist entrepreneur who funded artistic experimentation at the turn of the century. Her historical counterparts were indeed far more vital and interesting. For example, the Morozov family of Moscow imported French Impressionist paintings at a time when they were barely appreciated in France. Mme. Morozova organized a salon and supported the efforts of young artists and musicians.[67] The railroad magnate Savva Mamontov contributed greatly to modernist culture: he founded an opera company and developed the talent of the great Fedor Shaliapin. He invited artists to his estate outside Moscow to work and experiment and financed the lavish journal *Mir iskusstva* (*The World of Art*, 1898–1904). The Riabushinskys, a family of textile manufacturers, funded such modernist ventures as the Symbolist journal, *Zolotoe runo* (*The Golden Fleece*, 1906–1909).[68] The old guard to which Boborykin belonged were obviously alarmed by these changing cultural influences that were undermining the ethos of the old intelligentsia and violating all aesthetic standards.

Boborykin's last Nietzschean novel, *The Cruel Ones*, paints an extraordinarily unappealing portrait of a Russian Nietzschean. The hero, Matvei Prispelov, is a self-proclaimed Nietzschean who considers himself a "candidate to become an 'Übermensch'" (Zh, 2, 32). He possesses a "satanically egotistical" character but no ability or gift of any kind. He conceals this failing with the transparent lie that he has "no literary reputation because [he] refuse[s] to 'prance' before the public" (Zh, 2, 32). Prispelov worships Nietzsche, keeping a picture of the German philosopher in his bedroom. He shares the vulgar Nietzschean belief that "man is a god, there is nothing higher than his ego. He can dare indefinitely, there is nothing that is not allowed to him" (Zh, 2, 27).

As in *The Scum* and Boborykin's earlier novel, *The Pass*, vulgar Nietzscheanism shields petty and more often repugnant attitudes. In *The Pass*, racism is an issue. In *The Scum*, it is the license of art to produce empty and sometimes sadistic spectacles. In *The Cruel Ones*, the problem is the assertion of "will to power" through enforcing one's sexual influence over other people. In this last travesty of Nietzscheanism, Boborykin shows vulgar Nietzschean values as they are practiced in a society deprived of a moral code. Everyone in the new society, as Boborykin puts it, is in search of an ideal of "supersensuality." Hardheartedness and promiscuity are accepted as virtue. The novel's heroine, Polina Bezrukova, treats her dying husband with "Nietzschean" cruelty. She refuses to pity him in his suffering, viewing pity as a sign of disrespect (Zh, 2, 31–32). Meanwhile, she is dallying with other people, among them Prispelov. In this novel, everyone is having affairs with someone else, leading that person on, attempting through force of sexual attraction to overpower him or her. As might be expected, Prispelov would like to rule the roost, but much to his chagrin he finds that his powers of attraction are waning. As a last resort, he tries to gain influence through sexual blackmail, but no one is frightened or even impressed. Finally, this pathetic "superman" is so angry at being ignored that he decides to prove his superiority to mere people once and for all: he commits suicide after long meditation on Nietzsche's portrait.

Despite his attempts to discredit Nietzsche as a broad, popular influence, Boborykin counts as Nietzsche's most successful "popularizer." He spread an accessible if distorted version of the new philosophy to a broader audience than either Preobrazhensky or Mikhailovsky. Indeed, his novel *The Pass* popularized the popularizer Preobrazhensky. In 1900, Boborykin wrote that many of his readers had taken Preobrazhensky to be the model for Kostritsyn.[69] Boborykin most successfully "translated" Nietzsche's archetypes of the free spirit and superman into Russian equivalents, modeling them particularly on Bazarov. Under the rubric of Nietzscheanism Boborykin revived what might be called the "endgame" mytheme of Russian moral rebellion: the protagonist's revolt against society and God ends inevitably in failure and even suicide. Unlike the other *real* popularizers, he did not stop to distinguish between Nietzsche and his Russian precursors or to use the Russian tradition of moral rebellion better to define the originality of the German thinker's work. Still, the fact remains that his oversimplification was easy for a broad audience to understand. Most importantly, Boborykin's three Nietzschean works would exert some influence on the development of popular literature. They provided character types and narrative strategies that would be appropriated by younger best-selling authors to considerably different purpose. The central character in both places would be a visionary and a spiritual mentor who combined the inspirational tone of Zarathustra, the arrogance of Bazarov, and the resoluteness of both. Just as Kostritsyn lectures on the new Nietzschean gospel, Pereverzev flaunts his Nietzscheanism before Olga, and Prispelov yearns for total power over his peers, so the popular Nietzschean protagonist would gather around him a following, to whom he would preach. The fundamental difference in the ways the Boborykin archetype and Zarathustra would function as spiritual mentor illustrates different kinds of moral consciousness. Zarathustra encourages *self-discovery* in his "disciples." He sets himself up not only to be mentor but to be rival and even "enemy." Thus, he fosters spiritual independence and real self-searching. Boborykin's protagonist functions more like the ascetic priest who imposes a ready orthodoxy of so-called self-creation on his following. For Boborykin, there is only one pattern to follow, that devised by the mentor. This kind of moral rebellion could end in two ways: either in the protagonist's ultimate reconformity to traditional norms or in ruin.

Both Nietzsche and his most important Russian popularizer, Preobrazhensky, died in 1900. Although it is true that Nietzsche had been insane for eleven years, it seems ironic but perhaps fitting for the new cult that his death was noticed less than that of his popularizer, Preobrazhensky. Most adherents were looking for a new, ready-made purpose for their lives, not for painful self-examination. Such a purpose was given them by Preobrazhensky and, to an even greater extent, by the vulgarizing fictional travesties that surrounded him. The only acknowledgment of Nietzsche's death given in the Russian literary press was a memorial in *Mir iskusstva*. Preobrazhensky's death, on the other hand, was remembered by many of his colleagues as well as writers and critics. The September-October issue of *Voprosy filosofii i psikhologii* was devoted to Preobrazhensky. It is here rather than in the memorial to Nietzsche that the concept of "Nietzscheanism" was crystallized. Two commentaries, by Petr Boborykin and Kotliarevsky, are particularly illuminating. Both men admire Nietzsche's work in the abstract and appreciate the power of his human vision. However, both view "Nietzscheanism" as the dangerous destruction of moral standards. Boborykin defines Nietzschean morality as a mood of "absolute negation of the divinity" and anticipation of a "dawn of a new world of truth, light, [and] liberation [from] . . . the predominant morality."[70] Boborykin repeats the opinion common to Nietzsche's detractors that practiced Nietzscheanism is narrowly self-serving: "The formula 'beyond good and evil' has been circulated in the last few years by various petty predators . . . of both sexes. The cult of the self is a convenient way to mask the unbounded egotism [conveyed] in the current free-for-all of appetites, the stir of vanity, sensuality and disorderliness."[71] Boborykin suggests, moreover, that Russian Nietzscheanism has potentially dangerous political implications. This popular philosophy, he says, supports the view that might makes right. Nietzscheans, in his view, condone "any crime against the social order [as] a manifestation of strength seeking an outlet."[72] Kotliarevsky is, if possible, still more sweeping than Boborykin in his condemnation of Nietzscheanism. He hesitates to call Preobrazhensky a Nietzschean "lest a reader, not knowing [him] personally, attribute to him certain qualities which he might have noticed among his 'Nietzscheanizing' acquaintances." Kotliarevsky recognized this "Nietzscheanizing" type in a whole gallery of offensive persons:

> Anyone who is tormented at times by his own moral insignificance; anyone who indulges in all possible appetites, and sometimes very base ones; anyone dissatisfied with the way things are, who is looking for something for which he does not hold himself responsible; any neurotic nature that yearns for the sublime, but has no ability to create it; and finally, anyone prevented by the nearness of a neighbor from doing things in a big way—all these people now prefer to say that they are "Nietzscheans" rather than call themselves by their real names.[73]

Nietzsche's Russian detractors, thus, saw the mark of "applied Nietzscheanism" in a variety of shocking trends among what anachronistically might be called a "me generation." Nietzscheanism, as it would be practiced by its devotees, as it was brought alive in popular fiction, and as it was recognized by literary critics, indeed would become known as a general rejection of conventional ethical virtues of selflessness, kindness, and consideration. These were replaced with a hardness and single-mindedness that critics condemned as callousness and arrogance.

Russian vulgar Nietzscheanism was a worldview taken from a mixture of contemporary issues, events, and moods that were already in the air. Nietzschean catchwords such as "beyond good and evil," "love of the distant," "superman," "master," and "slave" were used to make sense of this mixture. They lent the image of youthful revolt a sharper profile and a desired spice and notoriety. Fiction would play an enormous role in the process of giving Nietzsche's difficult ideas a concrete human form. Literary heroes who read Nietzsche, quoted his catchwords, or modeled their lives according to some "Zarathustrian" principle, immediately became the carriers of a popular worldview that bore only the crudest resemblance to Nietzsche's actual thought. These heroes turned words and ideas to action and thereby themselves became role models in the Nietzschean cult.

So far we have seen a reception process largely resistant to Nietzsche. The appearance of Nietzsche's works and their Russian adherents called forth among older populists, liberals, and idealists a large number of negative responses in the form of polemic and satire. Although in general these vulgarizations were designed to exclude Nietzsche's thought as an influence from Russian culture, they actually went a long way toward russifying it, particularly the idea of the superman. Moreover, the views of older intellectuals reveal an interesting ambivalence in their own cultural consciousness. It is not by chance that Turgenev and his hero Bazarov were broadly revived in this discussion. In the vulgarization of Nietzsche fathers were fighting back against children. Nietzsche's reception highlighted a deep schism between fathers frustrated with their own moral insufficiency and children who underscored the failure of the fathers' values by completely turning away and insisting on an anarchic kind of freedom. The fact that these fathers received Nietzsche's moral thought with an odd mix of curiosity, fascination, and alarm suggests a process in their own minds of casting around for vital values. The new philosophy clearly raised in their memories the heady hopes of the 1860s and 1870s, the discussions of egotism and *lichnost'* (selfhood, personality) of those times, the search for a balance between self-interest and social interest. On the other hand, the older generation as a whole was unwilling to see the virtue of the inner self with its blind instincts and passions. We see over and over in their commentary on Nietzsche the concern that these impulses unreined must lead to a foolish, inconsequential egocentricity at the very least, and to domination, oppression, injustice at the worst. In the minds of people as different as Tolstoi, Mikhailovsky, Boborykin, Grot, and Solovyov the social "other" loomed much larger as a moral impulse than the private "self."

The new generation became for these intellectuals a moral alter ego. The elders saw in the Nietzscheanism of the young the "evils" of their own generation. Their quest seemed like a farce of the radical nihilism of the "new men" of the 1860s. Although in deed there was strong interaction between the generations, morally a chasm opened between them. If their elders looked to communality as the source of value, the young gave this role to the self. The older generation saw wrongdoing on all fronts where the younger generation would see noble striving toward self-overcoming. The forms of arrogant and selfish behavior that aging liberals and populists abhorred were for young people part of a rite meant to generate the transfiguration of human nature and ultimately of society. The travestied picture of Nietzschean-ism given by older intellectuals failed to grasp the heart of the cult: the fervent hope and the almost religious faith in trans-figuration that led the young to look inward and concentrate their energies on themselves. Popular Nietzschean fiction be-came a ritualized enactment of a private myth of self-creation. Because these books were purchased and read in unheard-of numbers, some in tens of thousands, they are evidence of the shifting popular moral consciousness of the early 1900s.[74]

The child is innocence and forgetfulness, a new beginning, a sport, a self-propelling wheel, a first motion, a sacred Yes.

Yes, a sacred Yes is needed, my brothers, for the sport of creation: the spirit now wills *its own* will, the spirit sundered from the world now wins *its own* world.
—"On the Three Metamorphoses,"
Thus Spoke Zarathustra

Yes and *no:* here everything is mine,
I will accept pain as mercy,
I bless existence,
And if *I* created a desert,
Then its grandeur is mine!
—Konstantin Balmont, *Burning Buildings*, 1901

The only reality . . . is man's love for himself, his love for his beautiful body, for his mighty brain, for his infinite variety of feelings. You tell me—who's closer to you than yourself? No one. In your private universe you're king, you're the god of everything living.
—Aleksandr Kuprin,
The Duel, 1905

4

From Populist to Popular Art
Superman and the Myth of Self-Determination

Living the Myth

Boborykin's Nietzschean new men, as two-dimensional as they may seem, stirred a lively literary response in the years after 1900. Popular writers ranging from the relatively respectable Andreev and Kuprin to the scandalous Artsybashev and Verbitskaia used these and other popular stereotypes as a point of departure to create their own narratives of self-determination. What was meant to warn youth away from destructive self-centeredness had by all accounts the opposite effect. Particularly in *The Pass* and *The Cruel Ones*, Boborykin had produced a remarkably stable plot structure and protagonists. Inspired by the heady romanticism and the lust for life of Balmont and Gorky, younger writers polemicized with but nevertheless appropriated aspects of Boborykin's Zarathustra-like protagonists and their adventures. The older writer's work seemed to have the effect of challenging younger writers to go one further: to dispel his negative, reductionist attitude and create three-dimensional heroes who like them believed in the new world to be discovered within.

The myth of self-determination developed in two phases and with two different narrative structures. The earlier is what I will call *living the myth*. In the form of a confession a narrator very close to the protagonist or the protagonist himself tells about his efforts to achieve inner transformation.[1] The reader follows the protagonist through his inner struggles and watches these struggles lead to a different view of the world and the rationalization of a new ethos. The second phase is *teaching the myth*. Here the protagonist, who considers himself liberated and has a vision of future humanity, takes it upon himself to propagate his vision. The result is an outwardly directed adventure story in which the protagonist "travels" from encounter to encounter and encourages the people he meets to change their lives according to his vision.

Three works show the breadth of the search for self-realization. They are Andreev's "Story of Sergei Petrovich" ("Rasskaz o Sergee Petroviche," 1900), Kuprin's *The Duel* (Poedinok, 1905), and V. Ropshin's *The Pale Horse* (Kon' blednyi, 1911). These writers do not belong to any one school. Nor are they linked by much more than their parallel quests for a moral view beyond nihilism. It is true that both Andreev and Kuprin were connected through the Moscow *Sreda* literary meetings and their close association with Gorky. Both contributed to Gorky's *Znanie* almanacs. However, the impact of this common tie was insignificant. It is true that Gorky was a supportive reader of Andreev's early stories, such as the one under discussion. He was sure that Andreev was destined to be a great writer. Gorky also played an important role in 1904 and 1905 in persuading Kuprin to finish *The Duel*. Kuprin's novel gave for its time a stunningly candid view of army life in the provinces. The shame of the Russian defeat at the hands of the Japanese was painfully fresh, and Gorky wanted to publish *The Duel* in a timely way so that its exposé of the Imperial Army would have the desired impact. However, although all the writers of the *Sreda* group were pressed by Gorky to follow his revolutionary romantic vision, none of the major talents did.[2] Instead, each pursued his own particular style and worldview. Andreev arrived at a stark, "expressionist" style that allowed him to explore the dark moral despair and psychic imbalance that he saw through the cracks of moral liberation. Kuprin turned away from the topical, social issues of his earlier work, *Moloch* (1896) and *The Duel*. He developed a delicate impressionist style and treated more personal, private themes. After Gorky went into exile in 1905, he was intensely disappointed by their turn away from social-political struggle. They, along with so-called modernists and decadents, became the objects of his critical assaults in these years.³

Ropshin had no connection with the other two writers. Throughout the prerevolutionary period, he was active under his real name, V. Savinkov, as a Social Revolutionary terrorist. He plotted the assassination of the Grand Duke Sergei in February 1905. After fleeing into exile, he became acquainted with the Symbolists Merezhkovsky and Gippius, who were residing in Paris. He enjoyed the particular favor of Gippius, who admired political anarchism as a form of martyrdom. It was Gippius who chose the pseudonym "Ropshin" and the title of his novel.⁴

Although all three writers sold many copies of their books and were extremely popular, they cannot be counted merely as authors of bestsellers. Their work reveals a drive to achieve a literary voice that is characteristically their own. They set themselves apart by polemicizing with popular writers. For example, in their Nietzschean works, they polemicize with vulgar Nietzschean stereotypes. On the other hand, it is impossible to consider them "strong" writers as, for example, Gorky, Blok, or Belyi were. They are unable fully to master their literary and philosophical precursors, to sublimate influence in their own literary personality. The result is that these works retain an imitative quality that is apparent in their responses to Nietzsche.

Andreev, Kuprin, and Ropshin are of particular interest for our subject because of their relative stylistic and philosophical distance from one another. Their work is evidence of a broad attempt among young writers to see the human self as the seat of moral valuation and existential meaning. In the three works discussed here emerges a mythos of inner quest and self-realization. All share a mythic fabula that starts with revolt and develops through an inward search for self-transfiguration. The resolutions to this quest are also remarkably similar and speak of a definite attitude toward change in general and inner transformation as a mode of change.

The protagonists of all three works are significantly dissimilar. All they have in common is a contempt for their present life and for "normalcy." Andreev's Sergei Petrovich is the most mediocre of university students, a person, as Andreev puts it, "typical of our time." He tries to change his boring, gray personality when he discovers the idea of the superman from a friend and struggles through *Thus Spoke Zarathustra* with his pathetic knowledge of German. As Andreev wrote in his diary, his protagonist "has realized that he has a right to everything that other people have and rebels against nature and the people who take away his last hope for happiness."⁵ Kuprin's Georgy Romashov is an officer in a provincial army camp who finds himself slowly being ruined by the mediocrity and boredom of army life. Although he has come to the provinces eager to improve himself, he now feels his desire to make something of himself seep away and is horrified by the prospect of becoming as unfeeling and indifferent as other officers. As a last, desperate attempt to shield himself from the effect of this debilitating life, he considers the idea of the superman: he tries to believe that he can change himself and the benumbing conditions under which he lives. Ropshin's George is a terrorist who plans and carries out political assassinations. His newest plan is to murder the governor-general of Moscow. His goal is to overturn all society as it now exists. George hates any political system that turns people into slaves. He also despises all utopian schemes as forms of slavery.

Unable to accept life as it is, each character looks for a strategy for change. Each searches within for the seeds of an alternative consciousness and discovers some dream of personal transfiguration that he then tries to realize. All of these dreams hinge on the idea of the superman. Sergei Petrovich's discovery of the idea of the superman seems typical of the way in which an educated Russian reader might have apprehended Nietzsche. Sergei tries to read *Zarathustra* in the original, because there are no translations, but he becomes too confused by the Fraktur letters and the difficult grammar to gain anything more than some vague idea. He learns more from his Kostritsyn-like egotist roommate, who thinks of himself as a "new man" and is appropriately enough named Novikov (*nov-* means new). However, Sergei decides that Novikov has not understood the spirit of Nietzsche's thought and sets out to find his own interpretation. What emerges is the product of his own Russian imagination and almost completely without basis in Nietzschean texts. The promise of spiritual freedom inspires Sergei to look within. He is set afire by the "vision of the superman, that unattainable but [still] human creature that had realized all the potential within him and [now] by rights possesses strength, happiness, and freedom" (SP, 246). The vision shines "painfully bright in his eyes and heart," and it seems "miraculous and unattainable" yet "simple and real (*real'no*)" (SP, 246). Sergei's life takes on a new dimension. He appears to himself "completely new and interesting like a familiar face in the glow of a fire" (SP, 246). He believes that he will be transformed.

Romashov in *The Duel* encounters his own version of the superman that promises to lift him out of the stagnation of army life. His dream echoes Balmont's passionate belief in the self and its ability to create its own worlds. Romashov's friend, the officer Nazansky, is his teacher. Crushed by a routine provincial love affair that he took too seriously, Nazansky has retreated into a life of alcoholic phantasms. He believes that he will be transformed into a radiant, powerful, self-reliant human being of the sort that Balmont celebrated in his verse:

> The only reality, Romashov, is the love of man for himself, the love of his beautiful body, of his mighty brain, of his infinite variety of feelings. You tell me—who's closer to you than yourself? No one. In your private universe you're king, you're the god of everything alive. Take whatever you wish then. Fear nothing because there is no one equal to you in the whole universe. There will come a time when the great faith in *I* will shield people's heads like the holy spirit. Then men will become gods and our very bodies will become powerful and beautiful and . . . I believe in it like I believe in the evening sky above my head. (D, 183)

Nazansky believes that the new individual will be a god who can make his own rules; his self-love will guide him to do what is best and most beautiful.

As he plans his next political assassination, Ropshin's protagonist George formulates a justification for his act, a vision of the free person. He rejects all political loyalty and religious faith as forms of slave morality. He scorns both autocracy as it exists and other intellectuals' dreams of a rural socialism. "If I could," he writes, "I would kill all the bosses and all the rulers. I do not want to be a slave. I do not want there to be any slaves" (KB, 7–8). Then he attacks socialist ideals of land reform: "those old tales seem ridiculous to me, and the idea of my own fifteen acres of land does not fascinate me. . . . I do not want to be a slave" (KB, 11). What comes through most clearly in George's worldview is negation. George is most concerned with tearing away whatever bonds actually exist in his life. He has no strong, positive convictions of his own. Here, just as with the other two versions of the dream, is no real, well-anchored concept of self.

The only real "good" for George is total freedom, that is, the absolutely free play of his own will. Anyone or anything that demands commitment of him must be pushed down. More importantly, anyone more powerful than he who threatens or attracts him or captures his admiration must actually be destroyed so that he will not become "enslaved." Reasoning thus, he murders some—the governor-general of Moscow as well as a successful rival in romance—and psychologically crushes others—his present mistress and a former love.

Although the dreams of self-transfiguration bring results for the three protagonists, it is significant that none of them succeeds in any way in realizing his dream. None actually creates himself anew or builds a better life. Rather like some of their "superfluous" precursors, they waste themselves in futile ways. Nonetheless, their search is tragic, and in many ways they stand out as being better than the bored, arrogant, complacent people around them. For example, Andreev's anti-hero, Sergei Petrovich, comes to a clearer, harder view of himself. He realizes that his spirit is not the stuff of which the superman is made. Indeed, the vision of the superman opens to him the emptiness and grayness of his own character:

> He saw a person named Sergei Petrovich for whom everything was closed that made life happy or bitter but [at least] profound, human. Religion and morality, science and art did not exist for him. Instead of a burning and vital faith, the kind that moves mountains, he sensed within himself a formless lump in which ritual was bound together with cheap superstition. (SP, 249)

Sergei realizes that he has no will of his own and no pressing vision to spur him on. He understands that he is capable only of becoming some faceless paper-pushing bureaucrat or business person. He is like a self-aware Akaky Akakievich who has realized that he is a nobody but has learned to resent the oppressive lack of choice and the narrow hierarchy within which he must live out his existence. He realizes that he loves the simple pleasures of life. He likes simple work but not when he must perform it for others. He recognizes, finally, that he loves the power of money. The worst part of his dilemma is that he understands that he ultimately has no choice to do good or evil because nature bestowed upon him a feckless, will-less character. The only choice he has is to be useful to someone else or to be superfluous. Neither alternative has any appeal. Again referring to *Zarathustra*, he decides that if he cannot determine his own life, then he must kill himself. The final solution is suicide.

The result in Kuprin's *The Duel* is equally problematic. Romashov must fight a duel with the husband of his lover, Aleksandra Nikolaeva. He considers leaving the army and seeking his fate elsewhere but cannot make up his mind. He consults his friend Nazansky, who presents to him another alternative: a philosophy of self-love. This philosophy is meant to bolster Romashov's resolve to resist the insidious tradition of dueling. It is meant to provide a new meaning to the word *honor*, one closer to "self-reliance" and "honesty" than to the traditional hubris and bravado. However, Nazansky's solution has no basis in physical reality. The bright dream of self-determination has done nothing for the clever, fair, and seemingly self-reliant Nazansky. In his self-imposed isolation he has turned into an alcoholic who suffers from half-insane visions and nightmares. He has not overturned bad reality: bad reality has ruined him. Nazansky's ideal agitates Romashov, but the younger man regretfully dismisses it as "just a dream, a fantasy" (D, 183). This realization leaves Romashov with one avenue to follow, to sacrifice himself according to Aleksandra's wishes in a senseless duel.

The outcome is even more destructive for the more decisive, aggressive terrorist-hero of *Pale Horse*, George, who for the sake of total self-determination kills and kills and kills, only to end with the same solution as Sergei Petrovich and Romashov, suicide. The will to absolute freedom, in Ropshin's view, is ultimately self-destructive: George's willingness to kill destroys his will to live. After his final murder, he passes judgment on himself. "Blood breeds blood and vengeance lives on vengeance," he writes. "I killed not only [my rival]. . . . Where will I go and where am I running?" (KB, 134). By killing the man who married his beloved, he has ruined her life. He has trampled the beauty, pride, and aloofness that he had admired in her and reduced her to the "merely human," a suffering, contemptible woman. Through this murder, he has killed his last "higher" feeling, his last goal. The resulting loss of values is stated in Nietzschean terms of the "distant" and the "near." In George's life, all difference between the "near" and the "distant" has been erased. The real nature of nihilism, its valuelessness, becomes clear when George can see no differences. Everything is contemptible. His disdain for everything human makes his life unbearable: "I am bored with life," he writes. "The days, weeks, years drag on monotonously. Tomorrow is like today, today like yesterday. The same milky fog, the same gray routine. The same love, the same death. Life is like a narrow street: the old houses, the low, tight roofs, the corpses of factories" (KB, 139). All that George has now is the "near," the containing—everything he despises. Ironically, in striving for "distant" goals that are by nature earth-denying, he has killed everything: his lofty vision, his ability to evaluate, and most importantly his own best feelings. Finally his will to freedom turns on itself and applies its terrible methods against the one cherished value that still exists, life itself. His final act is suicide.

Nietzsche's detractors saw only one side of the new cult, its apparent amorality. What they could not understand were the desperate feelings of discontent and equally desperate hope for change that motivated what by most standards would be called nasty, destructive behavior. The ethos that emerged in middle-brow literature is interesting as evidence of a widespread reconsideration of social values and standards of permitted behavior among the educated reading public. The previous ethos of self-restraint and care for others gave way to another mode of social comportment.

The strongest shared traits among the three protagonists discussed here are a decisive rejection of the ethos of neighborly love and a militant, uncompromising arrogance. Sergei Petrovich's mentor, Novikov, spurns the "weak and poor in spirit"

(SP, 225). Sergei Petrovich himself soon learns to turn up his nose at his university comrades while he probes himself for signs of superhuman self-will. Their "selves" clearly are not so capable of seeking and thus so privileged as he is.

In *The Duel*, Romashov's friend Nazansky has a much more radical but understandable distaste for compassion. Despite his unpromising exterior, Nazansky is by far the most sensitive and morally conscious person in Kuprin's novel. He hates the waste and cruelty of army life: he hates the way that officers torment soldiers and strut their empty "honor" among themselves. His manner of compensating for his own inability to change these attitudes is to strike out against what tortures him most—his feeling of useless compassion. He pictures compassion as "sick":

> let someone show me what I share with my "neighbor," who may be a low, contaminated idiot! Of all the legends the one I hate most is that of Julian the Charitable, to whom the leper says, "Lie next to me, I am cold. Put your lips to my contaminated mouth and breathe into it!" Oh, I hate it! I do not like my neighbors, and I loathe lepers. (D, 182)

Compassion is too weak to heal suffering. It is the insufficiency of this virtue and the hold that it has over Nazansky that makes him turn so brutally against it.

George in Ropshin's *The Pale Horse* is most uncompromising in his scorn for the "near." He despises anything or anyone who makes claims on him. For example, he scoffs at his mistress, Erna, mistaking her affection for a kind of slavery. He calls her a "little beggar" and is irritated by her large hands and protruding lower lip. It is surprising, then, to realize George can only tolerate the ugly: everything sublime and powerful threatens his sense of superiority and must be destroyed.

The alienation from other people generates obviously callous behavior. These seekers seem insensitive, much like their forebears, the superfluous men. However, now callousness seems more broadly acceptable than in earlier novels. Extreme, even illegal, behavior—self-isolation, drunkenness, murder, and finally suicide—are all more widespread. The particular pervasiveness of suicide raises the question as to why it is a logical or acceptable outcome to the Russian myth of self-creation. In these three works suicide becomes the only "heroic" solution for a protagonist who is unable to accept the abyss of naked earthly reality. The dreams of self-determination that Sergei, George, and Romashov weave have no roots in this life. These characters suffer from the same fatal rift between the ideal and the real as the superfluous men did and are condemned to face much the same fate. All of the seekers find in death an escape from existence; for none does the act of suicide express *amor fati*. Suicide is a further negation of earthly existence.

Nietzsche's role in this moral revolt now becomes clear. Masked by the overt appropriation of popular Nietzschean themes we find a response to the Russian and particularly Dostoevskian tradition. Here is a rereading that revalues Mikhailovsky's reductionist view of Dostoevsky as morbid, clinical psychologist. Nietzsche's philosophical terminology functions as a foil for the moral dilemma raised by the most important literary precursor, Dostoevsky. Each work gives clear evidence of this confusion. For example, Sergei Petrovich in Andreev's story justifies his suicide with a proverb from Zarathustra, which he misquotes twice in a revealing way. He says: "Esli zhizn' ne udaetsia tebe, esli iadovityi cherv' pozhiraet tvoe serdtse, znai, chto udastsia smert'" ("if you do not succeed in life, if a poisonous worm eats at your heart, know that you will succeed in death," SP, 250, 265). Sergei Petrovich interprets the line to mean that he will find ultimate freedom and victory in death. When he cannot overcome his own nature in life, his only alternative is suicide.

Sergei Petrovich's "motto" comes from the section entitled "On Free Death" in which Zarathustra exposes his ideas about the meaning of death. He says, "Die at the right time." Death should be a fitting dénouement to a rich life. In dying, Zarathustra argues, a person should affirm his own life and urge others to live. Suicide is never mentioned in this section; indeed, the subject is raised only once in all of *Thus Spoke Zarathustra* when Zarathustra attacks his enemies, the Christian "preachers of death." The kernel of their message, he says, is "kill yourselves!" These alleged ministers of true faith hate life because their own lives are miserable. They resent happy people and secretly want to punish them. They claim knowledge of a "true" life, a life after death, when all people will be judged and punished. For such people, death has become a way to avenge a wretched life. The quotation Sergei Petrovich cites from "On

Free Death" refers to these people, the "preachers of death." Zarathustra says in German: "Manchem mißrät das Leben: ein Giftwurm frißt sich ihm ans Herz. So möge er zusehn, daß ihm das Sterben um so mehr gerate ("For many a man, life is a failure: a poison worm eats at his heart. So let him see to it that his death is all the more a success," Z, 98). Zarathustra urges the wretched to view death not as revenge, but as a form of self-fulfillment. Even here, Zarathustra does not advocate suicide: he feels that death is the completion of life, not its bitter and vengeful discontinuance.

Sergei Petrovich's interpretation of Zarathustra's idea is closer to the idea of free death propounded by Kirilov in Dostoevsky's *The Devils*. Kirilov believes that "free death" means freely willed suicide. People, he says, suffer because they anticipate and fear death. Life on earth would be joyous and free if the fear of death could be overcome. Kirilov dreams fervently of a "man-god," liberated from anxiety: "man is not yet what he will be. A new man will come, happy and proud. To whom it won't matter whether he lives or not. He'll be the new man! He who conquers pain and fear will himself be a god."[6] Kirilov believes that the liberation of all humanity will come through the freely willed sacrifice of one person. He conceives of a paradoxical solution to his dilemma: he must give up the very life he loves—or wishes to love—in order to liberate himself and others. He is compelled to commit suicide. Sergei Petrovich thus follows Kirilov, not Zarathustra, in believing that freedom is gained through suicide.

Kuprin in *The Duel* confuses Nietzsche and Dostoevsky in another way. Nietzsche is conjured up as the overt influence on the ethos of the army camp. His is the only nonfictional name to be mentioned in the whole book (D, 79). Nazansky, a Nietzschean voice, recognizable at least to a Russian readership, unfolds a critique of the ethics of love of one's neighbor that, the reader is conditioned to believe, is also Nietzschean. However, his diatribe against compassion (D, 182) is a misquotation from *The Brothers Karamazov*. In the chapter "Rebellion," Ivan says:

> I must admit one thing . . . I could never grasp how anyone could love his neighbors . . . I read somewhere about John the Charitable . . . that when a hungry and frozen passer-by came to him and asked him to warm him up, he took him into his bed,

he embraced him and began to breathe into his infected mouth, foul from some horrible disease. . . . In order to love a person, that person must be hidden, the moment he shows his face, love is lost.[7]

Nazansky confuses John the Charitable with Julian the Charitable. Both he and Ivan show the same squeamishness in the face of human failing. Nazansky, however, is clearly the weaker intellect of the two, just as Kuprin is clearly under the shadow of his Russian precursor, Dostoevsky. Whereas Ivan is able to objectify and generalize his moral revolt, Nazansky becomes confused and embroiled in his own fastidiousness. His closing observation, "I do not like my neighbors and I loathe lepers," seems to be a silly personal remark rather than the basis for moral revaluation.

Finally, in Ropshin's *Pale Horse*, George's moral revolt confuses Nietzsche with Smerdiakov in *The Brothers Karamazov*. George's comrade, Vania, himself a Christian visionary, recognizes George's dream of self-determination ironically as the dream of a slave. In Vania's view a person must find something valuable in the here-and-now if he is to transform earthly life and free humanity:

> Everyone dreams of the superman. You simply have to think: the superman. And, really, people believe that they have found the philosophers' stone, the solution to life. In my opinion, that is all Smerdiakovism. They say, I cannot love my neighbors, but I do love those who are distant. How can you love those far away if you bear no love for those around you? (KB, 31–32)

Here Vania counterattacks George's disdain for life and human nature as they are. In order to improve life, Vania implies, one has to evaluate and not merely reject what already exists.

George is indeed closer to Dostoevsky's slavish rebel, Smerdiakov, than to Nietzsche's superman. Both characters seek an elusive freedom that, once achieved, only confuses and throws them into despair. Zarathustra warns against the pursuit of freedom for its own sake: "Alas, there are so many great ideas that do no more than a bellows: they inflate and make emptier" (Z, 89). One of them is the desire for freedom. He asks that the man who wants freedom not say what "yoke" he has cast off, but "for what" he has cast it off. "There are many," he says, "who threw off their final worth when they threw off their bondage" (Z, 89). Those who seek freedom for its own sake become empty and spiritually lost: they are the true nihilists. George is such a type. The idea of the superman meant for Nietzsche the attainment of a deep self-knowledge out of which new, constructive life goals would become apparent. In the process of coming to know himself, an individual apprehends a will deeper than his self-will or conscious impulse. This deeper will becomes his "fate." Dostoevsky's idea of the man-god, however, made the self-will supreme. In Smerdiakov and George this idea is distorted altogether. Both view freedom simplistically as the destruction of all masters. This kind of purposeless moral anarchy leads only to the void. Once their vanity is satisfied, they are faced with their own insignificance. They are lost.

The identification of Dostoevsky's moral rebels with Nietzsche's idea of the superman had important consequences for the reception of both authors. The renewed fascination with the psychology of the alienated, nihilistic superfluous man meant an end to the reductionist Populist view of Dostoevsky and signaled the start of an era of existential searching, this time among a much broader readership. This hidden rereading only helped the reemergence of Dostoevsky as a vital Russian writer. The brunt of the disastrous moral revaluation was borne by Nietzsche. And it helped to discredit him as a popular philosopher. All these characters were recognized in the press as Nietzschean types. The terrible fate that met each was seen as the natural consequence of belief in the superman. Some critics blamed Nietzsche for ruining the young; others blamed young writers for vulgarizing Nietzsche.[8] In any case, most agreed that this particular philosophical-moral encounter was not good for public mores.

The mode of misreading employed by Andreev, Kuprin, and Ropshin has further implications for their place in the literary spectrum of their epoch. If one end is held by authors of potboilers and newspaper feuilletons and the other by writers struggling with literary and philosophical forebears to carve out a unique literary personality, then these writers occupy some middle space. Clearly they stand apart from mass literature in the sense that they work out their own characteristic "signature." They consciously polemicize with the clichéd style of writing and thinking typical of potboilers. They appropriate as literary models precursors from high literature. They consider time-honored literary themes and difficult moral questions. On the other hand, they lack the acuteness and originality to distinguish one precursor from another, and they are unable to absorb and displace the mentors' personality in their own.[9] Thus, their work always bears the imprint of imitativeness and distortiveness.

These works were ideal for the propagation of ideas among the middlebrow intelligentsia, those who did not necessarily bother with original philosophical or scientific texts but read literary journals and wanted to be abreast of current intellectual trends. Kuprin, Andreev, and Ropshin succeeded in arousing discussion in the press and thus in spreading the mystique of self-determination.[10] As readers of the middle intelligentsia received it, this idea was radical and tantalizing but tragically self-defeating. These protagonists never succeeded in upending the prevailing style or moral view to explore other, more productive paths. Their explorations concluded with a sense of being trapped: the existing conditions were unacceptable, yet human nature offered none of the resources necessary to break through to another form of consciousness. The only heroic alternative was seen in the struggle to know oneself clearly and to define one's goals, to live and finally to die by them.

Teaching the Myth

> "I love him who wants to create beyond himself, and thus perishes."
> —"On the Way of the Creator," *Thus Spoke Zarathustra*
> —Epitaph on the grave of the anarchist Jan in Anastasiia Verbitskaia, *Keys of Happiness*

Mass Nietzschean literature emerging in the years after 1905 offered brighter prognoses for self-realization in this life. Self-liberation and self-determination now became a program propagated by characters who already possessed a liberated consciousness. In these novels the range of possibilities seems broader: the teacher has seemingly survived the ravages of despair and the suicidal tendencies of earlier seekers. He has found something to affirm in human nature. He knows a way to overcome the misery and stagnation of the present and to open vistas to the realization of human potential.

This popular literature addressed a specific readership: educated young women from the middle layers of society.[11] The 1860s and 1870s had produced a few visible women intellectuals and activists, but now by the early twentieth century educated women could expect more active participation in intellectual and political life. In this period a large number of women were gaining greater stature in the literary world as well as elsewhere. If they had been important as readers in the nineteenth century, now women were becoming active as writers and critics. They were helping to create taste and consciousness. If Boborykin in his novels and plays had created heroines who were the bearers of conventional mores, now there was clearly a market for more stories about women who sought more than a traditional way of life and realized talents other than child rearing. In the three works discussed here the teacher is always a man, but the major disciple is a woman. The form of self-realization usually combines sexual liberation with some discovery of artistic or intellectual gifts.

This category of popular writing is more cohesive in its development than the earlier phase of the myth. The main reason relates to the stereotypic nature of mass literature: all these works were built on the same basic adventure plot in which the protagonist wanders from encounter to encounter, and the encounters grow in intensity to a dramatic climax at the end. The model for this kind of literature is entirely different from that of the first phase. That group of works was centered on an introspective, confessional mode of writing, whereas this category originates in an extroverted "picaresque" mode. The most recent model for this mass literature was Boborykin's Nietzschean novel. *The Pass* and *The Cruel Ones* were constructed around the same string of "adventures in moral revolt" of a protagonist-mentor who imposed moral revaluation on other characters, often women.

98 The Revolution of Moral Consciousness

The three works considered here are Mikhail Artsybashev's *Sanin* (1907), Anatoly Kamensky's *People* (Liudi, 1908), and Anastasia Verbitskaia's *Keys of Happiness* (Kliuchi schast'ia, 1909–1912). They hold together as a group in the sense that Artsybashev's novel was the immediate model for the other two. Verbitskaia even quoted *Sanin* in her novel as a great piece of popular literature. One critic invented for her the fatuous title "Sanin in a skirt."[12] Kamensky made no overt reference in his novel but clearly patterned his protagonist Dmitry Vinogradov on Sanin as a preacher of sexual liberation.

None of these writers ever achieved real literary "respectability." All of them made their names as writers of quasi-pornographic fiction. Even Artsybashev, who had been a minor contributor to Gorky's *Znanie* almanac and who knew Andreev and Kuprin, made his name writing popular, sensationalist prose. Ironically, the least respectable, Verbitskaia, may have the greatest social significance for her treatments in her novels of topical family issues and women's liberation. This type of literature as a whole has a special significance for this study because, of all the work considered here, it best reflects popular taste and the ways in which Nietzschean thought penetrated and took root beyond the bounds of the cultural elite. These novels sold in record-breaking, multiple editions of thousands and tens of thousands of copies. Verbitskaia's novels sold beyond all imagination, coming by 1914 to a total of over a half million copies sold.[13]

In the best-sellers the mythos of self-determination is worked out through a constellation of characters who discover something valuable within themselves. The hope of change seems justified. There seem to be an internal "self" to be realized and a way to realize it in society. The realization of the self becomes the pretext for interaction between teacher and disciple. The extent to which the disciple can absorb the new philosophy and break free to follow her own needs and develop her own gifts will show the extent to which real change is believed possible.

The teachers in these novels are all self-made men. They have overcome the nihilism of the "superfluous men" by playing out their beliefs in the social sphere. All are independent, but none is oppressed by a social and governmental hierarchy that oppressed or ostracized their superfluous predecessors. Artsybashev's hero, Vladimir Sanin, for example, forms his philosophy of sexual hedonism in relative freedom. There is no hint of the ressentiment of the underground man. He is soft-spoken and attentive to the people around him. Neither is Sanin destroyed by his isolation. He is full of fight and an infectious zest for life that is lacking in the lone individualists. During the summer he goes home to visit his family's provincial estate and immediately becomes the center of attention. He gradually unfolds his hedonistic outlook and welcomes debate with rival ideologies such as Tolstoianism and radical socialism. A clone of Sanin, Dmitry Vinogradov in Kamensky's *People* develops in much the same way. His brand of sexual liberation is proselytized in Petersburg homes and salons where he reveals his acquaintances' sexual inhibitions and encourages sexual experimentation. Both Sanin and Vinogradov work in the sphere of personal lives and private bedrooms. Verbitskaia's teacher in *Keys of Happiness*, by contrast, works on the larger plane of broad political change. Jan is a revolutionary who goes to the beautiful Belorussian countryside to foment revolution. His character combines the hatred of slavery of Ropshin's George with a refreshing Preobrazhenskian vitalism. Unlike George, who is escaping *from* slavery, Jan wants freedom *for* the realization of his vision of individual flourishing.

A dynamism emerges in the interplay of teacher and disciple. While one tries to impose his new philosophy, the other, intoxicated with the possibilities that lie within, fights free of her mentor's influence. Typically the first stage of the rebellion is to succumb to blind sexual drive. Thus, in Artsybashev's novel, Sanin's beautiful and talented sister, Lida, falls (against Sanin's advice) for a brutish but handsome soldier with whom she becomes pregnant. Her attempts at self-liberation are all too short lived. Kamensky's heroine in *People*, Nadezhda, resists the advances of her mentor Vinogradov but discovers the joys of sex with other men. Verbitskaia's heroine Mania Eltsova in *Keys of Happiness* avoids the usual night of passion with her "teacher," Jan, only because he drowns while saving a young boy in a lake. Before his death he had tried to teach Mania about the pitfalls of love and the dangers of becoming a slave to a man. Aware of Jan's warnings but unable to help herself, she succumbs to the cruel, reactionary but compellingly powerful and handsome landowner, Nikolai Nelidov. Like Lida she too becomes pregnant. However, unlike her predecessor, she does not let this inconvenience stop her. After considerable agony and anguish, she has her child and goes on to become a great dancer.

The attitude to existence in these works is buoyant and uplifting. These simple protagonists have none of the withering self-irony or misanthropy that characterizes the more introspective rebels. Thus, the heroines typically survive their disastrous first experiences with self-liberation and go on to make something of themselves. Of the three novels, *Sanin* is the least hopeful, but even here almost everyone survives. Sanin's sister, Lida, does try to end her life, but her brother saves her. Her spirit of adventure is crushed, and she gets married, reverting to the existing life of stagnation and boredom. The second heroine in Artsybashev's novel, Zina Karsavina, is perhaps more successful, although she too ultimately turns back to a traditional set of values. Karsavina is already using her talents as a schoolteacher. She is also a gifted singer. Although she is devoted to a kind of populist, reformist idealism, she too is aroused by the sexual awakening around her. She and her Social Democrat beau try to make love, but he turns out to be impotent. Sanin later seduces her in the bottom of a rowboat. When her real beau commits suicide out of desperation, she is far from defeated. She angrily rejects Sanin's callous hedonism and blames him for the death. Thus, although it is not the kind that Sanin had in mind, Karsavina does attain a new sense of selfhood by defending her own worldview. The major problem with her values is their traditional nature. They cannot, Artsybashev implies, provide a model for vital and urgent change.

Nadezhda, in Kamensky's novel, *People*, goes further than either Lida or Karsavina in turning sexuality toward productive, life-affirming goals. She and Vinogradov, each separately, survive the anarchistic stage of sexual liberation. Eventually they learn not to reject sexual energy, as nineteenth-century fictional precursors might have, but to channel it toward higher aims. Mania Eltsova in *Keys of Happiness* also learns to separate the physical urge, which has the power to enslave her will, from sexuality sublimated as creative drive. She renounces Nelidov and goes with one of Jan's disciples to Western Europe, where she develops her gifts as a dancer. Verbitskaia suggests that it is the higher affirmation of sexual drive in art and culture, and not the brute instinct itself, that can truly transfigure earthly life.

These stories of self-determination all suggest a real shift in social mores and behavioral patterns. Change in all popular (as well as middlebrow) Nietzschean works starts with a negative phase, a rejection of conventional values, and leads to vile behavior and eventually to inner discovery. The mentor-figure points out to his following the emptiness of accepted morality. For example, Sanin interprets his philosophy of hedonism as an answer to the traditional ethos of self-effacement and service to society (VS, 167–168). People, as Sanin sees them, have passed through a period of "revaluation of all their feelings, needs and desires" and now demand physical freedom (VS, 275). After centuries of denying their bodies and physical urges, people are at least ready to grant that they are a legitimate part of human nature. Sanin dreams of a time when each person will fully liberate his body, "when nothing will stand between man and his happiness, when man will give himself freely and fearlessly to all the pleasures accessible to him" (VS, 276–277).

Dmitry Vinogradov in *People* characterizes self-denial as form of hypocrisy. His highest value is honesty at any cost:

> I think in general that if an abscess has developed in one's organism that one must help it to burst as soon as possible. When people have already started to feel all the heaviness surrounding them and, most importantly, the lie inside of them, then sometimes the least push is enough to explode this lie . . . all you have to do is push a little. And I really consider that [to be] my sacred mission. We don't need to think but to do, because we have already thought our way to a great variety of liberties a long time ago. We just need someone brave to come and yell [at us].
> (L, 16)

Vinogradov reserves for himself the role of "yeller"! He is harsh in his general moral outlook as well. Predictably enough, he scorns weak, herdlike qualities of human character and loves strong-willed people.

102   The Revolution of Moral Consciousness

Jan in *Keys of Happiness* is the most outspoken of all the mentors in his disdain for the ethics of pity and neighborly love. He feels that these virtues repress the productive aspects of human nature and warns Mania to avoid them:

> Oh, this pity! Mania, never let this parasitic plant grow in your heart! It is the weed of the soul! It is the cocklebur which ruins the field of golden corn. Its kingdom has no end! If only you could count how many people have perished, how much potential has not been fulfilled because of this deadening feeling—the world would shudder from horror. (KS, I, 104–105)

Jan is more hard-hearted than most "Nietzscheans" in his distaste for wretched and pitiful people: "The weak latch onto the feet of the strong and drag them back. The weak and pitiful drag after us like a weight on the leg of a prisoner, slowing the flight of our soul, breaking the wings of our dream with the weight of their love and their demand for compassion" (KS, I, 105). Love, in Jan's view, usually enslaves one person to another: it is only the rarest form of love, self-love, that frees a person and allows him to give genuinely to other people and to love them. All the teachers of self-determination agree that pity negates the drive to assert oneself and explore one's inner wealth. They replace this virtue with hardness of character, forcefulness, insistence on one's own right to live, grow, and become powerful. Again here Jan is the most convincing spokesman:

> Out of fear of public opinion, that is, the opinion of people who are strange and distant from us; from a sense of duty to those near us . . . all of us trample and disfigure our souls . . . where mysterious and beckoning voices sound. We must listen only to those voices. We must believe only them. *We must be ourselves!* (KS, I, 107)

A prominent behavioral trait in the myth of self-determination is a romanticization of violence. Both mentors and disciples in *Sanin, People,* and *Keys of Happiness* are drawn by taboo or illegal behavior. The new people assert themselves particularly through political terrorism and sexual aggression. Sanin gives succinct expression to this drive:

If [the natural man] sees a thing which does not belong to him, but which is pretty, he takes it: if he sees a gorgeous woman who will not give in to him, he will take her by force or deceit. It is completely natural to do so because the need for and the understanding of pleasure is one of the few qualities which sets the natural man apart from the animals. (VS, 26-27)

Sanin raises an important point here: violence is not condoned merely for its own sake. A person's ability to realize his or her potential to the greatest extent and to take pleasure in life hinges in part on a sense of personal power. Pleasure and power are closely linked. Self-realization does not mean only the intense development of one's gifts and the transfiguration of personality in a vacuum. It does mean, at least in the popular literature, a shift in the power relationship, whether by winning freedom from some oppressor or more positively by making one's will felt in some context. Mere violation of the law is not the aim here: the consolidation of personal power and the enjoyment of that power in oneself and in the lives of other people are. The result in these novels usually extends well beyond debate of moral values in the abstract to mildly shocking behavior, to terrorist acts, and to heinous crime.

The desire for power underlying the new myth is particularly highlighted in sexual relations. Here there are no equals, only masters and slaves. The idea of sexual liberation as the first step toward self-realization conceals the irony that not everyone can realize himself—someone always remains a victim of his own sexual passion or of another person who plays on his sexual vulnerability. Thus, only women who fight their way free of sexual attachments and control their own desires become really able to realize their full potential. Even the most radically self-willed and egocentric of the liberated women, the dancer Mania Eltsova in *Keys of Happiness*, constantly fights with a dark, destructive passion for the racist, archconservative landowner Nelidov. It has a more profound hold on her psyche than do personal ambition and aesthetic inspiration. She is unable to withstand the power that Nelidov holds over her. She abandons her dancing career and returns to the province to him. Finally they both commit suicide. The only woman to free herself fully is Nadezhda in *People*, who resists Vinogradov's sexual advances and insists on finding her own way in life. She discovers her own sense of values, educates herself, and develops her considerable intellectual talents. At the end she even discounts Vinogradov's philosophy of ruthless honesty: "I want to be afraid, I want to lie, I want to hear and say untruths. . . . I've had enough of your revelations . . . . Why should we push the falling man down, why should we meddle in someone else's affairs!" (L, 167). She comes later to the view that disciplined work and study are the truest way to overcome the social and moral lie with which people have lived so long. Eventually she brings Vinogradov himself to modify his views.

There is intriguing ambiguity in the popular ideology of self-realization. Its concept of change, although founded on a belief in the will as a guiding principle and the self as a wellspring of life-giving energy, is essentially change from above, and not from within. Here the mentor incongruously *imposes* an ideology of so-called self-discovery upon a disciple. Successful self-realization, these novels tell us, is mediated through an influence external to the self. The lack of confidence in internal strength and will is also shown in these works by the inevitability with which the "liberated" characters return to some kind of situation in which there is a mentor or even master over them. Lida Sanina is married; Nadezhda marries an older writer before she leaves him and rediscovers Vinogradov; and Mania Eltsova returns to the oppressive Nelidov. As with Ropshin's George, these characters are not sure where to go with their freedom once they have won it. The habit of living under a master is still strong.

The mentor-disciple relationship is carried beyond the fictional situation to the relationship of the bestselling author and to his new mass readership. Indeed, didacticism is an important characteristic of popular literature as it evolved in Russia. As the critic Kornei Chukovsky noted in a 1908 article wryly entitled "Intellectual Pornography," sexual liberation was being received by readers as a "doctrine" on a par with Populism or Marxism.[14] Middle- and lowbrow readers clearly were interested in entertainment, titillation, and adventure. However, they were also showing intellectual pretensions. They wanted to be "educated," and were willing to be "taught" by these novelist-mentors. These readers were aware of the high value placed on ideas among the intelligentsia and welcomed intellectual fare that kept them abreast of contemporary ideational fashions. For example, a reader who immersed herself in the six volumes of *Keys of Happiness* could vicariously travel through Southern Europe, become acquainted with the Roman Forum and other monuments of classical antiquity and the Italian Renaissance, and overhear conversations about Spencer, Darwin, and Nietzsche, as well. In this literature is an ideological streak that does not appear on an equivalent low artistic level in Western literature.[15] The popular craving for ideas would rather appear to be an inheritance from the ideological novels of Turgenev, Dostoevsky, and Chernyshevsky, carried on and vulgarized by writers like Petr Boborykin. Pechorin's thought that the logical outcome of an idea is action finds a new realization here on the level of the mass reader. Ideas of major thinkers are brought to life in vulgarized form through the heroes and villains who practice and preach them.

This method of moral and cultural education of the mass reader by the novelist has decided implications as well for the process of cultural reception. The mentor-apprentice relationship that describes the early stage of influence in highbrow literature does not exist between precursor and best-selling author. Neither is there any of the serious if confused effort of middlebrow writers to discredit vulgarizers and arrive each at his own understanding of the original philosophy. The process is rather one of packaging familiar, easily grasped, though certainly inaccurate ideas that are then stamped with the name of the thinker or easily identifiable flag words. For example, Sanin is labeled as a "superman" (VS, 263). Vinogradov ironically calls himself a "Nietzscheanizing lazybones" and a "salon Zarathustra" (L, 88). Jan can frequently be heard quoting *Zarathustra*; moreover, he is busy writing his own imitation of *Zarathustra*, which after his death one of his followers then tries to publish. When he drowns in an accident, the identification with Nietzsche is reenforced with an epitaph taken from *Zarathustra* for his gravestone: "I love him who wants to create beyond himself, and thus perishes" (KS, I, 138).

The essential difference in the use of a philosophy such as Nietzsche's between best-sellers of the 1910s and early vulgarizers of the 1890s is one of evaluation. If earlier writers were negatively disposed to Nietzsche, these writers accept his writing as a legitimate part of the outlook of their generation. Altogether lacking is a strong prohibitive censure of vulgar Nietzscheanism such as there had been in the 1890s. For example, Sanin's personal philosophy echoes in positive tones what Max Nordau perceived as Nietzsche's dangerous ideal of the "laughing lion." His physical appearance exudes the great health and energy of the "magnificent beast of prey": he has a "tall, fair-haired, broad-shouldered figure" and a "tranquil, slightly mocking expression" on his face (VS, 3). Although he is aloof and well behaved in society, Sanin is fundamentally a kind of "natural" man, much like Nordau's concept of the master. Although restrained among his friends, he vents his primal instincts when alone. During a thunderstorm, "feeling life and strength with his entire being, Sanin spread his arms and gave out a . . . prolonged and happy cry" (VS, 250). His idea of willful, violent hedonism seems a positive copy of Nordau's vision of the blond beast's unreasoned drive to do "what gives him pleasure even when . . . it harms . . . others."

Another example is provided by the contrasting treatment of anti-Semitism in Boborykin's novel from the 1890s, *The Pass*, and Verbitskaia's *Keys of Happiness*. In Boborykin's novel Nietzschean thinking is seen as racist and therefore is judged abhorrent. In Verbitskaia's, Nietzschean/Social Darwinist anti-Semites are treated ambiguously and are even romanticized. In *The Pass* the protagonist-mentor, Ivan Kostritsyn, paraphrases fragments of *Genealogy of Morals* in an outrageous, exaggerated way that helps Boborykin to discredit anti-Semitic sentiment:

> Where did the poisonous stream of hatred, spite, envy, thievery come from if not from the Jews—from those preachers of pity for the insulted and the spurned, for the wretched and the poor, for the leprous and the revolting. . . . They, their prophets and teachers, destroyed a healthy, age-old concept of good and evil. According to their teaching, everything that had always been thought good, in other words, what was strong, brilliant, rich, gifted, magnanimous, courageous, they took to be evil and vicious. (P, 218–219)

Kostritsyn's words are as ugly as his thought. Although he eventually does discredit utilitarian ideals, the reader is made to feel that his racism is in no way a moral alternative.

From Populist to Popular Art   107

In *Keys of Happiness* Verbitskaia makes no attempt to question either the validity of Boborykin's association of Nietzscheanism and racism or the moral value of racial prejudice. Anti-Semitic views are held by the most appealing characters. Jan, for example, loves his Jewish entrepreneurial friend, Mark Steinbach, but feels that he is exceptional as a Jew: Jan observes that Steinbach has the "soul of an Aryan"! Nelidov, Verbitskaia's handsome villain, is a rabid anti-Semite. Everyone recognizes that he "hates Jews" (KS, II, 17) and that he blames the "Kikes" (*zhidy*) for the moral weakness of the 1880s. Moreover, he supports the Black Hundreds and their pogroms. Despite his reactionary, dangerous view, Nelidov is powerful and appealing. Verbitskaia does not judge him as Boborykin does Kostritsyn. On the contrary, the reader encounters him largely through the eyes of Mania who, despite her misgivings, is hopelessly in love with him. She romanticizes his hard, violent character: "Like Achilles, he should be naked. Fight at Troy. Drag the body of the defeated Hector around by the hair. Take women and booty for himself. Talk to the gods as an equal. And with people as their master. The world was made for people like him. The pitiless, arrogant, rapacious" (KS, II, 19). It is Nelidov's brute attraction that compels the reader to continue despite moral indignation. Nelidov's central structural role in the story as the villain whom "everyone loves to hate" and the lack of a strong moral antipode both give him a kind of legitimacy. His views are never disproved as Kostritsyn's are because there is no one in this novel with the moral authority of a Prince Ilarion.

If early vulgarizing novels of Boborykin had the unintended effect of spreading Nietzschean thinking, what influence did the popular novels of self-determination have on Nietzsche's reputation in Russia? The best-sellers helped primarily to embellish and reenforce Nietzschean stereotypes already in the reader's mind. Ironically, these novels that had celebrated Nietzschean self-sufficiency helped to generate another wave of discreditation of the philosopher in the years just preceding World War I. The German philosopher had subtitled his most popular work *Thus Spoke Zarathustra*, "A Book for All and None." Here he suggested that his book would be accessible to all, that is, everyone could read its words and understand something of the issues put forth. However, no one, it is further implied, would be able either to interpret the book in its most profound intended way

108   *The Revolution of Moral Consciousness*

or to resolve the problems Nietzsche raised. The popular Nietzschean craze in Russia supports this interpretation of the subtitle. Readers who wanted to find generally applicable principles could find them in Nietzsche's work. Thus *Spoke Zarathustra* became for such people a handbook of "new" ethics. However, as the critic Evgeny Anichkov noted, for most readers Nietzsche's real philosophy remained locked "behind seven seals."[16] With time, it became clear that Nietzsche was not the philosopher of all, but of the very few, the artists and thinkers who had their own personal dialogue with him. The symbolists and revolutionary romantics would combat vulgar stereotypes at an early stage of their own process of literary-philosophical self-definition.

Our final task is to ask what "precious realities of cultures and inner worlds" became apparent in the popular response to Nietzsche. What cultural and moral values revealed themselves in popular writers' distortions of Nietzsche thought? The phenomenon of popular Nietzscheanism shows how rebellion against moral standards spread beyond the intellectual elite to other levels of literate society. It is important to point out that popular Nietzscheanism at first advertised itself as fundamentally "democratic": it suggested that *every* person could be a "superman" if only he perceived in himself the desire and will to "know" and see himself as he is and then to push beyond himself. It promised that every striving, searching person was valuable, and that every such person possessed great creative potential. On the other hand, popular Nietzscheanism as enacted in fiction undermined its own promise: it finally cast doubt on the value of the lone, independent, self-determining, self-made individual, without suggesting some other sufficient life purpose. Having spurned other value systems, it left the reader with no firm moral ground to stand on.

Despite the democratic implications of the popular Nietzschean myth of self-discovery, it never became functional as an ideology for a whole social group. Vulgar Nietzschean writing gave no clear perception of social order. It was merely critical of all social ideologies and of social reality. Its anarchism contributed to the general instability of a society undergoing a process of rapid industrialization. It is true that Boborykin in his early satires of Nietzscheanism had identified this new intellectual trend as the natural ideology for the emerging bourgeoisie. However, popular Nietzschean literature suggested precisely the opposite evaluation. The entrepreneurial world did not present an opportunity for self-realization to the popular imagination. On the contrary, business and money were considered to be part of the "bad present." Sergei Petrovich condemns himself when he admits that he is good for nothing but to be a businessman or bureaucrat. At first attracted to the "terrible and powerful force" of money, he soon realizes that wealth only deepens life's problems (SP, 263). Similarly, Dmitry Vinogradov in *People* resists the idea of settling down to work at a dull urban job as a contractor, teacher, or dentist. In *Keys of Happiness*, money and entrepreneurship are scorned. The wealthy businessman, Mark Steinbach, is a good, kind person but he has no verve. His wealth cannot be the vehicle for realizing his own dreams because he has none. Rather he puts it at the disposal of others with pressing dreams: he gives it to Jan, who wants to bring about the revolution, and Mania Eltsova, who wants to dance. Thus, business, industry, and material wealth, Boborykin notwithstanding, are not admired and are seen to belong to the realm of stultifying normalcy. In the popular Russian literary imagination they are very far from the dream of self-realization.

Nietzsche, unlike other moral rebels such as Marx, did not succeed as a champion of a cause. Despite attempts to simplify and codify Nietzscheanism, too much ambiguity was associated with his philosophy. The ideas of the superman or the free spirit did not solidify into a real popular ideology the way that Spencerian thinking did in the United States or Marxism did in Russia, or, indeed, as vulgar-Nietzschean ideas did in Germany. Thus, when the youthful craze for personal revolt passed, popular Nietzschean "supermen" acquired the reputation of enemies of public mores. Nietzsche's most accessible concepts eventually entered the common parlance as pejorative terms. The idea of the superman, most easily grasped at least in an oversimplified form, was subject to the most pervasive vulgarization. The German word "Übermensch" sounded strange and even comical to Russians. The critic M. Nevedomsky reported that it was quickly deformed to "iubermensh," a conglomeration of near-obscene sounds which "evoked a crooked smile."[17] The Russian word for superman, *sverkhchelovek*, was acceptable, but its anachronistic, Church Slavonic plural, *sverkhcheloveki* (never "*sverkhliudi*"), could have sounded incongruous if not ungrammatical to Russian ears. A large variety of epithets were derived on the model of *sverkhchelovek*, for example, *sverkhbosiak* (supertramp), *sverkhnegodiai* (superscoundrel), *sverkhpatriot* (superpatriot), or *sverkhsobaka* (superdog).

The word *superman*, like the term *Nietzschean*, came to be used ironically to mean either an unscrupulous person or a person with an inflated sense of self-worth. Boborykin's "candidates to become supermen" illustrated this definition. Critics used the term in a similar way. For example, Mikhailovsky spoke of Merezhkovsky's Leonardo da Vinci as a "superman ... who would as soon build a bordello as a church."[18] Lenin, in his article, "Party Organization and Party Literature" (1905), caricatured "bourgeois" writers as "literary supermen."[19] Minsky ridiculed Gorky's "supertramp" heroes, who professed a "new provincial Nietzscheanism" that would be far beyond the mental capacity of ordinary tramps.[20] The word *sverkhchelovek* first appeared in the fourth edition of Dal's dictionary, published in 1911. Here the literalist, vulgar definition was given final authority. *Sverkhchelovek* was defined as a "person who considers himself something higher than human."[21]

Despite the final discreditation of Nietzsche's thought in the popular mind, we can speculate that it did have a strong impact. Popular Nietzscheanism added to a general mood of questioning and challenge. Along with popular Marxism and other ideologies of revolt, it helped to cast doubt on conventional standards and lend credence to widespread aesthetic, social, and political ferment.

We have discussed shifts in social behavior that were highlighted through the popular appropriation of Nietzschean thought. In addition, a distinct pattern of evaluation of self, of society, of the world, of tradition and change emerges in these stories. In popular Nietzscheanism we see an orientation inward toward irrational, subliminal life and its effects in conscious life, that is, in perception, intuition, will, passion. These phenomena of the psyche are given radical valuations. "Good" is the unique, aesthetically pleasing, heroic, powerful. "Bad" is moral, ordinary, normal. Nietzschean literature shows a fervent desire for the total, immediate transfiguration of the self from its "bad" present form to a "good" potential form. At the same time, ethical sense is paralyzed because it is reviled as part of the "bad," and thus all sanctions against certain kinds of behavior are removed.

Popular Nietzscheanism, in my opinion, shows the deepening in the public consciousness of an extreme mentality that could respond positively to social upheaval. This mentality is based on a profound moral-metaphysical malaise. In the six works analyzed in this chapter, the Nietzschean protagonists fall into two categories: teachers (Zarathustras) and seekers (potential supermen). The five teachers (Novikov, Sanin, Vinogradov, Jan, and potentially Nazansky) convey a view that the world and human behavior as they exist now are totally false and contemptible and a promise that from the "liberated" psyche will come fresh love of life, perception, creativity, and sense of self. The key, in their view, is to unleash irrational "life" forces—sexual drive, passion, instinct—through looking inward and candidly facing the subliminal self. It is worth taking another look at the relationship of the teachers to their followers because it offers a key to how personal change was to happen. All of the teachers are at least kind but condescending and at most scornful of their followers. The means by which they advocate liberation is force: less often through inner compulsion, more often through forms of physical violence. Moreover, the teachers generally are not morally committed to their gospel or their followers: they take no responsibility for the results of the experiments they perpetrate. They disappear (Novikov) or escape (Sanin) or die (Jan), with the one exception of Vinogradov, who "gets his girl" in the end. In the name of discovering a higher form of being, these teachers abandon all moral values.

The seekers, three men and four women, are typically dissatisfied or bored with the roles they have assumed in life. Following the teachers' prescription, they learn to scorn the "normal" life (with the exception of Nadezhda) and believe that they will find new selfhood within. In their experiments, only one of them, Mania in *Keys of Happiness*, finds true self-realization. All of them eventually despair at the limitations of their inner endowments. Having torn down the surrounding edifice of ethical values where at least they had a place, they are left to survive on the shaky foundation of a hatred of the present world and a scorn for themselves. Many either ruin themselves or commit suicide. The one real exception is Nadezhda, who "gets her boy," Dmitry Vinogradov. Having gone through with their Nietzschean quest for self-discovery and self-determination, both Nadezhda and Dmitry are ready to settle down with each other. Neither regrets anything or feels stifled by the other. Each knows and accepts himself. They have modified the nihilistic Nietzscheanism in themselves. Their example of moderation and gradual development, it bears repeating, is the exception that reveals the widespread taste for extreme solutions to spiritual malaise.

Against all expectation, the valuations implied in popular Nietzscheanism are self-destructive. A credo that promised that the good life could be found within eventually led to personal ruin. In the new individualism lurked the same "idealist" duality that Nietzsche felt was at the root of nihilism. There is a fateful, unbridgeable abyss between the "near" and the "distant," the dismal life of the present and the promised cultural riches of the future. Accepted human behavior and codes of valuation are perceived as "bad." The "good" lies beyond the here and now. It is the very opposite of what we *are*. It is important to stress that, in distinction to Nietzsche's own moral consciousness, ultimately the popular Nietzschean mentality admits no continuum between the bad and the good, the low and the high, death and new life. Members of each pair exist in separate spheres. The only connection between the two is total, radical transformation. Finally, the seekers come to view *themselves* as completely "bad" when they realize that they cannot throw off their human failings. Any realizable concept of the good is thus destroyed. All that remains is the bad. The idea of the self as a sufficient creative principle has been discredited. Thus, these popular Nietzschean heroes and heroines end up precisely with the "nihilist" outlook that Nietzsche diagnosed as the sickness of the age. The choice facing them is between two bad alternatives—absurdity and destruction—and they choose destruction. The words of Sanin capture the underlying despair: "I would prefer world catastrophe now to a dull and absurdly rotten life" (VS, 168).

Now, in the absence of all valuative perspective, the most violence is done in the name of transfiguration. In the popular Nietzschean works, it is violence to self. The only "good," heroic act is to deny the bad in oneself through self-destruction. It would take very little—indeed, the justification offered by some credible "higher" ideal—to turn the will to destruction outward toward high culture, toward society at large, toward all human nature.[22] The hatred of the present and the thirst for extreme transfiguration would be answered in two literary movements of the prerevolutionary period, Godseeking with its myth of the Dionysian Christ and God-building with its myth of the promethean masses.

a Christian who is at the same time an artist does *not* exist.
—Twilight of the Idols, 72

For a whole group of Russian Symbolists Nietzsche was a transition to Christianity. Without Nietzsche our neo-Christian philosophy would not have evolved.
—Andrei Belyi, "The Present and Future of Russian Literature," 1907

the true essence of Nietzsche is not the paradoxical affirmation of demonic evil over human good, it is the completely true . . . affirmation of "superhuman"—or "divine-human" [*bogochelovecheskii*], to use Solovyov's term—religious values which lie "beyond" human good and evil.
—Dmitry Merezhkovsky, "Revolution and Religion," 1908

It is terrible to see that Nietzsche penetrates to Dionysus the suffering god only as he is becoming insane—as if unconsciously and at the same time prophetically. . . . In a certain letter he calls himself the "crucified Dionysus." This belated and unexpected acknowledgment of the kinship between Dionysianism and Christianity, until now so harshly rejected, unsettles my soul.
—Viacheslav Ivanov, "Nietzsche and Dionysus," 1904

5

The Mystical Symbolists
The Making of Dionysian-Christian Culture

Dmitry Merezhkovsky's New Christ: The Synthesis of 'Spirit' and 'Flesh'

For several reasons, it seems unlikely that Nietzsche's thought could serve as a catalyst to renewed Christian mythopoetry. The philosopher himself was the proclaimed enemy of everything "Christian." He attacked every facet of Christian ritual, morality, and faith. Christian piety, as Nietzsche saw it, was the very antithesis of human creativity because it repressed the sensuous, the artistic will to celebrate existence. Even Pascal, whom Nietzsche praised as a great Christian, was an "antiartist" who made life seem "leaner" (TI, 72). Positive support for the Symbolists' religious seeking in their art seemed much closer at hand in the Russian tradition. Among the writers of the Populist era were great religious thinkers. Solovyov, Dostoevsky, and Tolstoi were major precedents for the new forms of religious consciousness that emerged at the turn of the century in Russia.

Indeed, Solovyov and Tolstoi lived to challenge Nietzsche's philosophy, and they helped to impart to it the stamp of vulgar amoralism that was central to popular Nietzscheanism. But the Symbolists saw something quite different in Nietzsche's thought. Merezhkovsky rejected the vulgar view propagated by Solovyov and Tolstoi that Nietzsche reversed good and evil, and he brushed aside the popular cult of Nietzsche as a "childhood disease fatal to adults." He treasured in the original philosophy a penetrating search for a "ruling idea," for existential meaning.[1] Belyi mocked the popular Nietzscheans' tendency to reduce Nietzsche's thought to a list of aphoristic rules and commandments, but valued Nietzsche himself as a thinker of Christ-like stature.[2] Nietzsche's thought served in the relationship between the Symbolists and their Russian precursors as an outside point of reference, a kind of mirror that allowed the younger writers to perceive the Russian tradition anew. It transported them beyond the established judgments of radical civic ideologies that had ignored aesthetic and religious issues.

For all the considerable differences between the Symbolist poets, Merezhkovsky, Ivanov, Blok, and Belyi shared much the same orientation in their separate responses to Nietzsche: all were drawn to the religious-mythical aspect of Nietzsche's inquiry, his overarching vision of life and the role of human creativity in it. Although they disagreed with his harsh, seemingly total rejection of Christianity, all responded most strongly to what they saw as Nietzsche's deeper yearning for spiritual regeneration. Most importantly, the Symbolists' readings spurred each of them to the definition of personal outlook: distinguishing features of the moral consciousness of each writer emerge in the process of appropriation of Nietzsche's thought.

Dmitry Merezhkovsky's response to Nietzsche must be treated first because he first expressed the mystic mood of the 1890s and created the context of existential inquiry to which other religiously oriented Symbolists would respond. Although he was at best a mediocre novelist and a hazy thinker, Merezhkovsky was of inestimable importance as a critic, editor, and organizer, as the intellectual who asked the questions and posed the religious-aesthetic challenge to which later writers would delineate their own resolutions. He exerted a personal and broad cultural influence that the others had to confront and overcome in their search for a literary identity. Ivanov belonged to the same generation as Merezhkovsky and was nearly of the same age. Both went through a similar infatuation with Populism (Merezhkovsky called Mikhailovsky and Gleb Uspensky his "first two teachers").[3] This youthful enthusiasm was then eclipsed by a discovery of classical philology and history. However, during the 1890s, the decade when Merezhkovsky and others were probing toward a Symbolist poetics and metaphysics, Ivanov was in Europe pursuing an education in Roman history. Encouraged in part by Merezhkovsky, he returned to the Russian scene early in the 1900s and would then have a strong if belated impact.

In the late 1880s Merezhkovsky experienced the moral rebellion that eventually led to the formulation of his ideal of a great religious culture. He had grown up in the waning years of Populism with its semipositivist ideology, its ascetic morality, and its fading civic orientation to art. Late in the decade, Merezhkovsky experienced a deep spiritual crisis.[4] He had long felt the insufficiency of positivism and searched for some deeper significance to human life. The Populist devotion to the *narod* (the people) did not sustain him. Many early poems convey his sense of weakness and futility in the face of the terrible sufferings of the people.[5] The crusading fire that had once driven intellectuals to dedicate their lives to the welfare and enlightenment of the masses had turned to ash. The ideal of the civic poet with his small, self-effacing voice was a painful reminder that the movement was dead. Merezhkovsky remembered meeting the most famous poet of the 1890s, Semyon Nadson. Their long conversations centered on two topics: Nadson talked about death and Merezhkovsky about religion.[6]

In the early 1890s Merezhkovsky cast beyond Russian culture for inspiration. During his university years he read his way backward from Spencer and Comte to Schopenhauer, the "decadent" poets Baudelaire and Poe, to classical tragedy. He absorbed Carlyle's love of ancient heroes. With Jakob Burckhardt he held antique and Renaissance culture as the pinnacles of human achievement. In the culture of ancient Greece and Rome was an answer to the populist aesthetic that condemned high art as vain, frivolous, and ultimately immoral. In 1891, Merezhkovsky and his wife, Zinaida Gippius, travelled to the Mediterranean. The

Acropolis, the churches and palaces of Rome and Florence astonished him as the work of superhuman heroes.[7] Here was a real alternative to populism, a vibrant life-affirming religious consciousness. The faith that had inspired the monuments of antiquity celebrated human creative genius rather than subsuming it to a social imperative as the populist ethic had. It was in this context that Merezhkovsky encountered Nietzsche's work.[8] He was immediately overwhelmed, indeed "shaken," by his discovery.[9] As he would write in 1900, Nietzsche's thought seemed to be a modern-day rebirth of ancient Greek culture and the harbinger of a coming great religious epoch (LTD, 4). In religious art of other ages the young Merezhkovsky thought he had found the answer to his own metaphysical malaise.

This personal reawakening was first felt in Merezhkovsky's literary work in his pathbreaking article "On the Reasons for the Decline" ("O prichinakh upadka," 1892). Here Merezhkovsky condemned his populist predecessors. He lamented that Russia had no real high culture and announced that great cultural works would emerge only where there was living religious consciousness. Using New Testament imagery, Merezhkovsky wrote that vital culture could only thrive "where two or three are gathered together."[10] The two or three he meant were poets and critics who understood the deep, mystic nature of art. Moreover, the great work of art, he suggested, was a kind of sacrament, revealing eternal truths through perceptible signs and comprehensible only to those initiated into the mystery.[11]

Merezhkovsky's purpose now was to find in high art the depths of religious meaning. The relationship between culture and religion would be reversed in later years, particularly after 1905. Then Merezhkovsky would be most concerned with defining a Christian consciousness that embraced and celebrated earthly life and thus nurtured heroic acts and creative works. Throughout, his interpretation and reinterpretation of Nietzsche would reflect the stages of his own thinking. The German philosopher would provide early on perhaps the most important model and later a provocative rival in Merezhkovsky's quest for religious consciousness.

Merezhkovsky's "Nietzschean" period has typically been limited to the 1890s.[12] It has been argued that Merezhkovsky appropriated an aestheticist, anti-Christian point of view from

Nietzsche.¹³ However, when in 1899 he had a religious change of heart, denied Nietzsche, and returned to Christianity, his new Christianity had a strong Nietzschean sensuality and individualism. Throughout, there is clearly a deep relationship between Merezhkovsky and Nietzsche, a relationship motivated by Merezhkovsky's continuing search for religious values that answered metaphysical need but honored and celebrated earthly life. Merezhkovsky's early criticism of what he called "historical Christian" ethics and his sensuous "pagan" moral consciousness may be seen as just the first imitative stage, a period that has much more in common with popular Nietzscheanism than with mature Symbolism. Still, even now in what has been called his "aestheticist" period, Merezhkovsky's concern with Nietzsche's thought was motivated by desire for vital religious values. In 1900, he hailed Nietzsche as the European thinker who revived the "graveyard" of Europe by rediscovering the Greek gods Apollo and Dionysus (LTD, 4). What links the two decades before and after 1899 in Merezhkovsky's thinking is a persistent meditation on the idea of "resurrection" that he found in Nietzsche's work.

There is no doubt that Merezhkovsky dissociated himself completely from the popular Nietzscheanism that critics pinned on him. Even as early as 1897 in the poem "Tranquility" ("Spokoistvie") he remarked on the moral confusion of his generation who looked for "truth in lawlessness" and "harmony in chaos" and "good in evil."¹⁴ These mistaken searchings could lead only to despair. After 1905 he again condemned Nietzscheanism as a "childhood disease which like scarlet fever is fatal to adults."¹⁵ But this harsh attack on vulgarization cannot be seen as rejection of the source itself. In "Revolution and Religion" (1908), Merezhkovsky distinguished Nietzsche's moral consciousness from the wrongheaded confusion of popular Nietzscheanism.¹⁶ He insisted that the philosopher meant something quite different from the "affirmation of demonic evil over human good" that the vulgarizers saw in his writings.

In this period around 1900 and after, Merezhkovsky entered a new and more productive stage of maturation. Now the Russian author engaged in a concerted effort to overcome his philosophical mentor. He reached his goal not by vulgarizing and denigrating Nietzsche but by "putting him in his place" historically as a precursor to himself, Merezhkovsky. True to the mentality of future anxiety, which sees itself as competing with precursors as equals to create the future, Merezhkovsky saw the great minds of the past as further from the final, perfect synthesis of all historical ages in the coming era of the "Third Testament." Thus, Nietzsche and other great nineteenth-century thinkers could only provide the shoulders upon which present intellectuals would stand to anticipate the future.

Another way in which Merezhkovsky overcame his mentor was to Russify his most influential ideas, that is, to fuse his thought into the Russian religious tradition. Thus, in the article "Not Peace But the Sword" (1908), Nietzsche was pictured as one of many, mostly Russian, moral rebels, including Bakunin, Tolstoi, and Dostoevsky, who set the stage for Merezhkovsky's new Christian faith.[17] In "Revolution and Religion" (1908) he was equated with Vladimir Solovyov, and the idea of the superman, with Solovyov's "God-man."[18] Underlying this placement of Nietzsche in Merezhkovsky's own national family tree can be seen a vital process of reading and rereading that extends well beyond the pre-1899 "pagan" aestheticist stage of religious search. This literary-philosophical relationship would play an essential role in Merezhkovsky's own formulation of a neo-Christian myth.

Merezhkovsky's religious thinking mediates between two valuative poles: aestheticist, earthy "paganism" and moralistic, ascetic "historical Christianity." In the earliest stage of Merezhkovsky's inquiry the pagan impulse receives most attention. Underlying his obvious love of earthy sensuousness is an important reconsideration of Christian ethics that leads Merezhkovsky to his own formulation of the failings of traditional religion and beyond to a new religious consciousness. Here Nietzsche's own critique of Christianity provides a model. In his early historical novel-trilogy, *Christ and Antichrist* (1895–1902), Merezhkovsky makes a vulgar, literalist version of the slave psychology the basis for what he calls the "historical Christian" mentality. The historical Christian type is typically self-denying but resentful, like Nietzsche's "preachers of death." He scorns earthly life, the human body, and the senses and directs all his repressed energy toward undermining and degrading them. For example, in Merezhkovsky's first novel, *Julian the Apostate*

Mystical Symbolists 121

(*Iulian otstupnik*, 1895), the Byzantine Emperor Julian struggles against entrenched Christian influence to reestablish pagan rites. One of his priestly opponents captures the historical Christian mentality when he asks the following: "Should we not be ashamed to be human, to be flesh, to be filth?" (J, 59). These Christian believers, Merezhkovsky shows, are false: although they preach compassion and tolerance, they viciously attack dissenters and resent those who try to celebrate earthly existence. In Merezhkovsky's view, such people are miserable, destructive, and incapable of real love. In the trilogy's second novel, *The Romance of Leonardo* (*Voskresshie bogi*, 1900), Merezhkovsky describes the renegade Florentine monk Girolamo Savonarola as a morally ugly, resentful fanatic: "Beneath the low forehead, sunken eyes burned like coals. The ugly lower jaw jutted out, giving an expression of devilish hatred and pride" (LV, 235). Savonarola is an enemy of paganism and the earth. He forms a crusade to eliminate the "demon of pagan enchantment" that he finds in the art work of great Florentine masters such as Leonardo and Botticelli (LV, 238). His only concern is to destroy, because he is too spiritually impotent to create anything new.

After the Revolution of 1905, when he lived in self-imposed exile in Paris, Merezhkovsky continued to draw attention to the failings of historical Christianity. These views show a surprising consistency with early objections if we keep in mind that Merezhkovsky had meanwhile experienced a religious change of heart in which aestheticist "paganism" was overturned in favor of neo-Christian mysticism. Now he felt the need to acknowledge and affirm the "earth," the senses, the body, the will but in the context of religious faith.[19] Christianity traditionally made the earthly the moral opposite of the heavenly, thus creating an irreparable psychological breach. In "Not Peace, But the Sword" (1908), Merezhkovsky put the problem this way:

> Christianity always did one of two things: by denying all realization, it turned the Church, the Body of Christ, into a disembodied abstraction, into the denial of all real existence, so that the Church became not only invisible but even non-existent; or by attempting to realize [the Church], it turned the Body of Christ into the Body of the Beast, the Leviathan of the State; it replaced the inward union of love and freedom with an outward

bond of coercion and violence which in the final analysis are
always murder, fealty to the Devil, the primordial murderer.[20]

Traditional Christian morality has found no practical solution
to the problem of earthly existence. The two alternatives seem
to be total asceticism, to the point of nonbeing, or physical coercion and spiritual repression. In this article, Merezhkovsky identifies the key issue for a healthy religion and vital culture as
sexuality. The Church as it exists cannot cope with sexual drive.
It represses or mishandles sublimated forms of sexuality in art,
philosophy, political action, scientific inquiry. In "Revolution
and Religion" (1908) Merezhkovsky appears to agree with Nietzsche's challenge that a person cannot be both Christian and artist because one cannot at once deny and affirm sexual drive:

> if sex is the crucial point, the most real and yet mystic affirmation of existence-in-God, then the denial of sex is at once the
> most real and yet mystical denial of existence, of "this world,"
> the phenomenal world, the earth, flesh. "My kingdom is not of
> this world [John 18:36]. Love not the world, neither the things
> that are in the world. . . . For all that is in the world [is] lust of
> the flesh, and the lust of the eyes, and the pride of life. . . [1 John
> 2:15-16]." That is why all attempts to include in Christianity
> the flesh of the world with its growth and flower-culture, science, art, public life—never come to anything. Returning to the
> world, humanity naturally leaves Christianity, becomes pagan;
> and conversely, returning to Christianity, it leaves the world.[21]

Merezhkovsky's literary, critical, and journalistic effort in the
period discussed in this study undergoes many shifts in emphasis, but it is consistently aimed at achieving a synthesis of what
he calls "Spirit" (*Dukh*) and "Flesh" (*Plot'*)—the Christian and
the pagan—in a fresh religious worldview. This new religion
must overcome the ruinous opposition between divine and animal, spiritual and sexual that Nietzsche had identified.

Merezhkovsky attempts to link all his writings of the prerevolutionary period to a mythic metanarrative that tracks the
way from failed ascetic Christianity to what he calls the "Third
Testament," the Christian-Pagan synthesis of the future. Like
other mythopoetic responses to Nietzsche, Merezhkovsky's narrative is apocalyptic. However, by contrast to best-selling au-

thors and to other Symbolists, Merezhkovsky is unfailingly optimistic. He anticipates the radical self-overcoming of human religious consciousness in the very near future. Merezhkovsky's myth appears pointedly unmystic and even positivist in its epic, historicist bent and its obvious concern for historical fact. His approach is "naive" in the sense in which Nietzsche defines the Apollonian (BT, 43). He sees in events a pattern and a play of superhuman forces that can be rationally known, understood, and predicted. Merezhkovsky puts himself in the role of witness to the mythic events of the present and the prophet of the coming Third Testament. He sees himself as the creator of new values much in the same way as Nietzsche thought of himself. Just as Zarathustra points out the spiritual path to follow in order to overcome one's bad present, so Merezhkovsky is concerned to leave the imprint of his predictions upon the future.

The Apollonian historicism at the heart of Merezhkovsky's mythmaking is supported consistently in all facets of his belletristic, critical, and theosophical work. Central to his idea of history is a concept of time that synthesizes Dionysian cyclicity with a popular-Hegelian teleological temporality. In his novel trilogy, *Christ and Antichrist*, he views the history of moral consciousness as a series of conflicts between a *thesis*, the earthy, pagan impulse, and an *antithesis*, the otherworldly, Christian impulse.[22] In each ensuing conflict the contradictions between the two become more marked so that eventually one impulse completely overpowers and displaces the other. So it has been in Russian history. In the last novel of Merezhkovsky's trilogy, *Peter and Aleksei* (1902), Tsar Peter, who embodies the force of human will, murders his son Aleksei, who defends Christian otherworldliness. The pagan impulse triumphs completely, causing total moral upheaval. In contrast, in his literary-critical essays Merezhkovsky sees in Russian nineteenth-century belles lettres the opposite moral development at work: self-denial, scorn for human nature, resignation have taken the upper hand. Pagan vitality has been completely suppressed. These extremes of moral consciousness in the Russian tradition give Merezhkovsky reason to believe that the time for a final *synthesis* has arrived and that it will happen on Russian soil.

Nietzschean-Dionysian temporality is felt in the periodic, historical resurgence of one or the other religious impulse.

124   The Revolution of Moral Consciousness

Time, as Nietzsche sees it, moves cyclically, coming back eternally to the same forms of consciousness, situations, and experiences (Z, 237–238). Thus, Merezhkovsky asserts early on that gods and the myths and values associated with them are resurrected cyclically. Pagan vitality reasserts itself from epoch to epoch, and its clash with Christian otherworldliness creates the conditions for great religious culture. The Nietzschean model for this idea is underscored in the preface to *Tolstoi and Dostoevsky* (1900) when Merezhkovsky hails *The Birth of Tragedy* as just such a rebirth of the ancient gods and their earth-affirming worldview.

The combination of linear and cyclical ideas of time leads Merezhkovsky to a view of historical time as a kind of ascending spiral. Each resurrection of the pagan gods leads to a greater cultural-religious flowering than ever before. The final goal, he makes clear in "Not Peace But the Sword," is the Third Testament, the perfect synthesis of 'Flesh,' pagan vitality, and 'Spirit,' Christian love, and striving for spiritual resurrection. Merezhkovsky's historical consciousness appears to cease on this point. Once the synthesis is achieved, time is to stop altogether. Ironically the future is ahistorical.

The historicism of Merezhkovsky's myth is further supported by the type of belletristic and critical genres he uses most often and with greatest success, the historical novel and the lengthy literary-historical study. In his novel trilogy, *Christ and Anti-Christ*, he examines the resurgence of pagan values in three periods: the late Roman empire, the Italian Renaissance, and the Russian empire of Peter the Great. His religious-aesthetic analyses of Russian writers use belles lettres as documentation of evolving national moral consciousness. Here he finds patterns of moral consciousness leading to the final total synthesis of pagan and Christian and the resurrection of the human spirit. His most famous critical study, *Tolstoi and Dostoevsky*, comprises several volumes and approaches its subject comprehensively, linking biography, literary work, and religious thought to an epic scheme of moral evolution.

True to his Apollonian "naive" sensibility, Merezhkovsky emphasizes the sense of sight over other human senses. He uses an abundance of visual imagery to convey the impression that the historical evolution of moral consciousness is knowable and comprehensible. Works of visual art, such as sculpture, mosaic, painting, always provide the key to understanding the particular stage of the conflict between pagan and historical Christian moralities. For example, in *Julian the Apostate*, a fresco of Christ-Pantocrator expresses the predominance of otherworldly values in Byzantium at the start of Julian's reign:

> It was the Aryan image of Christ: a dirty, dark emaciated face in a golden halo and diadem, . . . he was almost like an old man with a long thin nose and lips severely pursed. With his right hand he blessed the world, in the left he held a book in which was etched, "Peace to you. I am the light of the world." He sat on a wondrous throne, and the Roman emperor kissed his feet. (J, 28)

Julian reopens the pagan temples and reasserts the primacy of human existence. Despite his efforts to revive pagan sensuality, his neopaganism is a tired reenactment of past grandeur. Its waning vitality is belied by Hellenic statuary: "Dionysus,— young, naked, and beautiful, in a half-reclining position,—lowered one hand holding a chalice, as if tired of the bacchanalia: panthers were licking up the remains of the wine. And the god who gave joy to all living things, watched with a kind and knowing smile, as the sacred power of the wine tamed the strength of the wild beasts" (J, 209). Dionysus seems to be neither the just leader nor the tyrant that Nietzsche saw in him. He is rather the tired hedonist who has lost his will to enjoy. For all its grimness the Christian art has greater inherent power. Throughout the novel it is Christian frescoes and icons that carry moral weight.

By contrast, *The Romance of Leonardo* and *Peter and Aleksei* both begin with the rediscovery of statues of ancient gods and the concomitant resurrection of pagan values. In *The Romance of Leonardo*, an apprentice to the great master digs up an ancient statue and marvels at its warmth and vitality. In *Peter and Aleksei* a statue of Venus is shipped in a crate to St. Petersburg to stand in Peter's palace garden. Now the reassertion of human will and reason, the rediscovery of the senses bring tremendous creative drive. In Leonardo's paintings (Merezhkovsky mentions "Bacchus" and "John the Baptist") Christian themes meld with pagan earthiness and seem to point to a higher cross-fertilization of the two traditions. Already here the ultimate synthesis is prefigured.

After his religious change of heart Merezhkovsky's use of visual imagery matures. In works such as *Tolstoi and Dostoevsky* (1900) and *M. Iu. Lermontov* (1911), sight is deepened into insight. Visible detail is no longer mere allegory for moral consciousness. Here the critic conceives of a new kind of sight that admits of disjunction between physical appearance and spiritual being. For example, the rich physicality of Tolstoi's characters—Platon Karataev's roundness or the parallel between Anna Karenina and the mare Fru-Fru—is belied by an earth-denying moral view. In contrast, Merezhkovsky senses in Dostoevsky's characters and in his later study in the poetry and "literary persona" of Lermontov a significant relationship between physical suffering and moral health. Sickness, madness, ugliness do not here signal denial of earthly existence: they mask deeper affirmation. As with Nietzsche's ascetic philosopher who can face the worst and find in it new strength, so Dostoevsky and Lermontov will provide for Merezhkovsky Russian models for life-affirming consciousness.

Evidence of the movement of history toward the Third Testament Merezhkovsky finds in the lives of these various historical figures. These people enact in their own microcosm the grand epoch-making shifts in moral consciousness. Each resembles in some ways Nietzsche's "higher man" in the sense that he contains within his psyche the colossal struggles between two moral viewpoints (GM, 52). All are outsiders to their own time who point the way to what Nietzsche called a *"new* greatness of man" (BGE, 137).

Five characters play out Merezhkovsky's rebellion against traditional Christian asceticism and otherworldliness: in his fiction, Julian the Apostate, Leonardo da Vinci, Peter the Great, and in Russian literary history, Lermontov and Dostoevsky. All share a Dionysian vitality that combines deep sensuousness with anarchic rebelliousness. Julian takes moral-religious power out of the hands of the darkly hating, malicious clergy by reopening shrines to Dionysus and the other pagan gods. Leonardo resists the influence of the world-denying monk Savonarola, who condemned Renaissance masterpieces as earthly "vanity" and had them burned. Peter is perhaps the most forceful and tragic of all Merezhkovsky's rebels. His battle with the Orthodox Church becomes a family feud. The most conservative churchmen have gathered around Peter's devout son, Aleksei. Peter delivers a crushing blow both to his political opponents and tragically also to himself when he murders Aleksei. In *Tolstoi and Dostoevsky* and *M. Iu. Lermontov*, Merezhkovsky finds further challenge to the deathly, nihilistic force of historical Christianity. Through his treatment of Lermontov and Dostoevsky he attacks the will to resignation and reconciliation that he finds in most nineteenth-century Russian literature. The Dionysian, Lermontov, he sees as the scapegoat of modern Russian letters. Lermontov has been debased and spurned for his metaphysical rebellion. Merezhkovsky revalues Lermontov as a writer and spiritual type, suggesting that in him is to be found the kernel of moral regeneration. By reviling him, Merezhkovsky argues, Russian writers have neutralized a force in themselves that is essential to great religious culture.

By contrast, the widely beloved Tolstoi embodies for Merezhkovsky the spirit of historical Christianity in the present day. Tolstoi epitomizes a ruinous Russian denial of the flesh. In Tolstoi Merezhkovsky finds the same self-contempt and otherworldliness that Nietzsche criticized in the slave psychology. His art reveals a breach between mind and body, spirit and flesh: here the spirit mortifies the flesh. Merezhkovsky argues that Tolstoi's strength as a writer lies in his "pagan" ability to evoke his characters' flesh and blood physicality. However, he implies that the "priestlike" nature of Tolstoi the moralist undermines Tolstoi the artist. An overwhelming self-hatred and a paralyzing fear of death ultimately compromise his love of life (LTD, 231). Tolstoi denies his own earthliness and that of his heroes and wishes to lose himself in the greater "truth" of peasant life. However, as Merezhkovsky points out, success eludes Tolstoi: he is unable to resolve his self-contempt, and this feeling poisons everything he undertakes. His awareness of the "abyss" overcomes him.

Merezhkovsky devotes his greatest attention to identifying a Dionysian impulse in history and particularly Russian history. He finds it but always in imperfect form. In the two earliest heroes, Julian and Leonardo, the Dionysian has been tamed and channeled and, indeed, has borne the fruit of great religious culture that Merezhkovsky seeks in his own time. When Merezhkovsky turns to Russian culture, he finds the Dionysian impulse in its raw, barbaric form. Its outwardly directed violence, embodied in Peter the Great, suggests that Russia is young and untamed and has the energy to produce great philosophical-religious flowering. Peter himself dreams Promethean dreams of creating a new race of people (PA, 152). However, the emperor's brutality and tyrannical, anti-Christian ardor are such as to endanger chances of any ultimate higher synthesis. He all but destroys the spiritual impulse in Russian life.

Lermontov is the first Russian writer to sublimate primitive Dionysian energy, to channel it without totally destroying it. Merezhkovsky imagines Lermontov the historical figure as well as his poetic persona in terms of the tormented character Demon (ML, 26). Just as Nietzsche's Dionysian Greeks use the mask of bright Olympian mythopoetry and the tragic festival to shield themselves from the horrors of the savage Dionysus, so Lermontov uses his vulgar buffoonery and rebellious poetic persona to mask a vision of the void, a vision that if fully understood by his contemporaries would have made him a complete outcast. When he probes behind Lermontov's mask, Merezhkovsky finds a dark, tormented spirit with frightening insight into the other life before the cradle and beyond the grave. This insight prompts Lermontov always to challenge earthly fate, to call into question God's purpose. Merezhkovsky compares Lermontov with Job, whom God loved but tormented and whose love for God and for life was reinvigorated through suffering. Merezhkovsky finds that Lermontov with his demonic, otherworldly perspective and his challenge to God arrives at a most valuable attitude to life: in his long poem, "Mtsyri," he expresses an "unearthly love of the earth" (ML, 48). In his search for life, his celebration of nature, his desire for love, he achieves what no other nineteenth-century writer does: he apprehends the "source of a new sacred object" (ML, 48). In Lermontov, Merezhkovsky concludes, can be found the primitive roots of a Russian religious renaissance.

Merezhkovsky finds something closer to the mature Dionysian spirit in Fedor Dostoevsky's life and art. Dostoevsky like Lermontov masks his real vision of existence. Now a terrifying disease, epilepsy, disguises a profound love of the earth. Merezhkovsky suggests that this disease is "overfull"—Merezhkovsky could easily have used Nietzsche's key word *pregnant*—

with "vital strength, refinement, sharpening, concentration of spirituality taken to the final limit" (LTD, 219). In Dostoevsky's sickness Merezhkovsky finds the promise of a new moral consciousness. In his art is his ultimate affirmation of existence.

As Merezhkovsky's search for spiritual renewal intensifies, his insight into his spiritual mentor Nietzsche deepens. Nietzsche is no longer merely the moral rebel. Merezhkovsky invokes the philosopher anew in his discussion of Dostoevsky, this time as literary critic and as religious psychologist. Nietzsche as critic gives Merezhkovsky the tools with which to achieve a startlingly new reading of a writer who had been only recently stereotyped by the Populist Mikhailovsky as a "cruel talent." Dostoevsky is now revealed as a great tragedian and religious thinker. Nietzsche's musical conceptualization of tragedy suggests to Merezhkovsky a fresh reading of Dostoevsky's novels. Decades before Bakhtin coined the term *polyphony*, Merezhkovsky noted the tonal attributes of Dostoevsky's work. We recognize each of Dostoevsky's characters by the way he speaks: they are distinguished by their voices, their idiom. We hear Dostoevsky's, whereas we see Tolstoi's characters, who live by their physical nature. Each of Dostoevsky's characters pursues his own tragic fate rather than "sacrificing" himself to some preconceived destiny as Tolstoi's do (LTD, 119). The personalities of Dostoevsky's heroes are deepened and enriched through their sufferings, which take them close to the "final, brilliant summit of spiritual being" (LTD, 119). Just as Nietzsche saw a more noble, life-affirming moral consciousness in Prometheus the rebel than in Adam who humbled himself (BT, 71), so Merezhkovsky sees Dostoevsky's tragic rebels as more vital than Tolstoi's epic "victims."

Dostoevsky as religious thinker is treated implicitly as the Russian parallel to Nietzsche. Merezhkovsky views Nietzsche's moral inquiry and his "solutions" as forms of "sickness" that signal regeneration. For each of Nietzsche's ideas Merezhkovsky finds a similar one in Dostoevsky's heroes. For example, the diseased frame of mind that drives Raskolnikov to murder the pawnbroker is the result of probing "beyond good and evil." Kirilov's search for the man-god resembles Zarathustra's dream of the superman (LTD, 134). Ivan Karamazov's struggle with metaphysical boredom parallels Nietzsche's flirtation with the idea of eternal return (LTD, 181). As he discusses Dostoevsky's ideas, Merezhkovsky anticipates their significance for his own time. It is by working through Dostoevsky's (and Nietzsche's) spiritual "pregnancy" that contemporary Russian intellectuals can break through from degeneration to regeneration.

The final stage of Merezhkovsky's metanarrative is the formulation of new religious consciousness. He attempts such a formulation through the synthesis of pagan 'Flesh' and Christian 'Spirit' in a new image of Christ. Typically in Merezhkovsky's novels and criticism it is artists and writers who either envision or embody the new Christ. In Merezhkovsky's first novel, *Julian the Apostate*, Julian's friend, the artist Arsinoe, frames the following vision of Christ: "People who mortify their bodies and souls in the desert are different from the meek son of Mary. He loved children, and freedom, and joyous festivals, and lush white lilies. He loved beauty, Julian! But we have forsaken him, our spirits have become dark and confused" (J, 336).

Merezhkovsky rejects the severe Christ of historical Christianity but discovers the true Christ, who loves and celebrates the earth. Leonardo presents a fresh synthesis of the pagan and Christian in his image of Christ. Leonardo considers himself a Christian although many think him a servant of the "Antichrist." He rejects the ethic of self-denial and obedience but reveres and practices more loyally than anyone else his own concept of love. He hates Savonarola, who himself despises the earth and fills his listeners with fear of the Last Judgment. Like Zarathustra he embraces a spiritual attitude of gaiety and lightness. Leonardo's ideal of goodness is St. Francis of Assisi, who, though a monk, preached love of the earth and something like the "gay science" of Nietzsche's philosophical asceticism. "St. Francis of Assisi," Leonardo remarks, "called despair the worst of vices and asserted that whoever wants to please God must always be of good cheer" (L, 379). Leonardo's Christian vision contains the seeds of future greatness, and his art affirms and celebrates both the human and the divine. However, Leonardo lacks the power to convince and inspire others with his vision. Even his pupils still judge him by historical Christian standards as Antichrist. In this view, Dionysus is really the Devil. As a result many of Leonardo's works are destroyed and he remains at the mercy of princely patrons and ecclesiastical judges.

In Russian history, the true forerunners of neo-Christianity are to be found among writers. At the threshold of his own time, Merezhkovsky attempts some synthesis of Dostoevsky and Tolstoi that would give both the artistic gift and the religious substance for a sustaining religious-cultural vision. Tolstoi is the pagan who suffers from his paganism. He sees it as vanity and finally turns to a priestly ascetic form of life. In contrast, Dostoevsky's characters are disembodied, his outlook seemingly otherworldly. Yet through his close brush with death, his suffering in the camps, his struggle with epilepsy he comes to a passionate affirmation of this world. Dostoevsky and Tolstoi, in the combination of their experiences, are the originators of the coming moral consciousness (LTD, 188).

Merezhkovsky's ultimate model of the higher man combines in himself both pagan and Christian but in a remarkably un-Christian mold. Merezhkovsky looks back beyond the Populist era that produced Christian seekers like Tolstoi and Dostoevsky to the balanced, harmonized "aristocratic" era of Pushkin. Pushkin, Merezhkovsky writes in 1906, represents the essential quality needed for the coming synthesis, the ability to uncover higher harmony in spiritual conflict: "The essential condition of all creativity destined to have universal-historical significance is the presence and interaction, in varying degrees of harmony, of two poles: the new mysticism, the denial of one's ego in God, and paganism, the apotheosis of one's ego in heroic acts" (Pushkin, 72). Like Nietzsche's philosopher, Merezhkovsky's Pushkin creates his own style and personality through conflict. He celebrates existence in himself. The difference is that Merezhkovsky's ideal human operates in a dualist metaphysical framework. If Nietzsche's philosopher carries on an inner struggle between master and slave moral-psychological impulses, Merezhkovsky's new Christian struggles between an idea of the eternal God and an idea of self as God.

Merezhkovsky's dialectical scheme never really jelled into plausible myth. Andrei Belyi compared Merezhkovsky's work to the Eiffel Tower, whose foundations are visible but whose summit is hidden in the fog.[23] The older Symbolist's work was confused and lost in abstraction. Although he sowed the seeds of mythopoetic thinking, he himself never succeeded in turning historical narratives into mythopoetry. His historical characters remained exemplars of a cosmic scheme and never became flesh and blood. His ideology lacked passion. Nevertheless, Merezhkovsky's vision was suggestive enough to invite a whole generation of poets to rethink their values. Merezhkovsky felt more keenly than anyone the nature of what the philosopher Berdiaev called "our renaissance": indeed, he was one of its major instigators.[24] In the years between 1898 and 1905 he was very active in organizing and orchestrating a revival of a religious culture. He collaborated in the neo-Idealist journal *Severnyi vestnik* when it pulled away from outlived civic-populist aesthetic dogma. He published in the early modernist journal *Mir iskusstva*. He and Gippius organized the St. Petersburg Religious-Philosophical Meetings from 1899 to 1904. Here a few members of the Church hierarchy, prominent thinkers, and writers all met to discuss theosophical and aesthetic issues. Merezhkovsky and Gippius edited two journals that formed the heart of early mystical Symbolism, *Novyi put'* *(The New Way)* and *Voprosy zhizni (Questions of Life)*.

Merezhkovsky succeeded in what had been a relative artistic wasteland in raising in writers' imaginations the possibility of a different kind of art, which heralded more than just itself or focused on themes other than human misery. More importantly, he probed a new way of thinking that motivated and nurtured all kinds of creative activity. The "mystical realism" of his neo-Christian thought replaced the otherworldly, antiartistic dualism of historical Christianity with a metaphysical dualism that celebrated earthly existence perhaps more than the eternal. Although God as an otherworldly idea had failed, the taste for the eternal lingered. With his search for resurrection in his own time, Merezhkovsky tried to satisfy both the desire to live and flourish and the need for metaphysical meaning.

We can return now to our original question about Nietzsche as predecessor to neo-Christian myth. Nietzsche's thought clearly provided a challenge to Christianity that spurred Merezhkovsky toward a more vital religious view. In his reading of the philosopher, Merezhkovsky found a moral consciousness, an orientation toward religion and culture, that suggested new insight into the Russian literary heritage. And, in turn, Merezhkovsky enriched Russian critical insight into Nietzsche's thought.

His reading pointed the way beyond the vulgarization of Nietzsche in popular art. Well before other critics Merezhkovsky hinted at the philosopher's close ties to the Christian tradition.

Although the Symbolists generally saw Nietzsche's moral consciousness as too aestheticist, they recognized in his work new religious sensibility. Merezhkovsky's reading of Nietzsche prompted him to look for a great religious idea in Russian literature, something akin to the spirit of rebirth in the Greek god Dionysus. He found it in Dostoevsky's and Solovyov's idea of the god-man, the human embodiment of the eternal.

Nietzsche's inquiry into moral consciousness gave Merezhkovsky powerful tools to undermine his populist predecessors, to reread Russian literary history, and to gain a new overarching vision. Populism in the person of Lev Tolstoi was devalued through comparison to the priest mentality. Tolstoi's denial of the body and the senses gives way to an "earthly mysticism." Even at its most abstract and schematic Merezhkovsky's writing is saturated with at least the desire to affirm human existence, sexuality, and the senses, particularly for their sublimation in creative activity.

Merezhkovsky's rereading of Russian literary history led to a total revaluation of the *raznochinets*-populist aesthetic. Now the socially committed writer is placed at the bottom. In terms of the representation of a great religious idea "naturalist," philosophically materialist writers like Gorky are considered nihilists and assigned to the bottom rung. Chekhov is situated only slightly higher. Gogol, who was highly prized by Belinsky, is valued by Merezhkovsky for a different reason: because he recognized the "evil" of materialism. Moral rebels are put near the top of Merezhkovsky's hierarchy. Of these the "Galilean" Tolstoi is the lowest because of his "priestly" denial of the 'Flesh.' At the top are "Dionysian" spirits, Lermontov and Dostoevsky. On the pinnacle stands the national genius, Pushkin, whom Populists and particularly the nihilists of the 1860s had dethroned. Pushkin clearly possesses the ability of the "higher man" to harmonize and synthesize in his works warring valuations of the pagan and the Christian, the Flesh and the Spirit, the earthly and the eternal. He is a prefiguration of the coming Russian Renaissance. Merezhkovsky's critical work with its aesthetic-religious revaluation of the Russian heritage was perhaps his most valuable and enduring contribution to the definition of a new moral consciousness.

Finally and most importantly, Nietzsche's philosophy of morals—and not Russian Christian mysticism—could suggest to Merezhkovsky a new religious view because it offered an orientation toward existence that seemed to be lacking in Russian letters. As Merezhkovsky put it, the greatest Russian moral rebels affirmed existence through negation of it: Lermontov and Dostoevsky brought an "unearthly love of the earth." If we may indulge in a characteristically Merezhkovskian reversal of terms, we can observe that Nietzsche complemented the Russian tradition with an "earthly love of the unearthly." That is, he offered a system of valuation that was not otherworldly and did not devalue human nature as such but that embraced opposite valuations and inspired higher striving. Nietzsche's dualism was founded in earthly realities and affirmed and bolstered earthly potentialities. His idea of cyclic self-overcoming bridged the gap between his earthliness and the Russian idea of resurrection in which Merezhkovsky found the essence of eternity. Ultimately, Merezhkovsky came through Nietzsche to his own set of this-worldly oppositions. In place of "earth-heaven" and "human-divine," he arrived at "Flesh-Spirit" and "human-God-man." The result was of a piece with the Russian tradition, but it had been enabled through the strange-making mirror of Nietzsche.

Christ in the Underworld: The Myth of Christ-Dionysus

Merezhkovsky's neo-Christian explorations spurred younger Symbolists to formulate their own religio-aesthetic views. His presence contributed strongly to an atmosphere of heightened expectation and metaphysical searching. Nonetheless, although Merezhkovsky helped to establish the terms of the new consciousness, he remained essentially a midwife to later, artistically more productive versions of neo-Christian myth. Younger writers felt the insufficiency of his outlook. Belyi identified one major weakness as the diffuse, abstract character of Merezhkovsky's writing.[25] Aleksandr Blok cast doubt on Merezhkovsky's central idea of synthesis of pagan and Christian impulses.[26] In his view, earthly and divine truths inherently contradicted each other. Life was conflict and paradox, and to synthesize and harmonize was to negate life itself.

Although it aimed at mythmaking, Merezhkovsky's theory never succeeded in becoming living myth, that is, a true narrative that linked human and superhuman, that established a "right" order of things on earth. It was too schematic, focusing on external historical patterns rather than internal experience. Despite Merezhkovsky's professed voluntarism, his historical heroes and, to a lesser extent, his literary figures remained marionettes controlled by a grand historical plan. In contrast to the work of two great precursors, Solovyov and Nietzsche, Merezhkovsky's theory set forth neither a religious attitude nor a psychology of creativity.

Merezhkovsky did succeed in establishing a distinctive trend within the much broader rediscovery of Christian spirituality among intellectuals at the turn of the century: he embedded Nietzsche's high valuation of creative drive within the Christian context. Many members of the Religious-Philosophical Meetings in St. Petersburg and the Solovyov Society in Moscow, for example, Sergei Bulgakov or Evgeny Trubetskoi, would decidedly have disagreed with this combination of seemingly irreconcilable moral views.[27] For them, Nietzsche was a misguided if brilliant nihilist, something like Ivan Karamazov. However, Belyi's observation holds: for a group of Symbolist poets and theorists Nietzsche was a bridge to new Christian thinking. Merezhkovsky had carried through his own idiosyncratic synthesis of 'Flesh' and 'Spirit.' Now the exercise of grappling with the paradoxical relationship between Dionysus and Christ led each Symbolist, Ivanov, Belyi, and Blok, to the formulation of his own particular mythos.

This treatment begins with Viacheslav Ivanov, who before he appeared on the St. Petersburg Symbolist scene had arrived independently at a Christian-Dionysian worldview. With much greater vitality and artistic-philosophical maturity than Merezhkovsky, Ivanov charted an inward "mystery" of spiritual-psychic renewal. Instead of a grand, imminent historical synthesis, Ivanov proposed a ritual of immanent transfiguration.

During the mid-1890s Ivanov conflated Vladimir Solovyov's idea of "sexual love" with the concept of the Dionysian in a myth of personal religious epiphany. He had discovered *Birth of Tragedy* in 1891.[28] Nietzsche's thought, Ivanov wrote in an autobiographical letter, helped him to redefine his own moral vision and, most importantly, his concept of love. This shift had an immediate impact on his personal life. It led him to break a marriage based on a traditional ethic of kindness and obligation to join in one of ecstatic, mystical self-discovery:

> Nietzsche became ever more fully and powerfully the master of my thoughts. This Nietzscheanism helped me—cruelly and responsibly but—honestly speaking—correctly to make the choice facing me in 1895 between a deep and tender affection . . . and a new, wholly gripping love which was destined from that time only to grow and deepen spiritually but which in those first days seemed to me and to her with whom I had fallen in love, just a criminal, dark, demonic passion. . . . Through the other each of us discovered himself and more than just himself: I would say we found God. (SS II, 19–20)

In this state of being in love resides the kernel of a mythic event of self-transfiguration, of rediscovery of a greater, wholer self and of a divine wholeness in the relationship with the beloved. This kernel would develop into a mystical-psychic rite of creative release in Ivanov's aesthetic theory.

Ivanov developed his Dionysian-Christian religious views first in a long essay entitled "On the Hellenic Religion of the Suffering God." He first read it as a series of lectures in 1903 in Paris. Soon thereafter Merezhkovsky wrote from St. Petersburg asking to publish the work in his religious-literary journal *Novyi put'* (SS, II, 21). Thereafter Ivanov's Russian audience drew him increasingly back to Russia after long years in Europe. In 1905 he settled in St. Petersburg and for a few years replaced Merezhkovsky and Gippius (who were at this time in Paris) as the center of Symbolist literary life. His literary Wednesdays helped to ferment a mystical Christian-Dionysian literary cult.

Ivanov criticized his German mentor Nietzsche for looking on the Greek god Dionysus only as an aesthetic principle.[29] His own interpretation made the god into the embodiment of sexual drive sublimated as mythopoetic creativity and religious feeling. He set the higher cultural aspect of the Dionysian in perspective as part of a mystic experience of achieving "ecstasy." With both Nietzsche in *Genealogy of Morals* and Solovyov in *On the Meaning of Love,* Ivanov sees sublimation as the psychological process by which brute, outwardly directed instinctual drive is channeled inward to become conscious, value-giving power. Raw sexual passion, for Ivanov, is the primordial ground from which springs spiritual consciousness and creative inspiration. In erotic passion is born what he calls "dangerous madness" ("opasnoe bezumie").[30] This force, turned inward and sublimated, is transfigured. Thus channeled, it becomes the life blood of fruitful higher activity.

When Ivanov first read Nietzsche in the 1890s, he embraced the archindividualism he sensed in Nietzsche's work. Visiting Solovyov in the late 1890s he announced arrogantly that he disagreed with everything that the Russian mystic had written. Solovyov's response was an affectionate hug and the observation that "you won't stop at Nietzscheanism."[31] By 1904, Ivanov had rejected the apotheosis of ego that had first attracted him (and most early readers) but had opened up another more profound aspect of Nietzsche's thought, his religious seeking. It is Nietzsche's effort to justify human suffering and his attempt through Zarathustra to overcome his greatest rival, Christ, that calls forth a deep affinity in Ivanov.

Through academic study of the Dionysian cult and through personal religious exploration Ivanov reaches his own interpretation of Christian myth. As Fedor Stepun points out, the Dionysian and the Christian are never identical in Ivanov's work. While Dionysus was indeed a god to the ancient Greek, for Ivanov he symbolizes a psychological state. However, the real object of faith and model for personal appropriation is Christ. Although Ivanov does give Christ some Dionysian qualities, it is still the Christian myth of crucifixion and resurrection that remains dominant in his moral consciousness. In "The Hellenic Religion," Ivanov views the Dionysian cult as a precursor to Christianity. Here he formalizes the parallel between Dionysian orgy and Christian crucifixion. Both rites ultimately celebrate human existence because they embrace its deepest paradoxes. They deny nothing. Here Ivanov sees the mythic union of opposites—vitality and destructive violence, self and other, male and female, human and divine. Christ and his mythic predecessor Dionysus represent life as overabundance and creative energy on one hand, and death, murder, and anarchy on the other. The human psyche's striving toward the god represents an affirmation of the self and an ultimate sacrifice and destruction of the self. As Ivanov writes in "The Hellenic Religion," "the passionate striving toward God shatters the limited individuality of a person: where love awakens, the ego dies."[32] Sexual orgasm is here the central metaphor for the process of seeking and encountering the god. In erotic frenzy, a person gives up his "ego" or what Zarathustra calls the "small reason" and discovers the deep-lying "Self." Now a person achieves a state of "ecstasy": he literally "stands outside himself" and experiences a fuller, broader consciousness. The human spirit encounters the god, and transformative energies are released: individual joins whole, profane becomes sacred, and the destruction of the ego unleashes a new sense of life.

Ivanov views the creative process as a mystical-orgiastic experience of seeking the god within. In "The Symbology of Esthetic Origins" (1905), he borrows Nietzsche's geometric and geographic images as a metaphor of the psychic landscape (SS, I, 824). If for Nietzsche the flat line—the plain, the desert, the sea, the horizon—is a symbol of "nature," meaninglessness, for Ivanov it represents the psychological and metaphysical singularity, the monism of materialist thought. This line, Ivanov writes, ignores the life of the psyche and has no relation to creative inspiration. For Nietzsche, mountains and valleys, ascent and descent are related to introspection, the quest for one's fate, and the creation of meaning. To Ivanov, the ascending spiral and ascending and descending lines symbolize the spirit's interaction with the god. This interaction, he writes, has three basic stages: ascent, return to earth, and descent to dark chaos.

The parallels between this mythic construct and its Christian model are clear. Christ ascends to Golgotha and is crucified; he is then carried down and buried and then descends into Hell. Just as the Christian passion brings resurrection, so the conclusion of Ivanov's mythic rite is to be spiritual transfiguration and creative release. In its first stage, the "ego" rebels against its earthly condition. Ivanov calls this stage *bogoborchestvo*, or "struggling with the god." Affirming itself and its power, the human ego ascends and challenges the god. Implicit in this challenge, according to Ivanov, is a tragic yearning to sacrifice the ego to the god: "The person who raises a sacrifice heavenward, also brings the divine to earth and becomes a bearer of the god (*bogonosets*). The god-wrestling and god-bearing passion of ascent results in fulfillment through sacrifice" (SS, I, 824). The god answers the striving spirit by descending to earth and becoming visible as beauty. Here Ivanov quotes from *Thus Spoke Zarathustra*: "When a power becomes merciful and descends into the visible world,—I call this descent Beauty." Creative transfiguration cannot take place without the third stage: descent into the "demonic" realm of Dionysus. This realm within parallels Zarathustra's idea of the "Self," the great subconsious life force (Z, 61–62). Out of anarchy, out of the limitless, tumultuous void comes intense energy that realizes itself in Apollonian form, in the creation of the knowable and perceptible. Ivanov stresses the role of sexual passion in this process:

> In these depths of pregnant night, where the profoundest roots of sexuality dwell there is no division of sexes. If ascent is masculine, and descent corresponds to the feminine principle,—if there shines Apollo and here smiles Aphrodite,—then chaos is the realm of the bisexual, male-female Dionysus. Here becoming joins both sexes in dark conception. (SS, I, 829)

Creative willing thus involves giving up one's ego and joining with the god. The creative person becomes the vehicle, the Apollonian form, through which the god is manifested.

The link between Dionysus and Christ is explored in Ivanov's work on several planes. On the level of mythic narrative, the torment of Dionysus and the crucifixion of Christ are seen as similar mythemes invoking the renewal of life. Another parallel can be seen in the role of erotic love in religious renewal. The same goal of *sobornost'*, the reunion of part with whole, is achieved through the ancient, brutal Dionysian orgy and the refined Solovyovian idea of "sexual love," the sexual union between Christ and Sophia (the principle of Divine Wisdom), spirit and flesh, lover and beloved. In contrast to Stepun, I believe it is evident here that Ivanov's image of Christ has shed its otherworldly aspect and has taken on a sensuous, earthly life-giving aspect. Ivanov's Christ has reappropriated its Dionysian heritage.

Ivanov's Christian-Dionysian myth implies a definite moral view. It has often been claimed that the Symbolists foresook ethics in their search for aesthetics.[33] This view does not hold for any of the mystical Symbolists, and particularly not for Ivanov. Throughout his essays on aesthetics he revalues and reappropriates conventional values. Although in "The Hellenic Religion of the Suffering God" Ivanov argues that "morality" as such is a sign of waning vitality, later, in "Nietzsche and Dionysus" (1904), he affirms instead that both Dionysian and Christian "ideas" are equally based on a "slave" morality (SS, I, 723). And in the article "Athena's Spear" (1904), he questions the widely held view that Symbolist artistic and religious searchings are "antisocial," which in the populist-civic tradition is tantamount to "antimoral." Art, Ivanov argues, has a strong "collective" (*sobornyi*) character: it strives to uncover what is essential and shared in human existence.

This vision of Christian myth gives new meaning to virtues of self-sacrifice and love. If traditional Russian Christianity is oriented toward personal imitation of the whole life of Christ, then Ivanov's focuses on enacting the moment of spiritual renewal, the point of self-sacrifice to the god and release from the small ego. In this connection, Ivanov revalues Christian love: if love of the neighbor traditionally implies fulfillment of obligation, then Ivanov's idea of love as discovery of the other is an integral part of self-discovery and brings about a release from the constraints of the small ego. Thus, instead of an ethos of externally imposed duty and self-denial, Ivanov conceives of a more compelling and organic ethos of love as mutual self-discovery and enrichment through interaction with the other.

Ivanov and the younger Symbolists would differ from their predecessors, for example, Merezhkovsky, Briusov, and Balmont, and indeed from the contemporary popular ethos in their evaluation of individual will. In "Nietzsche and Dionysus," Ivanov criticizes Nietzsche for giving too great legitimacy to the will. Concepts such as superman and will to power, in Ivanov's view, deify the narrow individual "Ego" and thus restrict interplay with the Dionysian "Self." Despite Nietzsche's injunctions to "love the earth," Ivanov argues that these chosen "guiding ideas" lay the philosophical groundwork for a new life-negating ideal.

A central difference between Merezhkovsky's and Ivanov's neo-Christian visions is the idea of the individual, the ego, and the value of personal perception and evaluation. Merezhkovsky values highly the self-conscious, striving "higher man." In Ivanov's writing, individual will is seen as something to overcome, to fuse with the greater whole. Even the creative act, in Ivanov's terms, is the result not of individual active will but of relinquishing ego and will to release the deeper life power of Dionysian forces. Willed rebellion, the "no-saying" act, is only the first negative stage of a mythic, cyclical pattern, leading to sacrifice of individual personality, union with the mystical collective, and eventual psychic regeneration. Thus, the Russian neo-Christian view evolves toward gradual discreditation of ego and will and replaces these focal points with combination of the idea of *sobornost'*, as Solovyov used it, and Nietzsche's idea of the "large Self."

Ivanov's myth was put into practice in a variety of ways. His first two collections of poetry, *Pole Stars* (*Kormchie zvezdy*, 1903) and *Transparency* (*Prozrachnost'*, 1904), contain many dithyrambic poems that read like ritual invocations of the god Dionysus.[34] A Dionysian mood of mystical expectation reigned at his weekly meetings in the "tower" across from the Tauride Palace in St. Petersburg. He and his wife Lidia Zinoveva-Gannibal, who was invariably dressed in a Greek chiton, greeted everyone with unassuming friendliness. By comparison to Merezhkovsky's and Gippius's circle, these gatherings were said to be much less ideologically constrained.[35]

Soon after the 1905 revolt, Ivanov became involved with a strange social movement known as "mystical anarchism." To its founder, Georgy Chulkov, Christ was the ultimate revolutionary and revolution the ultimate creative act.[36] He believed that revolution would usher in a utopian society guided by the principle of *sobornost'*, the union of self and others. Social relations would be guided by the spirit of *vliublënnost'*, or being in love. With Chulkov, Blok, and others, Ivanov envisioned a kind of Dionysian theater that would help to create the desired sense of social oneness.[37] The movement itself was not successful, but it is important to mention here because it drew attention to the ongoing Dionysian revaluation of Christianity.

Ivanov's Christian-Dionysian myth inspired response from the two major younger Symbolist poets, Blok and Belyi. During a short period in 1905 and 1906 both writers were frequent visitors at the apartment of Ivanov and Zinoveva-Gannibal. They were enchanted by the Dionysian mystique and the magical atmosphere of the all-night meetings in the "tower." Belyi objected to mystical anarchism, when it emerged, and soon broke off relations with its founders. Through the Moscow Symbolist journal *Vesy*, he spent the next two years contributing to an intense effort to discredit what was seen by many as a vulgarization of the spirit of Symbolism. Blok, on the other hand, remained very close to Ivanov until the death of Zinoveva-Gannibal in 1907.

Ivanov's impact is perhaps most strongly felt in Blok's cycle *Snow Mask* (*Snezhnaia maska*, December 1906–January 1907) in which the poet himself enacts the drama of the new Christ. We can see in this work Blok's antipathy toward traditional Christianity as well as a powerful attraction to Ivanov's myth of resurrection. Andrei Belyi aptly referred to Blok whom he called his brother in Symbolism the "unresurrected Christ."[38] Indeed, Blok's art of this period conveys an unrepentant thirst to live life in all its darkness and passion, to sacrifice himself to the earth and the elements. During 1905, the year of general revolt, Blok experienced a private rebellion against conventional Christianity. The first signs could be detected in a letter to his close friend Evgeny Ivanov. He wrote, "not for anything . . . will I go to Christ to be healed. I *do not know Him* and *have never known Him*. There is no fire in this denial, only naked rejection." And later: "In this self-negation, I feel healthy and wide awake."[39] Here he denied the traditional Christ of resignation, self-effacement, peace, and harmony. He felt an anarchic desire to live free of the heavy artillery of traditional moral sanction. During this period, Blok overthrew his early mentor, Vladimir Solovyov, calling his form of mysticism "boredom and prose."[40] He plunged toward an anti-Christian extreme, writing to Evgeny Ivanov: "If I had met you a few years ago I would, perhaps, have taken the sacrament from your hands with warmth. But I am blind drunk, I can perceive only the sharp corners of madness . . . you say that on one of the turnings I shall meet the Galilean—maybe! Only, for God's sake,—not now!"[41] In this spontaneous Dionysian mood of *bogoborchestvo* (struggling with the god), Blok was strongly attracted to the dark spirit of rebellion in Mikhail Vrubel's art. In the summer of 1905 he reread Dostoevsky's *Crime and Punishment*, which only bolstered his anarchic mood.

Blok's revolt had a vaguely political side. For the first time, during the strikes of 1905 he was drawn to the plight of the workers. They appeared to him not as victims and sufferers but as rebels much like him. His increasing social interest drew the criticism of his poetic "brother," Belyi, who admonished him for betraying the high mystical truth of Symbolism. Now Blok retorted that he was not a mystic, and in his work "The Puppet Theater" ("Balanganchik," 1906) he dethroned the St. Petersburg mystics, Merezhkovsky and his circle, who had encouraged him early on, as silly, beclouded fools.

In this bristling mood he made the acquaintance of Viacheslav Ivanov and Lidia Zinoveva-Gannibal. Blok had known and read about Ivanov for quite a while. In 1905, he had written a review of Ivanov's second book of poems, *Transparency* (*Prozrachnost'*, 1904). The next year he published another, longer essay entitled "The Creative Work of Viacheslav Ivanov" ("Tvorchestvo Viacheslava Ivanova"). The older poet attracted his attention as a talent who could help Russian poetry to move beyond the imitative lyricism of the "decadents," which Blok, borrowing Nietzsche's term, compared to the "Alexandrian" period of ancient Greek culture (SS8, V, 7–8). He sensed in Ivanov's art a mythopoetic "wellspring of pure poetry," a cultural "memory" capable of "reflecting the past, and the future, like a promise [*obetovanie*]" (12–13). Now, when Blok met Ivanov and Zinoveva-Gannibal in person, he was drawn to their spontaneous, "Dionysian" manner.[42] The first Wednesday he attended was devoted to the subject of "eros." Here people with the most diverse outlooks met and debated. The Marxist Lunacharsky, for example, talked to the classics scholar Zelinsky. The atmosphere was charged with energy without being divisive and dryly intellectual as in the Merezhkovsky and Gippius circle.[43] Blok despite his remonstrances to the contrary now embraced a form of mysticism that he clearly distinguished from Christian religion as such. The one he saw as a liberating force, whereas the other seemed a dry principle of regulation and limitation.[44]

Under the influence of Ivanov and Zinoveva-Gannibal Blok rediscovered *The Birth of Tragedy*, which he had read when it first appeared in Russian translation in 1900. Then it had held little interest for an idealist poet looking upward to the azure heavens for the mystical revelation of the Divine Sophia. Now he absorbed it wholeheartedly, copying down long passages in his notebooks. Attracted as he was to the Dionysian atmosphere of Ivanov's nocturnal gatherings, Blok himself seemed to come alive.⁴⁵ In a poem entitled "The God in the Brothel" ("Bog v lupanarii," SS, II, 327–328), Ivanov depicted Blok as a divine statue come alive, inscrutable and captivating. Blok's first biographer, Konstantin Mochulsky, affirms that during these months late in 1906 Blok indeed seemed to be revitalized. His eyes lost their "lifeless," "unmoving" gaze and his body its "woodenness."⁴⁶ He became ravishingly handsome. He lived for the hours between midnight and dawn, when he declaimed his newest poetry.⁴⁷ If we are to believe Boris Pasternak's description in *Doctor Zhivago*, the literary world lived and breathed Blok.

Late in 1906 Blok made plans and sketches for a drama to be entitled *Hyperborean Dionysus* (*Giperboreiskii Dionis*), in which he would invoke the god. Here he conflated Ivanov's myth with his own perennial search for Sophia. The female deity had shed her previous azure brilliance and here took on a dark Dionysian character. Blok was consciously trying to invoke Dionysus and striving to imitate the god's cycle of torment and renewal. In his notebook he remarked on Ivanov's warning that "One must not invoke Dionysus in vain. . . . If I am not transformed, I will die as I am, in torment."⁴⁸ The risk, he felt, was necessary: "maybe soon a new, fresh [poetic] cycle will come. And Aleksandr Blok [will come] to Dionysus."⁴⁹ In the night of 29 December, he wrote a sketch for his new drama. Blok made only a beginning, which enacted Ivanov's first stage of ascent. The setting is high mountains in the depths of winter. The central character is a youth who climbs into the mountains alone. He is chosen to become the bearer of the god.

The god descends to him in female form. And here the drama stops. It cannot progress to the hero's descent into the Dionysian chaos because the young man is unable to relinquish himself to the god. Instead he loses himself in abstracted musings about the "moral" character of this deity, whether she is good or evil. Thus, the mythic drama fades. This episode is worth mentioning because it reveals something of Blok's moral consciousness in this period. The act of moral judgment is opposed here to life and passion. Morality itself is understood as inhibition and prescription. The failure of this first mystical drama implies that one must overcome morality in order to release deep creative energy. In this sense Blok is quite different from and perhaps more primitively and naturally "Dionysian" than all the other Symbolists. It is interesting that in *Snow Mask*, one of his greatest cycles, the poet consciously abandons traditional morality as he gives himself over to his encounter with the female other. Only in this way, Blok decides, is it possible to live and feel to the fullest.

Blok created *Snow Mask* in the first two weeks of January 1907. Dedicated to the actress Natalia Volokhova, with whom Blok was smitten, the cycle is situated in the story of a love affair. It is divided into two parts, "Snows" ("Snega") and "Masks" ("Maski"). In the first part the poet experiences the courting of his beloved as a cosmic *bogoiskanie* (seeking the god) and *bogoborchestvo* (struggling with the god). The second part, "Masks," treats many of the same situations but this time in the diction of social satire. The humorous surface event, the "mask," is a routine social flirtation. With his ironic wit Blok ridicules social convention but does not touch the deeper, tragic interpenetration of human and divine. The contrast helps to place the mystic experience in another realm away from society. In the final poems the poet reopens the mystic drama when he finally sacrifices himself to the god.

In the first of the cycle's two sections, "Snows" ("Snega"), the beloved is revealed through metonymic detail as a Dionysian deity. In the cycle's first poem, "Snowy Wine" ("Snezhnoe vino"), she has Medusa's "heavy-serpentine hair" ("v tiazhelozmeinykh volosakh"), and her reflection in the glass of wine is curved and distorted in liquid serpentines ("zmeish'sia v chashe zolotoi"). In the beginning of the second section, "Masks" ("Maski"), the poet uses parallel imagery, but this time in a spirit of self-parody. Here the "masks" of social etiquette flatten and solidify the fluid, fleeting quality of the Dionysian images used in "Snows." For example, symbols of sexual passion, snakes and wings, are reduced to concrete, even crass objects, for example, a little snake sewn onto the toe of a woman's shoe (239) and a carved wooden bas-relief of a cupid on a bookcase (238).

The cycle is ordered along the lines of the Dionysian ritual described in Ivanov's essays. Here as in Ivanov's "Symbology of Esthetic Origins" the poet becomes a Christ figure who rebels, affirms his own will, invokes the god, and finally gives himself up to Dionysian androgynous chaos. Out of chaos emerges a new mystical-creative consciousness. This resurrection lasts only a short time. At the end of the cycle the poet admits with appealing self-irony that he is merely human, that in essence he is no different from any other lover. He accepts his final sacrifice on the "snowy pyre."

Throughout, the Dionysian rite of regeneration is framed with the spatial and temporal markers of the traditional Christian myth of crucifixion.[50] In addition to the vertical movements of ascent and descent, we note that the first section, "Snows," takes place in a span of three days. The third poem, "The Last Way" ("Poslednii put'"), marks the first sunset; the tenth poem, "Being-In-Love" ("Vliublennost'"), the second sunset; and the sixteenth and final poem of this section, "In the Snows" ("V snegakh"), marks the third. This time span is recapitulated in "Masks" when in the final poem "On the Snowy Pyre" ("Na snezhnom kostre") the female persona says that she was "true for three nights." Within these parallels of time and space, the poet contrasts himself with the conventional Christ and thus evokes the new consciousness of the earthly, as Belyi put it, "unresurrected" Christ.

One contrast between the conventional crucifixion and this one is its purpose. The purpose of the original crucifixion was to remind people of their eternal debt before God, a principle of absolute goodness. It had the goal of restraining and taming. This sacrifice celebrates rebellion against conventional moral judgment. The poet defies otherworldly measures of goodness as he enters the dark underworld of passion. In the cycle's third poem, "The Last Way" ("Poslednii put'"), he catches sight of another, considerably more sensual divine being as it rises in the distant sunset like Botticelli's Venus over the "snowy foam." Symbolically he casts off traditional moral sanctions when he watches as in the setting sun "on the distant church / The last cross faded joylessly" ("na dal'nem khrame bezotradostno / Dogorel poslednii krest," 214). The traditional symbol of human sin and sacrifice, the cross, has lost its meaning. The anarchistic Dionysian Christ enters through his "second christening" into a "new world" where conventional values are turned upside down: the "evil"—senses, sexuality, passion—leads to "paradise" ("Vtoroe kreshchenie," 216). He and his beloved enter the chaotic Dionysian night, where there are no limitations, only sensation.

In the cycle's second part, "Masks," the poet treats moral conscience with a more gentle irony. Ethical feeling is only a trapping of social appearance, as something superficial. It is relinquished in the first poem of this section, "Under the Masks" ("Pod maskami"), as the poet's inner firmament opens: "And under the mask it was starry. / Someone's story smiled, / The night whiled itself quietly away. / / And pensive conscience, / Quietly floating over the void, / Led time away" ("A pod maskoi bylo zvezdno. / Ulybalas' ch'ia-to povest', / Korotilas' tikho noch'. / / I zadumchivaia sovest', / Tikho plavaia nad bezdnoi, / Uvodila vremia proch'", 236). Here as in the first part the poet rejects all limitations—mind, moral conscience, rationality—in order to probe life itself: the mystical, the passionate, the unseen world of the psyche.

This dismissal of traditional moral valuations corresponds to Ivanov's first rebellious stage of ascent, *bogoborchestvo*. Another aspect of this stage is the poet's attempt to overpower the god. In the cycle's second poem, "Snowy Ligature" ("Snezhnaia viaz'"), he claims that the god is his creation, the "captive ligature of my verses" ("Ty-stikhov moikh plennaia viaz'," 212). He treats her with a certain contempt, claiming that "you are not the first to give herself to me on the dark bridge" ("Ty ne pervaia mne predalas' / Na temnom mostu," 212).

With this challenge the poet succeeds in invoking the god in "Caught By the Snow Storm" ("Nastignutyi metel'iu"). Her sublime presence is felt in the power of the blizzard, through her ability to turn his world upside down. Most importantly, she is known through the ecstasy she evokes in the poet: the poet has become *bogonosets*, the bearer of the god, and relinquishes his "small reason," his brash ego and his contemptuous arrogance. The poet is now thrust into the cosmic void and there discovers new sensation. The world becomes topsy-turvy: the stars are "black," and ships sail over the heavens. Now he gains a view into the deepest truth of cosmic chaos. Far from being tormented by it, he feels free. He has a sense of flying breathlessly over the void. He watches ships sail perilously over nothingness. He is in ecstasy.

The poet reminds us three poems later, in "Wings" ("Kryl'ia"), of where he has taken us—it is an inner world of passion. He uses images of the expanse of the ocean to convey the infinity of the Dionysian domain. Here, he reminds us, we are far from the limited, measurable, familiar "land" of the conscious, moral self. Its "tablets," its rules and sanctions, now are barely outlined in the mists (221). Nevertheless, the poet's ecstatic mood slowly fades into a vague consciousness of the ultimate limitation placed on human life, that is, death. Through the passion and exhilaration, he senses the fate that he is not yet ready to accept. He knows he will have his own "cross," his own crucifixion. He again asserts himself, defying his fate of torment and sacrifice. He wishes "that the fire of the flaming winter/ Would burn the threatening/ Distant cross!" ("chtob ogon' zimy paliashchii/ Szheg groziashchii/ Dal'nii krest!" 226). Instead, he desires "to fly like a ringing arrow/ Into the void of black stars" ("letet' streloi zveniashchei/ V propast' chernykh zvezd," 226).

The poet experiences a kind of resurrection near the end of the cycle's first section in the poem "Away!" ("Proch'!"). He is told that three days have passed, and he is called back from his languor ("istoma") to his "creative work" ("k sozidaiushchei rabote / Vorotis'," 227). This poem is filled with an Apollonian daytime light radiated not by one single sun but by several "suns." The close parallel to Christian experience is brought back. The poet is here more than ever a kind of self-denying Christ figure. He is compared to an ascetic in a "cell" or a "cave." He bears on him the "chains of snows" ("snegov okovy," 228). He realizes that three days and nights have passed since he descended into the void. Despite the parallels, the poet reminds us that he is not some otherworldly ascetic. He scoffs at the idea of any reality but the earthly one. It has it own depth, its own highs and lows. "Heaven" is treated here as some ridiculous fairyland. The poet refuses to ascend to heaven "to the gold-roofed mansions" ("v zlatoverkhie khoromy," 227) and tells the "daughters of paradise" to fly away "to the old door of dying paradise" ("Proch' leti, sviataia staia, / K staroi dveri / umiraiushchego raia!" 228). He wants no association with the "other world," with angels, their gifts, and their words of praise. He wants nothing of "Communion" ("Prichastie"). The poet affirms himself as the Dionysian Christ: he wants to stay here on earth in this existence, in this "dimmed cell" ("v pomerkshei kel'e,"

229), with all its hardship and suffering. He prefers his owls and wild animals to the angels. In an earlier poem, an archangel has threatened him with a cross made of two crossed swords. He answers now that he has in his cell his own swords from which he will make his own cross. His fate will come from this earth. He already sees the "signs of black days" and now gladly accepts them as his own fate: "my gaiety pours out in two rays" ("struit moe vesel'e / Dva lucha," 229).

In the final poems of "Snows," the poet supersedes Ivanov's mythic structure. He gains something like Nietzsche's concept of wisdom. He senses more than a way to deep creativity: he gains a vision of his own earthly fate. Thus, he sacrifices himself anew to the "snowstorms" of passion. He gives up his ego altogether. It is interesting to note that until the final poem in this section, "In the Snows" ("V snegakh"), the poet never uses the grammatical forms *I* and *me*. He has forfeited his ego and his will. His earthly self is objectified in the third person. The poetic consciousness balances many consciousnesses, "She" the Dionysian spirit and "He" the earthly self grappling with its fate. Her view is an eternal one, urging the living to strive beyond the vale of life, to the stars, to face the abyss and death. She embraces eternity and death. "He" lives the tragedy of accepting that there is no escape from death. In the section's final poem, "In the Snows," the poet, much like Zarathustra in his "Song of Intoxication," achieves the mythic link with eternity, with the superhuman. He looks at life *sub specie aeternitatis*. He compares himself to the Milky Way, stretched across the heavens. He addresses "Her" as "Eternity" and "Infinity." He sees the "dungeon of the world" as part of an infinite pattern (*uzor*) and affirms it.

At the end of the cycle the poet again greets and is glad of his earthly fate. He reaffirms, "I feel gay in perishing" ("pogibnut' mne veselo," 250). Here he sacrifices himself to the divine beloved. He is the "Crucified" on the burning cross. The final affirmation of earthly fate is to relinquish the fantasy of personal uniqueness. The final value is to have lived, to have experienced, not to fix the experience in its uniqueness as something higher, untouchable, unrepeatable. Although he laughs at himself with a renewed irony as one of the many indistinguishable "heroes" who have given themselves to her, even in "death" the poet affirms the quality of becoming. He lives Zarathustra's idea that death should be the fitting dénouement to life.

The question now arises, How does Blok in this period appropriate the myth of the new Christ? What does it show of his own moral consciousness? If Ivanov "dionysizes" Christ in a moderate way, then Blok does so in the extreme. Just as he earlier doubted that Merezhkovsky's harmonic synthesis of earthly flesh and heavenly spirit could ever really work, so he now defies and dethrones the otherworldly with its angels and gold palaces in favor of the daimonic, dark, unformed but passionate and alive earth. He prefers to perish, having lived, suffered, and known himself, rather than to await and prepare for some unknown future.

Another point regarding the issue that pervades Nietzsche's reception and the consciousness of the period as a whole must be raised: the relationship between aesthetic and ethical in this revolution of moral consciousness. Blok, more than many others, seems to fit the stereotype that the ethical was sacrificed to aesthetic interest. His letters and notes, as well as the cycle *Snow Mask*, convey anarchic rejection of any constraining form of moral judgment. He completely rejects morality as stultifying regulation. He seizes the freedom to rebel and destroy himself. In *Snow Mask* Blok underscores the superficiality and weakness of moral conscience in the context of our psychic nature as a whole.

In contrast to Ivanov, Blok ironizes the social and ethical aspect of the I-thou relationship. The act of relinquishing the ego and the discovery of the "thou" are seen as a form of true mystical experience. The ethical is actually harmful to the revelation of the inner realm. However, Blok's anarchism is very far from the crude egotism that vulgarizers criticized and Nietzscheans preached. It is reminiscent rather of the tragic Dionysian worldview that Nietzsche saw in the Prometheus plays: the poet commits the heroic higher transgression that ultimately affirms human life, that condemns external power as domination but nurtures life power within. Ultimately Blok reaches his own form of moral answerability: he accepts and affirms his own fate. He faces death without resentment.

Blok's cycle was one of several literary incidents that revealed the fissures in Russian mystical Symbolism. In 1906 and 1907, Belyi, Merezhkovsky, and Gippius used the Moscow journal *Vesy* to fire a barrage of criticism upon the Petersburg "mystical anarchists," Chulkov, Ivanov, and Blok. Although Chulkov's ideology with its earthy and sometimes vulgar sensuality and its populist overtones was the focus of attack, Chulkov was neither talented nor significant enough as a thinker to split the mystic Symbolists.[51] The real bone of contention was the Dionysian Christianity of Ivanov the theorist and Blok the poet, its orientation toward the senses and its affirmation of the erotic. The Moscow faction centered around *Vesy* felt that the Petersburg poets, and particularly Blok, diminished the fundamental symbol of Symbolism, the "Divine Sophia," the ideal of sublime beauty and wisdom.[52] They reviled their Petersburg opponents' "dirty and unkempt" eroticism.[53] Belyi, Gippius, and Merezhkovsky, by contrast, upheld a view of poetry as theurgy: the poet was entrusted with lofty mystic vision. Whatever the considerable differences that lay between them, and despite Merezhkovsky's overly intellectualized effort to embrace the earth, all three ultimately yearned for eternal truth. They awaited spiritual transfiguration through the impact of superhuman forces (whether "history" or the "transcendent") upon the human psyche.

Blok points out the dangers of this theurgic approach in his article of 1910, "The Present Condition of Russian Symbolism." He argues that the realization that these mystic visions are self-induced and that so-called cosmic forces are merely fabrication results only in nihilistic self-irony. Here as earlier, Blok agrees with Ivanov's view that spiritual transformation can happen only within the human psyche in the struggle of the self with the deity within.[54] The poet must travel through the artistic "hell" of internal discovery and release the elemental forces of life within himself. Instead of seeking to create the harmony of some supposed eternal realm here on earth, Blok speaks for "learning afresh from the world and from the infant who is still alive in our burned soul" (SS8, V, 436). Invoking Nietzschean images throughout his article, he imagines an earthly mystical Symbolism that can withstand the sharp light of the "hour of the great midday" (V, 425), that ironizes over the old transcendent reality (V, 429), and that celebrates the creative, Dionysian force of the "child" within (V, 436). "The Puppet Show" had been Blok's first, nihilist step beyond the transcendent. With *Snow Mask* he enacted his new mystic Symbolism.

Belyi and the Crucified Dionysus

Of all Nietzsche's Russian Symbolist adherents Andrei Belyi is the most divided and difficult. In his prewar prose work the rift between "earth" and "heaven" remains unbridged despite Belyi's passionate effort to reconcile the two. Indeed, in his two first novels, *The Silver Dove* and *Petersburg*, the contradictions between the two seem unresolvable. Belyi in the course of the prewar period overturns other mythic resolutions found by his precursors and contemporaries but can find none of his own. He is unable to accept the naive, life-affirming neo-Christianity of Merezhkovsky, the earthy Dionysian outlook of Ivanov, or the fatalistic irony of the unresurrected Christ figure Blok, who rejects the abstract and eternal idea of heaven in favor of the passionate and vital, if mortal earth. Unlike Blok, Belyi does not reconcile the crisis of metaphysical meaning with which all the mystical Symbolists have to grapple. Belyi's moral consciousness is split between a hope for fulfillment in earthly existence and a strong sense of irony and disbelief about earthly potential. "Earth" is too inviting of deprecation, too contemptible, and too grotesque to be a life-giving, regenerative force. By contrast, "heaven" is too distant, abstract, and unattainable to offer vitality and sustenance.

Belyi's essential and ruinous ambivalence appears in sharp relief in his repeated attempts to formulate a personal Christian myth of regeneration. At the heart of his dilemma is the question as to the ontological nature of myth. Is myth the product of human creative will and a celebration of earthly suffering and passion? Or is it rooted in a transcendent reality; is its truth absolute and immutable? Is mythical truth to be actively created, lived, and tested or passively perceived and known? Belyi's response to two major philosophical mentors of his early period highlights these contrasts. The work of Nietzsche and Solovyov, discovered at roughly the same time around the millenial year 1900, present two equally gripping but mutually contradictory alternatives to the young writer. They are alternatives that he cannot reconcile but that exacerbate the schisms in his own moral consciousness. Solovyov presents to Belyi's imagination the ascetic vision of a pure, saintly figure. He was historically and geographically close to Belyi. The young poet was good friends with the Solovyov family, particularly with Solovyov's nephew, Sergei. He had met the philosopher just a few times and, most importantly for his philosophical development, once in the spring of 1900. Deeper acquaintance was denied by Solovyov's untimely death later that year.[55] Soon thereafter a cult of Solovyov took shape, and Belyi was at the center of it. Belyi was attracted most to the apocalyptic aspects of Solovyov's thought. Whereas Ivanov admired Solovyov's philosophy of love and Blok pursued the transcendent image of Sophia, Belyi discovered special significance in the "prophetic" final work of the late philosopher, "The Story of the Antichrist."[56] Belyi captures the ethereal quality that attracted him to Solovyov when he calls Solovyov "merely a sound calling [us] to cast off from the shores of the old world."[57]

Nietzsche appealed to quite another side of Belyi's character, holding forth to the young writer the potential of creative will and the promise of earthly existence. When he discovered *Zarathustra* in 1899 as a first-year student at Moscow University, Belyi was smitten with a "crazy passion" for Nietzsche.[58] For the first time, as he remembered it in *On the Border of Two Centuries*, he felt completely alive. Nietzsche seemed a "creator [*tvorets*] of vital images themselves, the theoretical or aesthetic significance of which would be revealed only on the path of co-creation [*sotvorchestvo*]."[59] The discovery of Nietzsche appears to have been the deciding factor in his turn from science and a materialist-positivist worldview to art and neo-Idealism. As seems often to have occurred in Belyi's life, his infatuation with Nietzsche was undermined by an equally strong counterinfluence. Now Belyi's respected father, a well-known mathematician at Moscow University, could not understand the change in his son. To make matters more difficult, Belyi's chief intellectual-spiritual lifeline, the Solovyov household, was openly alien and hostile to his new idol Nietzsche.[60]

Belyi had read *Birth of Tragedy* when it appeared in Russian translation in 1899, but around 1904 he rediscovered it and with it a fresh orientation to Nietzsche.[61] Just as vibrant as before, Nietzsche's thought now appeared able to help him bridge the gap between his need for earthly self-fulfillment and his religious quest for higher meaning. In the image of the "crucified Dionysus," Nietzsche's thought promised Belyi an all-encompassing religious myth. In his article "The Present and Future of Russian Literature" (1907), he observed that Nietzsche's rebellion reawakened Russian Symbolists to Christianity.[62] In 1908 in his article "Friedrich Nietzsche" Belyi ranked the German philosopher with Christ as a great "teacher of life" who had founded a "religion of life."[63] The Dionysian idea of eternal return, Belyi wrote, was Nietzsche's "Golgotha" on which he had tested existence and perished. Just as Zarathustra had been a model for moral revolt that Belyi had imitated in his early belletristic work, now the "crucified Dionysus" became more than a symbolic image and indeed suggested to Belyi's mind a life goal. In his memoir of Blok he remembered that by probing this image he "came right up against Nietzsche's life story."[64] Later, in 1912 while practicing anthroposophic meditation in Basel, Switzerland, he experienced two aspects of the Dionysian-Christian myth: sacrifice and regeneration. He believed he was being crucified like Christ. At another time he felt as if he were physically being torn apart like Dionysus at an ancient Greek ritual.[65] Belyi was intensely aware of being in the place where Nietzsche had first suffered debilitating bouts of illness. The identity with this early mentor was overwhelming.

Despite his strong identification with philosophical precursors, Belyi is extremely insistent in all his writings upon his own originality. He reminds us in his memoirs that he was never any "-ist" or "-ite" and could not be labeled any of the long string of "Schopenhauerians, Solovyovians, Nietzscheans," and so forth.[66] This insistence becomes much stronger the closer physically, temporally, and ideologically a precursor stands. For example, Nietzsche is imagined in 1901 in Belyi's first published prose work, "Second Symphony," as a "sweaty coachman with a magnificent face, black moustaches and eyebrows hanging over his eyes" (SII, 134). Contemporaries would be subjected to much sharper criticism and unkind, if sometimes amusing, mockery. The need to be original will seem increasingly incongruous as Belyi evolves a radically ascetic moral view. However incongruous it may appear, this drive for complete originality remains, and it plays an enormously important role in the way Belyi ap-

Mystical Symbolists 155

propriates his philosophical mentors' thought in his literary work. Whether he wants to admit it or not, his interpretation of Nietzsche is less "original" than he would like us to think: to a great degree his reading is conditioned by the views of his Symbolist precursors, Merezhkovsky and Ivanov. They help reorient Belyi's moral search from a rebellion against positivism to a reappropriation of Christianity. The mythic constructs of these two men sharpen the opposition between creative will and transcendent being in Belyi's thinking. Through his polemic with them Belyi arrives at his own characteristic appropriation of Christian myth.

Merezhkovsky had a strong early impact on Belyi. It can be argued that of the two mentors, Merezhkovsky and Ivanov, Merezhkovsky was more personally likable to Belyi. As a precursor he was less psychically threatening and thus more easily overcome. The younger writer was drawn by Merezhkovsky's intellectualized approach to moral revaluation and by his untroubled, optimistic idea of a historic plan leading to a new Christian epoch.[67] He also liked Merezhkovsky's naive belief in human creative will.[68] Belyi noted in *On the Border of Two Centuries* that around 1900, Merezhkovsky was the master of his thoughts, who, along with Nietzsche, induced him to write his four prose "symphonies."[69] The two met in 1901 at the Solovyovs'. Soon Belyi was attending Merezhkovsky's Religious-Philosophical Meetings in St. Petersburg. Belyi was quick to acknowledge Merezhkovsky's power as a critic. Merezhkovsky, he wrote, was the first to discover Nietzsche and to reopen Russian nineteenth-century literature, reading Gogol, Dostoevsky, and Tolstoi "as no one else had."[70]

In his amusing satires of this first Symbolist precursor-become-rival, Belyi emphasizes the failure of Merezhkovsky's synthesis of the "two truths" of "earth" and "heaven." Both in the second symphony (1901) and in his article "Merezhkovsky" (1907), Belyi mocks his precursor's lack of spiritual focus. In the second symphony, Belyi composes a picture of existential boredom, showing a cityscape with people engaged in their absurd routines. Here a poet, a philosopher, and a priest all think disconnected thoughts and speak silly words. Into this setting comes not one but two Merezhkovskys. One is Merezhkovich and the other Drozhzhikovsky, whose name means "yeast" and

156 *The Revolution of Moral Consciousness*

who, Belyi later quips, does not provide the spiritual leavening needed for real regeneration (SII, 299). Merezhkovich preaches his historical correlative's beloved theme of "union of paganism and Christianity" (SII, 252). Belyi gets more mileage out of Drozhzhikovsky's attempts to prophesy moral-spiritual resurrection. Belyi points out the vagueness and incongruity of Merezhkovsky's thinking by providing a kind of absurd, prolonged list of all his satiric double's ideas. Thus, this "fashionable, rising talent" "resurrected extinguished giants; he connected their ideas; he saw the evolution of this thought" (SII, 206); he seemed ready to state a new truth (SII, 208); he talked about the "sacred meaning of the superman" (SII, 209); he "awaited spiritual renewal, . . . the possible synthesis of theology, mysticism and the church" (SII, 209–210); he "indicated three metamorphoses of the spirit" (SII, 210). Eventually Drozhzhikovsky is discredited by his lack of concrete focus and the lack of anything really new at the core of his personality. In 1907, Belyi gives a more succinct, concrete, and effective picture of Merezhkovsky as a "specialist without a specialty."[71] He sketches him sitting in the fog at the top of his intellectual "Eiffel Tower" raining pieces of paper down on the people below. His lack of coherence and concreteness, Belyi suggests, make his prophecies incomprehensible even to a large intellectual circle thirsting for prophecy.

Less intellectually containable and controllable was the impact of Viacheslav Ivanov. Belyi was clearly troubled as well as, for a time around 1905, bewitched by Ivanov. In contrast to his open appreciation of Merezhkovsky's contribution, Belyi was unwilling to admit Ivanov's much more far-reaching influence. Although he admitted that Ivanov "gave a deep foundation to our ideas," he was embittered and even nasty in his treatment of what he saw as Ivanov's shortcomings.[72] Ivanov's earthy, sensuous thought clearly irritated Belyi, revealing a surprising fastidiousness, even squeamishness and prudery.

Belyi must have read Ivanov's "Religion of the Suffering God" when it first appeared in 1903 and 1904. In his *Reminiscences on Blok*, Belyi claimed to have discovered *Birth of Tragedy* at this time and to be grappling with the problem of the "crucified Dionysus." Although he implied an independent discovery of Dionysus, he clearly appropriated Ivanov's general myth as his own when he wrote in 1904: "The cross appears . . . and with it the tragedy of the cross, resolving itself now in revolt, now in sacrifice," and elsewhere: "I was already [in 1904] posing for myself the problem of suffering and sacrifice: through the symbol of the crucified Dionysus I came right up against Nietzsche's life story."[73]

At a later time Ivanov played an important enabling role in Belyi's creative life. Despite their severe disagreements over mystical anarchism they made amends in 1908. Early in 1912 Belyi read some chapters from his second novel at Ivanov's Tower. Ivanov gave the work its title, *Petersburg*. When Belyi was staying in Basel later the same year Ivanov visited him there and even wanted to stay with him and practice anthroposophical meditation. Both spoke a great deal about Nietzsche, his life in Basel, and his early mental illness.[74] It is conceivable that these conversations with Ivanov intensified Belyi's dual psychic experience of spiritual resurrection through Christian crucifixion and physical Dionysian torture. Moreover, the same tribulations of the two protagonists in *Petersburg*, respectively, Nikolai Ableukhov and Aleksandr Dudkin, suggest that Belyi's Ivanovesque deliriums found their way as mythic narrative into Belyi's novel.

Perhaps because of Ivanov's centrality to his creative and psychic life, Belyi is very harsh when he criticizes his precursor. He resents Ivanov's "vulgarization" of Symbolism. He calls Ivanov a "poisoner of the air" and means by this that Ivanov clouded and confused the clear, lofty esoteric valuations inherent in "true" Symbolism.[75] Belyi dislikes Ivanov's *narodnost'*, that is, an urge to bring to the people ideas that inherently cannot be popularized. The result is a vulgarization of the sublime. Belyi cannot forgive Ivanov's imposing "something like an equal sign between . . . Christ and Dionysus, the Mother of God and any childbearing woman, the Virgin and the Maenad, love and eroticism."[76] Here we see Belyi's high estimation of physical purity and of the esoteric, and an unwillingness really to accept the physical, the fleshy, the sensuous. Belyi's concern with Ivanov's vulgarization was strong enough to inspire a parodic response in his first full-length novel, *The Silver Dove*. Here he wanted to show that Dionysus was not Christ, not every woman was the Mother of God, and eroticism was not true love.

Belyi's own idiosyncratic appropriation of Christian myth reflects his deep ambivalence. Despite his hostility to Ivanov, he shows a genuine attraction for the earthly moral rebel: the "unresurrected Christ," as he called Blok, and the "crucified Dionysus." He is also driven by a thirst for resurrection, which he imagines as ascetic purification and new, childlike innocence.

The major protagonists of Belyi's prewar prose reenact in varying degrees their author's dilemma. Their personalities contain elements of the Dionysian Christ: they often are driven to deny life as it is, because they believe in the power of their own creative will to regenerate the world. They believe that they know the way to regeneration. However, their dreams and imaginings sometimes contradict their belief in themselves: their highest goal is usually in some way ascetic and earth-denying. Instead of regenerating human nature, their dreams frequently reveal a will to dominate and quiet its violent aspects. Belyi's first moral rebel, Sergei Musatov, appears in the second symphony. Musatov, a feverish, golden-bearded ascetic, brings meaning to the absurd world of this work. He sees in separate details the signs of the Apocalypse. With Belyi's precursor Merezhkovsky, Musatov prophesies that the "Third Kingdom is at hand" (SII, 211). But in contrast to Merezhkovsky, who believes to some degree in creative human will, he tries to conjure and manipulate transcendent forces that will impose a future upon humanity. In this fashion he also appropriates Solovyov's apocalyptic vision from "The Story of the Antichrist" and Zarathustra's idea of eternal return.

Musatov's cosmic view reveals a naive, Merezhkovskian belief that earthly events and transcendent forces are allegorically related. "Earth" is a symbolic representation, a visible sign of "heaven." Thus, Musatov foretells a return to the events of 1900 years ago, the birth of Christ (SII, 253). He claims to have seen Vladimir Solovyov riding through Moscow warning of the end (SII, 280). He conjures a vision of the Solovyovian image of the Apocalypse, Sophia, the Woman Clothed in the Sun, and believes that a female acquaintance is Her incarnation.

The vision of the future that Musatov conjures discloses his preoccupation with dominative power. The Woman Clothed in the Sun, as he sees her, rides on eagle's wings, a symbol of political power. She is decidedly not Solovyov's Sophia, the force of Platonic wisdom, or the symbol of regenerating love. She bears with her a "male child" who reinforces an authoritarian vision:

the male child is foreordained "to shepherd the peoples with an iron rod" (SII, 248). Entirely lacking here is the voluntarism so evident in Ivanov's or Blok's brand of mysticism. Nietzsche's disdain for the herd is realized in the harshest possible way. Belyi's apocalyptic vision here is not only earth-denying and severe but positively dictatorial. The Apocalypse will bring absolutist denial and control, not human liberation and regeneration.

Belyi ridicules Musatov's desire to manipulate otherworldly forces. He makes his protagonist what V. Alexandrov has aptly called the "butt of a cosmic joke."[77] Musatov believes that a female acquaintance and her child are the earthly incarnations of his vision. He is deeply disappointed when he discovers that the child dressed to look like a boy is really a girl (SII, 299)! Musatov's yearning for a masculine cosmic order and control is clearly not in line with the powers that be. Nonetheless, the desire for order and control would be a subliminal motivating force for Belyi's moral rebels and their mystic visions. Another side to this preoccupation, the fear of being confused, manipulated, and ultimately destroyed by active superhuman forces of evil parading in human guise, would be disclosed in later works. Thus, despite his dreams of oppression, Musatov is in some ways the most optimistic and least unhinged of Belyi's protagonists.

Another character, Evgeny Khandrikov in "The Return: The Third Symphony" (1902), has a similarly ascetic, otherworldly nature. By contrast, however, he is pleasantly absentminded, never attempts to manipulate, and is free of visions of cosmic control. Khandrikov lives with a kind of higher consciousness of eternal return that gives everything around him in the aura of déjà vu. This symphony is divided into three "movements": the hero is first a child living with an old man by the sea, then he is a chemistry student, and finally he returns to the sea. With each new cycle he encounters the same personalities, situations, and feelings. Repeatedly he is overcome by a sense of metaphysical foreboding, a fear of hidden forces of destruction about to awaken. This sense leads him as he finishes a graduate degree in chemistry to revolt against his colleagues in chemistry and their narrow, contented materialist values and "liberal" social point of view, much perhaps as Belyi himself did when he first discovered *Zarathustra* and the "Symbolist" worldview. Khandrikov objects: "I do not see for humanity a peaceful future motivated by the development of the sciences, the arts" (SIII, 80). Unlike Musatov, Khandrikov is a passive observer of life whose quietude permits him deeper insight into cosmic being. However, he is driven to action by the fatuous, smug attitudes he senses around him. For his trouble he is declared insane and soon sent to a sanatorium run by a tall, old man reminiscent of Solovyov.

Khandrikov's otherworldly forebodings share one feature with Musatov's apocalypticism. Both devalue the earth—that is, human nature and human culture as it is—and, unlike Nietzsche, have little faith in human potential. Worldly life is devoid of inherent meaning: it is comical at best and grotesque at worst. Humanity's only redeeming feature is its yearning to deny and overcome itself. Without that it is hopeless. Nevertheless, despite this generally negative view, both these works end on a note of hope. At the end of the second symphony, Musatov's female acquaintance (the earthly mask for Sophia, the Woman Clothed in the Sun) hints that a real Christ Child may yet emerge. In the third symphony, Khandrikov drowns in this life but returns as a child to the existence of the first part with the old man by the sea. However, it becomes ever clearer that the breach between here-and-now and the eternal is unbridgeable. Resurrection in the context of human, earthly life seems less and less possible.

The best that will be possible, as Belyi shows in his two prewar novels, is retreat: one can hope to gain a clear conception of one's earthly condition through passive meditation. He comes to this conclusion through his own enactment of the tragedy of the crucified Dionysus. His protagonist plunges himself into earthly life, affirming it on the highest plane, only to perceive its fateful dangers too late to save himself. Petr Darialsky in *The Silver Dove* is just such a Dionysian character. Darialsky is a poet who has gone to the province to be with his Turgenevian fiancée on her estate. He becomes embroiled with a religious sect in a nearby town and abandons his betrothed for new mystical and amorous adventures.

In some ways Darialsky can be seen as a serious parody of Blok. At one point he quotes Blok's poem "It's as if we were in a new space" (SD, 306; SS8, II, 403, VIII, 305). Like Blok, he is capable of "giving himself blindly to the elements." His moral consciousness reflects a yearning for spiritual transfiguration shared by all the mystical Symbolists. He imitates Belyi's version of Zarathustra in his ambition to be more than a mere poet, to be an "artist of life." His creative efforts are focused on a search for a mode of "conduct befitting an as yet unfounded life" (SD, 134). He is trying to discredit age-old morality that evaluates violent, aggressive physical and emotional drive as the evil "image of the ancient beast." He dreams of creating a new sense of the good that will embrace all aspects of human nature, the aggressive as well as the submissive. He wants to find a "new human sanity." Darialsky shares the psychological weakness experienced by popular-Nietzschean heroes. Faced with complete metaphysical freedom, they are too weak to enforce upon themselves a code and a discipline that will foster constructive action. Like them Darialsky shows a will to self-destruction. His demeanor is repulsive to educated sensibility: he is rude, his smell is offensive, and he acts outrageously. Unlike his predecessors from popular literature he takes steps to stave off personal dissolution. He turns to a power he perceives to be greater than he. First he steeps himself in a Turgenevian gentry milieu. Then, finding that existence faded and insubstantial, he turns to the mysterious life of the "Russian people." It is important to realize that this *narod* is not the one of the populists: it is urban, formed from small-businessfolk (*meshchane*), not peasants. The name of the village to which Darialsky moves is *Tselebeevo*. The word *tselebnyi*, which suggests healing, particularly by organic, folk remedies, belies Darialsky's real psychic need. Although consciously he wishes to effect spiritual transfiguration on a national scale, he unconsciously yearns for salvation from his spiritual unease. The fact that he wants to be healed suggests that his revolt is motivated by spiritual "illness" of the sort that plagued moral rebels of the 1860s and 1870s; this illness, Belyi suggests, is not the Nietzschean concept of "pregnancy" that promises really new consciousness. He wishes not to reach beyond but to resolve his agony of straddling the abyss between the conventional and the new.

Darialsky's adventures enact Ivanov's myth of Christ-Dionysus, but now in Belyi's disapproving, vulgarized version of it. Now Belyi clarifies the distinctions in archetype that he felt that Ivanov had muddied: Belyi takes away the equal sign that he said Ivanov had placed between love and eroticism, the Mother of God and any childbearing woman, Christ and Dionysus. Here and in *Petersburg* Belyi admits of a relationship between the two but only in the sense that the person who possesses the "earthly" virtues—vital passion, regenerative energy, ability to suffer—has a greater chance than other humans of transcendence, of growing up to their ideal counterparts: higher love, tenderness, the will to spiritual resurrection.

Darialsky seeks in love something like Ivanov's sense of *sobornost'*, the spiritual and physical union of two selves and the breakthrough of a higher ecstatic consciousness. His pure, platonic relationship with the noblewoman Katia cannot satisfy that need. By contrast, with Matryona he discovers an all-consuming passion, and a lust for life that transports him beyond his narrow sense of self and gives him the sense of belonging to a life-giving whole.

In his affair with Matryona Darialsky experiences the Ivanovesque process of rebellion and sacrifice, followed by regeneration. The outcome contravenes expectation in that Belyi foresees not renewal but total moral and spiritual destruction. In *The Silver Dove* raw Dionysian passion is clearly related to the idea of Christian sacrifice of self to other. Darialsky possesses the brute rebelliousness and the blind passion of the Dionysian. He experiences the confusion, the loss of sense of self, and the subsequent loss of ability to judge as he gives himself up to the religious sect, the Doves. A result of this shading of the self into the other is an agonizing division in perception and feeling. The same experience of being in love thrusts Darialsky into a confusion of ecstasy and pain.

The Dionysian sacrifice of ego to powerful, subliminal forces is overlaid and given its ultimate tragic meaning through use of Christian symbols of crucifixion. Darialsky wears a red shirt. The color red, for Belyi, is a kind of New World equivalent to the purple of Christian passion and suffering.[78] As Darialsky awaits Matryona for their first love tryst he involuntarily weaves himself a crown from a prickly fir branch. The similarity to Christ's crown of thorns is clear. Soon after this incident Darialsky descends into the Christian "hell," that is, the threatening Ivanovesque nether realm of sexual passion. Unlike the protagonists in the two symphonies, Darialsky's consciousness is genuinely expanded through affirmation of the physical, emotional, and sensuous aspects of his nature. However, the result is neither the "new greatness of man" that Nietzsche wants nor the combination of creative release and spiritual wholeness that Ivanov seeks. Instead Darialsky stumbles onto a more traditional Christian view: that fleshly passion leads to moral enslavement and confusion of the will to truth. The highest good is the kind of compassion that liberates from sensuous desire and opens a person to the suffering and the beauty of another person's spirit. Thus, Darialsky sees Matryona's spiritual beauty as it shines through her physical ugliness. He loves her for a quality of passion mixed with compassion. She, in turn, understands his tragic fate. She gives him a copper cross, a symbol of his coming sacrifice. She too appears to break through to an expanded consciousness. She rebels against the psychic domination of her evil guardian, the chief Dove, Kudeiarov. However, both she and Darialsky are too vulnerable in their chaotic Dionysian condition to overthrow the designs of the demonically clever Kudeiarov.

In his search for vital consciousness Darialsky becomes tragically aware that he is too weak to prevail. He realizes that he is to be sacrificed to evil forces. Through his experience he does attain an independent moral consciousness, and one that goes beyond the conventional populist wisdom. If the populist *intelligent* sacrificed himself to the *narod* in its abstracted, iconic form, now Darialsky who has gained deeper wisdom sees the *narod* in its terrible sloth and ignorance, in its enslavement to the oppressive forces within itself. He clearly sees the evil power inherent in the *narod* that divides, confuses, and dominates. He has overcome the inner weakness that prompted him to seek moral regeneration blindly among the "Russian people." Tragically, as he gains this insight and is strengthened by it, he gains a clear understanding of his present vulnerability. He knows that he is doomed. He has the admirable fortitude to face the truth and to articulate his new insight into Kudeiarov. The narrator perceives him as a Christ figure who nobly accepts and blesses his coming crucifixion. Darialsky has learned here to evaluate—humanity's highest activity, in Nietzsche's view—and he has come to understand his own fate. His tragedy is that, although seeing clearly, he is too weak to act. He is the knowing victim who exposes the malice at the heart of Kudeiarov's enterprise, but he is unable to conquer it.

Belyi's appropriation of the myth of regeneration reflects his own aesthetic and ethical differences from Ivanov. He distances himself from mystical anarchism. He depicts small-town life of the "people" with Gogolian grotesquerie. As Alexandrov points out, Belyi agrees with the occultist position of "passive knowing" taken by Darialsky's friend Schmidt. However, the narrator seems very close and genuinely sympathetic to Darialsky's search: he presents Darialsky's story as a tragedy in the midst of grotesque vulgarity. Darialsky's desire to transport himself and subsequently others to a higher level of being, weak and misguided as it may be, inspires the narrator's admiration.

The greatest intellectual contrast between Ivanov and Belyi can be seen in each writer's evaluation of the Dionysian. Whereas Ivanov views it as pregnant chaos, Belyi cannot forget its terrible power to destroy. The force of rebirth that Ivanov sees in it is for Belyi merely a foil for a deeper unseen power striving to confuse and benight. Kudeiarov as the embodiment of that force is a new incarnation of Nietzsche's ascetic priest. He is transformed by inward power. Although he is a compelling personality, he uses his powers of attraction and persuasion to sow anarchy, to befuddle, and ultimately to repress. He is deeply resentful of generative power in other people, and he aims to manipulate and ultimately to destroy that power. Like Nietzsche's priest, although he is himself impotent both sexually and spiritually, he possesses the will to tame and to tyrannize others. Kudeiarov cannot himself sire the new Christ but must capture Darialsky to do his job. What he can do, as his name suggests, is to bewitch ("kudesnik" means "wizard"). Despite its seeming vitality the Dionysian can produce no true resurrection because it is too vulnerable to this kind of abuse. The dark, tyrannical side of Dionysus, in Belyi's view, must take the upper hand in the end.

In *Petersburg* Belyi comes to a decisive but still unsatisfactory resolution of his moral ambivalence.[79] Moral truth exists a priori and can be known only to sensibility that has been freed of forces of both Ego and Self. Myth that is intuitively generated and lived, Belyi shows in *The Silver Dove*, leads tragically to ruin and to the triumph of an active principle of evil. In his second novel Belyi replays Darialsky's story in that of the anarchist Dudkin. Now, however, a transcendent Christ-like deus ex machina intervenes and leads the moral rebel to a different, "better," although still tragic outcome.

Existence in *Petersburg* is the epitome of what Belyi considers evil: it is the manifestation of control of one earthly mind,

Mystical Symbolists 165

one self over all other selves. Petersburg is the geopsychological center of ascendancy of one self: historically Peter, and in the novel Peter's fictional, bureaucratic descendant, the senator, Apollon Apollonovich Ableukhov. The resulting symbolic oppression and obviation of all other selves also make Petersburg the breeding ground of Russian moral rebellion. Belyi mentions the statue of Peter the Great, the bronze horseman, as the symbol of Russia's division into two (P, 64). The horse rearing up from the rock is the separation of Russia's sons from their native soil. In this symbolic alienation is the crux also of Belyi's moral-psychological dilemma: here mind is severed from psyche, ego from body, spirit from senses.

The Petersburg of Belyi's novel is the construct of the mind of its most powerful inhabitant, Apollon Apollonovich. Like Zeus and Peter before him, Apollon "creates" the novel's other characters out of his brain (P, 20). Like his Greek and Russian predecessors, he is centrally concerned with consolidating and holding power. The rebels, Aleksandr Dudkin and Nikolai Ableukhov, respectively, Apollon's spiritual bastard son and his legal biological son, are the physical realizations of his fears about keeping his power. They represent the products of an all-powerful mind alienated from its "body," its greater "Self." This dominant, rational consciousness manipulates and controls the phobias that it breeds through a network of subterfuges. Apollon has a series of agents with Lippanchenko at their head. He does not know that they are actually *double* agents. They appear to feed and encourage dark rebellious forces but really work to reveal and destroy them. Apollon's power then is maintained through the agents' manipulation of the Dionysian medium in which the rebels exist: intoxication, delirium, moral confusion. Nikolai suffers from a sense of being torn apart (P, 127–128). Dudkin lives in a perpetual state of helpless drunkenness that Lippanchenko deftly abuses.

The double agents produce a bomb, which they wish to persuade the rebels to use to kill Apollon. Now it is questionable who has more power—Apollon, whose life is threatened; the rebels, who hope for new culture, a different social order, and their own power; or the middle men, who take advantage of both sides. Lippanchenko and his crew, like Kudeiarov in *The Silver Dove*, see and know everything. Apollon epitomizes the clear, rational world that is paralyzed with fear before dark subconscious forces and can control them only through repression. The double agents function in both worlds and can cold-bloodedly play one side against the other. They control the situation and stand to impose their own power on others.

The sabotage is revealed through the intervention of a higher force, the ethereal "sad and tall" Christ figure who appears to rebel characters, particularly Nikolai and Dudkin. In each of these Dionysian rebels the Christ arouses a latent moral conscience long unused and forgotten. Nikolai is horrified when he contemplates the crime he is preparing to commit (P, 127–128). Dudkin lives the passion of Christ. In the midst of his frenzied nightmares and his bouts of intoxication he calms himself by assuming the form of Christ on the cross: "When I have insomnia, my favorite posture . . . is to stand pressed flat against the wall with my arms outstretched to the sides" (P, 60).

The vision of Christ that Belyi takes as the epitome of moral truth is very distant from his earlier idea of the "crucified Dionysus," the archetype of regenerative creativity of Ivanov, or the life-affirming fatalism of Blok. The only very distant similarity is that the Dionysian rebels, Nikolai and especially Dudkin, are the only human characters in a book filled largely with metonymic caricatures. They are two of the three characters to be approached by the "sad and tall" figure. The Dionysian rebel, Belyi admits, is the only person able to perceive the real Christ.[80] The actual Christ figure represents disembodied and will-less clarity of memory and ability to judge. It has rightly been called "alienated."[81] It is as ethereal and otherworldly as the white shade of Solovyov that Belyi claimed to have seen or as Ivan Karamazov's Christ, who is nothing but a gesture. And it is not even so life-affirming as Ivan's Christ, who kisses the Grand Inquisitor as a gesture of forgiveness. Belyi's simply appears and accuses. Like Ivan's Christ, Belyi's apparition does not participate in the verbal delirium of the novelistic world, the bewildering network of parodic allusions, word play, sound association, trivialized dialogue, fragmentation of sound and meaning, subverbal sounds. He speaks only to accuse: "[A]ll of you deny me" (P, 119), and later, "You all pursue and persecute me!" (P, 220). Most of the time he remains silent but in his silence exerts a powerful, direct influence.

The effect of the "sad and tall" figure is to reawaken traditional, restrictive moral conscience. As a result of their encounters both Nikolai and Dudkin are able to reflect upon the momentous crime they are about to commit: they are about to assassinate their "father," Apollon Apollonovich. The Christ figure appears to Nikolai as a kind of daydream. He feels "as if someone sad . . . had entered his soul, and that the bright light of his eyes had begun to pierce him" (P, 220). Nikolai is starting to see clearly the pattern of his life. After this strange encounter he hurries to wrap up the bomb and throw it into the Neva. Although he does not succeed, his moral conscience and the ability to evaluate his condition have been awakened.

Dudkin's meeting with the Christ figure awakens not just the ability to judge actions but the clear knowledge of his position and the sense of who his real spiritual allies and who his enemies are. He understands that Lippanchenko has induced him to betray his "brother" Nikolai by giving him the bomb. Lippanchenko, Dudkin realizes, is a "traitor." Ironically, the motivating factor for Dudkin's murder of Lippanchenko is a moral judgment.

The encounter with the Christ figure is the first of three encounters with the supernatural that enable Dudkin to commit his tragic act. The second and third are with demonic characters, Shishnarfne and the Bronze Horseman. Shishnarfne, the Persian terrorist, is a parody of Zarathustra. He appears to Dudkin much as Ivan Karamazov's devil appears to him.[82] During this meeting Dudkin is purged of the delirium in his mind represented by the nonsense word *Enfranshish* and its reverse *Shishnarfne*. He regains his memory and his ability to reflect upon himself. He realizes that Lippanchenko and his network of terrorists have deceived him and bound him to them in a terrible conspiracy.

Lippanchenko, however, still holds the power of fear over Dudkin. He controls his will. Dudkin overcomes this fear through a phantasmagoric meeting with another demonic apparition, the Bronze Horseman. This figure combines a fantastic version of Pushkin's Bronze Horseman and Stone Guest with a reference to Merezhkovsky's characterization of Peter as the supreme expression of will. The reference to the glowing pipe (214) recalls the beginning of *Peter and Aleksei* in which Peter is seen as a towering, black silhouette smoking a pipe full of hot, red embers (PA, 25). The Horseman now fills Dudkin's veins with "metal," the will necessary to overcome and to kill Lippanchenko. Through his encounters with transcendent forces, Dudkin surpasses his fictional precursor, Darialsky. He overcomes the Dionysian oblivion that ruins Darialsky and threatens to ruin him. He finally has the "no-saying" decisiveness to cast off his chains and to act. He murders Lippanchenko, and the conspiracy fails. Dudkin himself then goes mad.

Dudkin's act, Belyi implies, is only a first step out of a terrible Dionysian deception. The revelation of Dionysus' dark side is a necessary negative act needed for the reinstatement of a "true" mode of valuation through the apocalyptic resurrection of a transcendent Christ. However, the worst has happened: the characters most able to perceive Christ, the illegitimate children of Apollon, the revolutionaries, are destroyed, and little else remains. The father himself is revealed as impotent. The birth of culture that Merezhkovsky had dreamed of has fizzled into trivialities. Ivanov's Dionysian cult produced its opposite: the sacrifice of self to chaotic Dionysian forces has led to the final destruction of everything. In the world that remains there is neither creative drive nor resurrection. Belyi's world, for all its fireworks, counts among the most nihilistic in the prewar era. It stands in its nihilism as a kind of demonstration of Blok's argument in 1910 that transcendent vision is insufficient to sustain Symbolism; one must embrace a Symbolism of the earth, a Dionysian Symbolism.

Belyi's novel, then, leads neither to a new nor to a traditional outcome of the Christian myth: neither to "renewal" nor to "salvation." Belyi only exacerbates the creative-moral rift in his own personality and in the received literary tradition of moral rebellion. He cannot synthesize vital Dionysian power with his hope for spiritual renewal and psychological wholeness, so he exorcizes the Dionysian. Like the Master in Mikhail Bulgakov's much later novel, *The Master and Margarita* (1940), he achieves peace but without wholeness or new life. Indeed, the terrible reality of eternal return, that "Golgotha" on which Nietzsche was "crucified," takes on a new and more deathly significance at the end of the novel.[83] Belyi and, through his novelistic solution, Russian literary culture return to an already lived past now faded and lifeless. Here on Russian cultural ground is reborn what Nietzsche saw as the decadent span of ancient Greek history, Alexandrian culture. Nikolai repeats Solovyov's pilgrimage to the

Egyptian desert. Solovyov had gone in 1875 at the bidding of the Woman Clothed in the Sun and had awaited there a blinding revelation. Nikolai simply repeats and thus "preserves" the ritual without the living faith. In essence, he fulfills for Russian Symbolism the role that the libraries of Alexandria filled for ancient Dionysian culture. After his father's death, Nikolai returns to the family estate in the country, dons a Tolstoian peasant blouse, and lives a quiet, regular, gray life of ascetic self-denial. Again he imitates a once-living myth, but now without feeling the urgency of the original.

The question must be raised, is this final greatest Symbolist novel an admission that Symbolist literature was never more than a mere Alexandrian library of quotations from other works and other ages? Did the mystic Symbolists, as Jutta Scherrer has asked, break through to a new consciousness or did the experiment fail?[84] Belyi starts his novel with the self-negating, Platonic view that art is "unnecessary, idle cerebral play" (P, 35). By the end he seems to concur with Nietzsche's comment that a "Christian who is at the same time an artist does *not exist.*" Has he chosen between the traditional moral asceticism of traditional Christianity and the demonic sensualism of art, and has he rejected art? If so, then we must return to our original question: why did he carry on such a passionate polemic with literary precursors and contemporaries, and why did he care so desperately about his own originality?

It is true that for all his fabulous verbal pyrotechnics, Belyi's moral consciousness was remarkably conservative, even archconservative in the sense that he carried traditional valuations to their divisive, destructive extremes. His literary personality contained much of the reactive, "taming" priest mentality. His prose was a well-aimed shaft directed against the sensual, the passionate, the willful—that is, life itself. His moral consciousness was atavistic: he insisted upon an absolute other, a principle of the good in the cosmic order. Partly from natural prudery, partly in order to counteract the strong influence of great contemporaries, Ivanov and Blok, Belyi's outlook became pronouncedly life-denying, world-belittling, otherworldly. What saved Belyi as an artist was his struggle to confront the "priest" in himself. He felt and lived through the tragedy of moral rebellion rather than denying or suppressing it. He objectified the priest in his personality through literary characters such as

170   *The Revolution of Moral Consciousness*

Kudeiarov and Lippanchenko. Finally, despite himself he realized a strange, earth-denying creativity. He insisted equally on his right to play, to make the world of the literary text in his own image, to innovate. Belyi might be called a radical mystic. His moral consciousness is perhaps less reminiscent of nineteenth-century authors than the fifteenth-century Russian ascetic, Nil Sorsky, whose Hesychastic form of mysticism was so radically world-denying and ethereal that he felt compelled to find new words to express his vision. The justification for Sorsky's "word weaving" perhaps is closest to Belyi's justification for originality. As Alexandrov has noted, Belyi points out the insufficiency of received language.[85] He uses his own innovations to undermine earthly power and to convey transcendent insight. In order to avoid playing second theorist to Ivanov and second poet to Blok, Belyi appropriated for himself the position of what Alexandrov suitably calls "amanuensis" to otherworldly forces.[86] As such, he performed the ironic work of Nietzsche's Christian "nonartists" of annihilating the world but in a masterful, marvelously ingenious way.

In conclusion, the mystic Symbolist appropriation of Nietzsche led to an array of really new visions that had never existed in Russia before. The Symbolists' struggle to find a religious-existential foundation for art led them to take up Nietzsche's challenge that Christian "nonartists" recreate life in their own "starveling" image and "impoverish" it. Thus, in varying degrees but always in remarkable, original ways most were able to resolve the antinomies that had ruined earlier Russian writers.

In this Symbolist mythopoetic process, Nietzsche played less the role of "master" than that of "enabler." His insistence that religious feeling and artistic temperament were irreconcilable challenged his mystic Symbolist readers to reconcile the two. Through the myth of the Dionysian Christ each of the Symbolists found his own answer to the nineteenth-century Russian void between the two. With the exception of Belyi, they redefined religion as a higher affirmation of earthly existence. Art was for each a mystic rite of life, enriching and celebrating it in the variety and originality of personal style and vision. Ivanov perhaps most fully reconciled the warring impulses to sensuality and restraint. He more than the other two practiced Nietzsche's moral psychology of sublimation in a religious view that celebrated earthly existence. He was able to balance two moral views, to weave together self-discovery and moral restraint. Blok, the "natural" Dionysian Christ, sublimated erotic drive as poetic inspiration. To a much greater extent than the others, he celebrated passion at the expense of moral restraint. Belyi is in a real sense the alter ego of other mystic Symbolists. He illuminated the dark, oppressive aspect of Dionysian consciousness.[87] He divided Dionysian and Christian impulses, but still he is essentially Symbolist in that he still finds some bridge between the two. Belyi's greatest Russian precursors, Gogol and Tolstoi, had been unable to reconcile the contradictions between eros and agape, the sensuousness of art and the asceticism of religious feeling. Belyi was also eventually ruined by his inability to find the mythic middle ground. After his third novel, *Kotik Letaev* (1916), his only works of note were memoirs and criticism. However, in distinction to his two Russian precursors, he continued to celebrate the "earth" as high art from the safe distance of a critic. His rich critical studies, particularly of Gogol, remain as Russian classics of the genre.

Belyi brought out the deepest moral dilemma of his age: even with the "death" of God and the failure of a transcendent moral principle, the taste for an external controlling power made itself felt. An essential characteristic of the revolution of moral consciousness was the polarity between the desire for spontaneity and self-realization and the doubt about the human potential to change for the better. The new faith in human creative powers was undermined by old moral habits that judged experimentation and deviation from tradition to be wrong, and limitations imposed from some external authority gave a sense of legitimacy. The popular writers showed this pattern in the many protagonists who either destroyed themselves in the quest for self-realization or submitted to some controlling external influence. Despite his celebration of the "earth," Merezhkovsky held to a vision of history as an overriding, controlling scheme. The revolutionary romantic writers, Gorky, Andreevich, and Lunacharsky, would also be susceptible to a coercive mode of valuation imposed on humanity by a single leader. In all these contexts, spontaneous, inner drive was perceived as the weaker of the two and ultimately the more vulnerable to distortion and abuse. Only two writers, Ivanov and Blok, threw off the idea of morality as externally imposed authority. For them the principles of dialogue held sway. The greater-than-human power of the Dionysian was for them a force with which the human will entered into discourse. In conflict, life energy was uncovered and existence made richer.

Finally we must draw some conclusions as to whether the Dionysian Christ really represented a revaluation of Christian values. The answer is certainly yes. Even in Belyi's radical rebuttal of it, the figure of the Dionysian Christ represented a significant reformulation of the traditional Russian literary archetype. In its Russian image the figure of Christ had always been "earthly" only in the sense that salvation was to be won through imitation of Christ in this life. Emphasis lay on the idea of resurrection as the purification of human consciousness in the here-and-now. Even the most radical kenotic outlook contained the idea that one could "perceive" the essence of God through right ascetic practice. By contrast, the afterlife never gave the comfort that it did in Western Christian systems. Still, the Russian Christ represented a strong denial of the subliminal "animal self." Here is an ideal of *umilenie*—mercy, tenderness, submissiveness, self-effacement, and determined repression of fleshly passion. If the traditional Russian Christ upheld a concept of denial, the Dionysian Christ represented a principle of sublimation. Ego, will, and sexuality were affirmed not in their raw, physical expression but as life energy channeled into higher human endeavor. Indeed, resurrection was now understood in terms of the inner process of sublimation of these "evil" drives. "Hell" gained a legitimacy as an inner realm in which the most secret process of spiritual transfiguration went on. The narrative of Christ's crucifixion now acquired new meaning. Christ was no longer the sacrifice and victim of human evil but assumed the positive, dramatic role of regenerator of the spirit. And crucifixion and resurrection were no longer viewed only as processes of emptying out and purification but of rechanneling and transfiguration.

Let us, first of all, eliminate the artists: they do not stand nearly independently enough in the world and *against* the world for their changing valuations to deserve attention *in themselves!* They have at all times been valets of some morality, philosophy, or religion; quite apart from the fact that they have unfortunately often been all-too-pliable courtiers of their own followers and patrons, and cunning flatterers of ancient or newly arrived powers. They always need at the very least protection, a prop, an established authority: artists never stand apart; standing alone is contrary to their deepest instincts.
— *On the Genealogy of Morals*, "What is the Meaning of Ascetic Ideals?" Section Five, quoted in a letter from A. M. Gorky to A. P. Chekhov, May 12–13, 1899

6

The Revolutionary Romantics
Social Rebellion and Mythopoetry

Gorky's Apotheosis of Creative Will

Maksim Gorky was the most popular figure in the Russian literary world at the turn of the century. Chekhov, who during the 1890s had enjoyed broad acclaim, felt that Gorky's star now outshone his own. He wrote wistfully and humorously to his potential rival, "I used to be our youngest writer, but then you came along—and all at once I aged, and now no one calls me the youngest anymore."[1] Gorky was more than just the next young writer to come along. For the educated Russian intellectual who sympathized with but had no clear concept of the "dark masses," Gorky's sudden and flamboyant entry onto the national literary scene was an event of apocalyptic magnitude. He arose before his audience, in Balmont's words, as the embodiment of sheer "Dionysian" energy.[2] He was a voice from the people, a link to some national "truth" more solid than the intellectuals' theories and dreams. Gorky's mood was invigorating. With a much greater vivacity than that of any of the Populist writers, he exposed and attacked the squalid social condition to which he had been born and the moral and mental numbness that went with it. He proclaimed to the world his ardent faith that there could be a better Russian society. Life, he urged, could be changed if each person self-consciously overcame his own complacency, greed, and cruelty and if people realized the great slumbering creative will within themselves.

The rise of Gorky's star paralleled the tremendous boom in Nietzscheana around 1900, and critics were quick to note a similarity of outlook between writer and philosopher. The Menshevik critic M. Nevedomsky saw the young writer as a "homegrown Nietzschean."[3] According to the critic Iury Aleksandrovich, Gorky was a Nietzschean prime mover: single-handedly he had transformed the mood of his time from resignation to belligerent cheerfulness. According to Aleksandrovich, Gorky's heroes seemed to cry out to readers, "Enough of Chekhov, enough of tears, groans and sorrow, hail to life, freedom, the brave, proud 'yes, to life'!"[4] Despite the clear parallels between writer and philosopher most critics denied the possibility of an influence. It seemed unthinkable that a provincial writer should be familiar with a foreign thinker whose ideas had only recently attracted attention in the capitals. Nikolai Mikhailovsky voiced an opinion shared by many when he argued that each man had sensed the mood of the times independently of the other.[5]

Nevertheless, there is plenty of evidence that the writer was very much interested in Nietzsche and even used the popular cult of the philosopher to accelerate his own debut into mainstream literary life. Memoirs show that Nietzsche was among the first subjects Gorky raised with people he wanted to impress. Vladimir Posse, the Marxist editor who recognized Gorky's potential and helped to boost him to national fame, recalled his first visit to the writer in the Volga River city of Nizhny Novgorod in 1898. His host entertained him by reading from *Thus Spoke Zarathustra*. After reading for a while, Gorky would interject enthusiastically, "This, brother, is well said"![6] Another memoirist, Nikolai Tumanov, reported a rare meeting in 1899 between Gorky and his archenemy-to-be, Merezhkovsky, during which the two argued heatedly about their common mentor, Nietzsche.[7] Several letters from this same period to leading writers and critics show that Gorky frequently quoted and discussed Nietzsche.[8] Indeed, here Nietzschean turns of phrase were often used to support Gorky's own views. The apprenticeship to Nietzsche is clear.

Nietzsche figures prominently in the late 1890s in Gorky's earliest efforts to make a national name for himself. The young writer went to considerable lengths to become a best-seller, to market his product in such a way as to appeal to a broad span of readers.[9] His collected stories were published in three volumes in 1898 and 1899 and were organized in such a way as to give prominence to stories inspired by Nietzsche's thought. For example, the lead stories in volume I were "Chelkash" and "Song of the Falcon" ("Pesnia o Sokole"), and the final ones in the other two volumes were important Nietzschean programmatic statements, "The Mistake" ("Oshibka") and "The Reader" ("Chitatel'"). His effort went so far as to persuade his publishers, Dorovatovsky and Charushnikov, to commission a well-known critic, Andreevich (Evgeny Solovyov, 1863–1905), to write a book that would help to advertise his name and product.[11] The result was *A Book on Maksim Gorky and A. P. Chekhov* (1900). Author, publisher, and critic apparently agreed that a strong association with Nietzsche could only boost sales. Near the beginning of his study, Andreevich made an explicit connection between writer and philosopher: "Nietzsche's superman is much nearer to us than one might first think. [The superman] knows no mortal terror and acts on the dictates of his own nature. He does not lie to himself, he is naive and bold. . . . Naive and bold as a child or a genius . . . Gorky's tramp is also something of a 'Nietzschean'" (MG, 28–29).

Gorky's reputation as a Nietzschean was not limited to Russian circles. It spread abroad when he went into exile after 1905. During his visit to the United States in 1906, he welcomed the chance to discuss Nietzsche.[12] When in the same year Nietzsche's sister Elisabeth Förster-Nietzsche received word that Gorky liked her brother's work, she invited him to visit the Nietzsche archives in Weimar.[13]

Given Gorky's typically open and enthusiastic praise for Nietzsche's thought, it is hard to understand why at certain times he chose publicly to vulgarize and discredit his mentor. At three points in his career—the revolt of 1905, shortly after he was sent into a second exile abroad in 1923, and soon after his final return to Stalinist Russia in 1930—he described an image of Nietzsche's philosophy as an authoritarian and arbitrary social doctrine. In 1905, Gorky wrote in "Notes on Philistinism" ("Zametki o meshchanstve") that Nietzsche's "bourgeois" philosophy attracted unscrupulous individualists (SS30, XXIII, 344–345). In 1923, in the third volume of his autobiography, *My*

Universities (*Moi universitety*), he compared Nietzsche's moral views to those of a ruthless Kazan policeman he had known when he kept company with students from the University of Kazan. This "vulgar Nietzschean" character saw the quality of pity as a "harmful thing." He argued that society "should help strong, healthy people so they don't waste their strength" and considered helping the weak wrong because they could never become a source of strength. They would only drag down the rest of society (SS30, XXVI, 73). Finally, in his article from 1930, "Conversations about My Trade" ("Besedy o remesle"), Gorky called Nietzsche's moral philosophy a "morality of cruelty" that taught that the "true purpose of life is the creation of people of a higher type, of 'supermen,' for which slavery is a necessary condition." He finished his tirade with a misquote from his mentor. In "Of Old and New Law Tables," Zarathustra asserts: "That which is falling should also be pushed!" (Z, 226). His thought refers to valuations that have outlived their time. Gorky anthropomorphizes "that which" as a considerably more callous "he who." Nietzsche's moral view, Gorky wrote, could be summarized with the motto "Push the falling man down!" (SS30, XXV, 320).

Are we to interpret these attacks as a rivalry of artistic imaginations on the model offered by John Burt Foster in *Heirs to Dionysus*? Are they part of a recurring deliberate misreading that allows Gorky the epigone to establish himself as a unique and original writer? We can certainly see some aspects of this pattern. However, I believe that another phenomenon is at work here, something that stands closer to the essence of Gorky's creative imagination. Gorky's strongly divided response to Nietzsche reflects in microcosm a larger breach in his moral sensibility. Here it is possible to see the conflict in terms of private and public literary selves. In private correspondence Nietzsche's thinking supports a personal ecstatic belief in human self-creation, but is seen in public polemic as the deadly enemy of the morality prevalent among radicals of self-sacrifice in the name of the people. In a well-known letter from 1898 to the editor F. Batiushkov, he quotes the refrain from *Thus Spoke Zarathustra* that "man is something which should be overcome" and finishes with an enthusiastic profession of faith: "I believe, I believe he will be overcome" (SS30, XXVIII, 33). In correspondence with the artist Ilia Repin, Gorky suggests that human nature contains a vast wealth of latent creative potential that awaits liberation (SS30, XXVIII, 101). Here he refers to Nietzsche although in a guarded way through reference to one of his own Nietzschean stories, "The Reader."

By contrast, Gorky's public mention of Nietzsche is at first glance very antagonistic and indeed vulgarizing. In this context Gorky poses as the defender of social utilitarian values of pity for the weak and recognition of the rights of the working masses. This ethos is in part genuine but, in my view, is highly glossed for the benefit of radical critics and patrons who took a strong interest in the proper development of Gorky's social views. It is significant that Gorky assumed this public posture only at critical moments in his career when his future as a writer depended heavily on support from radical politicians. For example, after the revolt of 1905, Gorky was sent into exile and his early popularity with Russian readers was in jeopardy. Meanwhile, his relationships to Bolshevik activists such as Lenin and Lunacharsky was growing in importance. After the Civil War, in 1923, his connection to the Russian press and readership had again been severed by foreign exile, this time strongly endorsed by his former companion in exile, Lenin. His relation to the young Soviet regime was unclear. The growing oblivion that became the fate of many émigré Russian writers threatened him as well. By 1930 Gorky had returned to the fold and had been honored as the "stormy petrel" of the revolution and had been handed all the honors—his name all over the new Soviet map, automatic if well-controlled "influence," and a broad readership—but all at a cost. In all these cases radical, authoritarian power had helped either to take away or restore literary reputation and influence. The price exacted was to relinquish at least his public profile of artistic and ideological independence.[14]

Gorky's acts of public rejection of Nietzsche hint at a basic incongruity in the writer's moral sensibility. Deep down he did struggle between two human views. Although he yearned for mass self-transformation and believed strongly that people were capable of self-determination of a kind, he also suspected that the individual "selves" that constituted the "masses" did not possess the ethical qualities necessary to turn that inner energy to broad social and cultural renewal. Given the freedom

180 *The Revolution of Moral Consciousness*

to act, real-life individuals would serve themselves and fritter away collective potential in narrow self-enrichment. To achieve the goal of massive, social transfiguration, personal energy must be controlled and guided by external, ideological sanction. Implicit in Gorky's two responses to Nietzsche is a delight in spontaneous human power mixed oddly with a mistrust of the kind of change that that power, left on its own without guidance, might bring.

Gorky's moral outlook is given more subtle shading in yet a third set of private references to Nietzsche. He used Nietzsche to support his own contempt for the smugness and torpor of human nature. In two letters from 1897 and 1910, Gorky upheld Nietzsche's "antidemocratic" views as an expression of disgust at contemporary society.[15] It is difficult from these remarks to see on what Gorky founds his belief in human self-creation. Unlike Nietzsche, who valued a few rare qualities in present human nature, Gorky found no redeeming features in contemporary man.

The mixture of aggressive vitalism, utopian dreams of universal compassion and harmony, and secret contempt for the "human-all-too-human" that emerges in Gorky's remarks on Nietzsche reveals a strange moral consciousness. It resembles something as incongruous as a Nietzschean priest preaching the productive self-creation of the ascetic philosopher. The question of the impact of this divided sensibility on Gorky's art and of what literary resolution, if any, was found, now arises. The significance of this rift for his art was best expressed in the letter of 1899 to Chekhov in which Gorky cites Nietzsche's thought that artists are involuntarily the "valets of some morality, philosophy, or religion" and the "cunning flatterers of ancient or newly arrived powers." This thought sounds in two ways. It expresses Gorky's challenge to himself to overturn the reigning radical utilitarian aesthetic of art in the service of ideology and to make art an independent force of social self-definition and self-determination. It also sounds as an anxious warning that spontaneous creative drive and its expression in art alone may lack the vision and will to motivate the transfiguration of society. It may be the fate of art to serve social ideology rather than to formulate and create new consciousness. What make Gorky's art and his personality vital and interesting is the tension between vitalist and social utilitarian impulses and his refusal ever completely to submit to the one or the other.

The salient feature of Gorky's earliest stories from the mid-1890s is his vitalist rebellion against all moral sanction. And it is with these early stories that he helps to shape the vulgar Nietzschean conception that evil is good and good, evil. Gorky is openly infatuated with what Preobrazhensky defines as "evil": fearless independence and strong personality coupled with aggressiveness and a will to violence: they are a sign of inner integrity and self-reliance. Petr Pertsov, who later became a prominent editor in Symbolist circles, remembered this belligerent mood in Gorky's writing as early as 1892, and he associated it with Nietzsche. Gorky submitted some of his earliest stories to the provincial journal *Volzhskii vestnik* (*The Volga Herald*), where Pertsov held his first editing job. Pertsov remarked, "I remember [seeing] in one of those stories some rather bold verses written in that Nietzschean spirit which was so characteristic of the young Gorky:

> Life is an instant:
> Sensation is
> The essence and meaning of all life.
> Less than all else
> Should one censure
> Crime.

(Zhizn'—mgnovenie:/ Oshchushchenie—/ Sut' i smysl zhizni vsei./ Vsego menee/Prestuplenie/ Poritsat' dolzhno v nei)."[16] Crime here is a sign of vitality. Clearly "moral judgment" as restriction and "life" as liberation are opposed, and "life" is the preferred value.

While groping for a way to social transfiguration and renewal, Gorky explores three major human archetypes. Two, the criminal and the dreamer, are inherited from his populist precursors.[17] The criminal illustrates the insufficiency of existing social mores. The dreamer has the attitude necessary to transcend existing social conditions, but he lacks vision. The third archetype, the artist-leader, represents Gorky's mastery of the populist tradition and his bid to establish a new socially engaged aesthetic. This type possesses the powers of the other two but combines them with the explosive, extroverted energy necessary to marshall and convert other people to his cause.

Many of Gorky's tramp stories, such as "Malva," "The Rogue," and "Chelkash," have as their central character a "noble" transgressor. All of them appear to have chosen to be outlaws because it is preferable to being slaves. In the "normal," good existence dignity is vulnerable, the mind is dulled, personal integrity is violated. Criminality is a protest against the deadening nature of socioeconomic conditions and the moral perversion that they spawn. Each of these protagonists considers returning to the regular life but then is convinced by some event that his present life is indeed better in the sense that he controls his own destiny.

In "Chelkash," Grisha Chelkash defies the benumbing life of the Odessa shipyards. Life here is oppressive: men are enslaved to machines, their lives squandered in the hold of some ship. By contrast, Chelkash lives for his own freedom, stealing what he needs for survival. He enjoys stealing for the challenge it offers him. His robbery seems justified as a kind of rebellion against the huge machines and as a reaffirmation of his own humanity. Chelkash indeed has a kind of moral integrity lacking in others. He keeps the few promises he makes. He does the jobs he pledges to do and generously repays his partners in crime.

Chelkash starts to doubt his life as a thief when he meets a young peasant, Gavrila. He "employs" Gavrila to help him take some contraband from a ship lying offshore. The two talk as they row back with their load. Gavrila dreams of having his own farm and a measure of independence. He has come to the docks to earn the money he needs to buy a plot of land. As he listens to Gavrila, Chelkash wistfully remembers his own village and wonders whether he should settle down. However, he reconfirms his preference for the free life as he begins to know Gavrila better. As the younger man is forced to take risks in his crime, he proves himself to be weak-hearted and disloyal. Later when they divide up the spoils, Gavrila is overcome with greed and nearly kills his partner in order to take all the money. Chelkash shows himself to be the more honorable of the two.

Gorky's youthful enthusiasm for the free, self-willed "noble" criminal moderates (but by no means disappears) when he frames the criminal and the harm he does in social perspective. In "Kain and Artem" (1898), we find a parable about the moral relationship between the powerful and the disenfranchised in the "jungle" of city life. A local South Russian hooligan, Artem, and a Jewish street peddlar, Kain, strike up a relationship when Kain saves Artem's life. In appreciation Artem protects him from the regular insults and injustices of the street but eventually decides that he, like the rest, scorns Kain and can no longer be his bodyguard. Although handsome, graceful, and free, Artem bears the brutish, repressive, wantonly violent character of Nordau's vulgar-Nietzschean "master" type. He is the "ancient animal self." His resemblance to the "laughing lion" is brought out in his frequent comparison to a cat. He is savage and cruel, beautiful and self-assured. His behavior is feline: he "warm[s] himself in the sun, stretching like a cat" (R, III, 131). When he strolls down the street, he is "morose, silent and wildly beautiful—like a great beast" (R, III, 135). Nordau describes the master as a "freely roaming solitary beast of prey, whose primordial instincts were egoism and lack of any consideration for others."[18] Artem resembles the master in his solitary way of life: "his comradely feelings were undeveloped and he was not drawn to associate with people" (R, III, 133). He always works alone, and he never shares his booty. He is cruel like Nordau's master, who "attacks weaker men to calm his destructive urges and his thirst for blood."[19] Artem often "hunts" in the street: he knocks over people's wares, breaks their tables, and steals whatever he wants.

Artem appears to be able to change his moral character after his brush with death. Kain's pity and kindness seem to have affected the stronger man: Artem promises to protect the person who has saved him. Eventually, however, he becomes dissatisfied with the arrangement and withdraws his promise. Tenderness and consideration, he decides, are not part of his character, and it is dishonest for him to pretend that they are. Even this barbarian has his own severely limited sense of integrity. He realizes that he has no compassion for anyone and feels that it is better to admit such a thing than to lie. Artem sends Kain away with the thought that "one has to act according to truth . . . according to one's soul" (R, III, 164).

In a naive, literalist way, Gorky "discredits" Nietzsche's moral view by supporting Nordau. He agrees with Nietzsche's vulgarizer that it would be impossible for the slave type in society to "control" the master, to make him question his strength and induce him to act less brutishly toward others. It bears repeating that these early stories helped to vulgarize Nietzsche by reenforcing the idea that Nietzsche was a social philosopher who advocated a crude ideology of "might is right."

In the course of the 1890s, Gorky returned to a traditional ethical view: the self-willed "transgressor" type is repressive, immoral, and unjust when he wields economic power without social conscience. For example, the rich merchants of *Foma Gordeev*, Iakov Maiakin and others, make their money by swindling, robbing, overcharging the poor. They support a social system that oppresses all but the very few. Gorky wrote to Leonid Andreev in 1901 that the world is divided between the masters and the slaves: the masters oppress and the slaves dream of liberation.[20] However, it is essential to point out that although Gorky accused his social adversaries of immoral behavior, he himself ultimately would not uphold the same ethical norms that he imposed on them. For him, the breaking of boundaries for the purpose of releasing deep creative energy would loom larger than the establishment and enforcement of just ethical norms.

Gorky's inherent attraction to the powerful, lively, self-willed aspects of human nature persisted. Gradually, these qualities became sublimated and synthesized with an overarching utopian vision of a free, just, and productive society. In his "dreamer" characters, violent, transgressive urges are turned inward. Like Nietzsche's man of "bad conscience," this type turns his energy and his violence against himself: he ruins himself to satisfy an inner yearning to test existence, to go higher, to be more than laws of necessity say he can be. This testing, questioning, challenging, for Nietzsche and Gorky, is the prelude to deep, world-altering creativity (Z, 90–91). By pushing beyond the bounds of moderation, by sacrificing himself to his inner drive, this person ennobles and regenerates all humanity: he gropes his way to what Nietzsche called a "guiding idea," some large, existential goal that sustains the human spirit and provides a justification for world-shaping acts. The best examples of Gorky's dreamers are the falcon in "The Song of the Falcon" (1895) and Foma Gordeev in *Foma Gordeev* (1899). The dreamer shares a rebellious quality with the outlaw type: he protests the falseness inherent in conventional morality. He possesses the élan, the will to sacrifice, the *amor fati*, but he does not yet have the "guiding idea" that the creator-hero will have. It is interesting that here Gorky no longer relies on popularized interpretations of Nietzsche but interacts with primary Nietzschean texts. If popularizations and vulgarizations provided character types and themes for his outlaw stories, now it is clear that Gorky is making his own direct readings, particularly of the recently translated *Thus Spoke Zarathustra* and *Birth of Tragedy*.

In "The Song of the Falcon" Gorky dramatizes the concept of *amor fati* in the character of the falcon.[21] The song celebrates the "madness of the brave," those who dare to strive even in the face of death. A falcon soars over the cliffs that line the ocean's shore. Although he is wounded, he flies upward into the azure one last time before plunging into his death in the ocean. The other personage in this allegorical tale is a grass snake, the falcon's moral opposite, who prefers the safe, cozy life of basking in the sun. The daring falcon and the prudent grass snake parallel Zarathustra's allegorical representations of virtue: his proud eagle and clever serpent. Zarathustra relies on both traits to carry him forward to self-overcoming. In the chapter "The Convalescent," his animals save him from utter despair. From them he learns a new philosophy of eternal return. Two letters give evidence that Gorky was thinking of Zarathustra's animals when he wrote "The Song of the Falcon." He clearly had in mind not a falcon, but an eagle because in both letters he refers to the bird as an eagle, and to his story as a "feuilleton" about a "Grass Snake and an Eagle" (PSS, II, 386). Gorky's animals are similar in character to Zarathustra's. The two serpents are prudent, wise, and clever. The two birds of prey are proud and brave. Zarathustra welcomes his eagle as "the proudest animal under the sun" (Z, 53). The ocean heralds the falcon's brave last flight as "the call to the proud [to strive] toward light and freedom" (PSS, II, 242). Both the falcon and the eagle possess the mad daring needed to strive beyond the familiar to the unknown.

Gorky radicalizes the relationship between the two virtues. The snake with his narrow-minded vision of the world becomes the less attractive figure, if not exactly the adversary. Although Zarathustra's animals fly together, the snake wrapped around the neck of the eagle, Gorky's snake dozes comfortably on his rock. His cautiousness seems less the virtue that it is in *Zarathustra:* whereas Zarathustra's serpent is able to adapt, Gorky's is observant but staid. This snake has perhaps more in common with Nietzsche's last man and Gorky's later petit-bourgeois characters. In addition to Gorky's own deformation of these two virtues, we see here the secondary impact of the Russian tradition. The idea of regeneration through suicide rather than through striving seems closer to Kirilov's view of self-overcoming than Zarathustra's.

Through the devaluation of the same prudent serpent and the preference of suicide to struggle, Nietzsche's idea of eternal return is lost. It is replaced by an anarchistic, nihilistic heroism. In his first novel, *Foma Gordeev,* Gorky creates his first larger-than-life tragic hero. Here for the first time is evidence of Gorky's interest in *The Birth of Tragedy,* which appeared in 1899 in N. N. Polilov's translation and which Gorky had in his library in Nizhny Novgorod. He clearly envisioned Greek heroes as a model for his own protagonist. He described Foma as a Hercules who wants to break the bonds of the merely human. In Foma's character Gorky emphasizes Dionysian rebellion rather than Apollonian vision. As with his other early characters negation of existing order is perceived as heroic. However, Foma is the first of this type to worry about the purpose of his rebellion. The son of a wealthy, self-made, shipping magnate, Foma himself possesses almost superhuman energy and strength. He is isolated in the merchant community in that he is gnawed by social conscience. He is appalled by the heartlessness of other merchants. His way of protesting, however, is ineffective: he destroys himself, drinking and squandering his wealth. When it is too late and he has been branded an outcast, he bursts out, making well-founded accusations against his fellow merchants. His rebellion against the social injustices of merchant life on the Volga is powerful but undirected, and it finally ruins him. Foma's actions are guided by blind passion. Unlike Nietzsche's tragic hero, who possesses a clear, Apollonian dream of a new order, Foma as pure Dionysian lacks the imagination and reason to channel his passion and to conceive of a better social order.

Like Nietzsche's tragic hero, Foma commits a "crime" against nature. The young merchant's rebellion against natural law is couched in socioeconomic terms: harsh economic conditions encourage the wealthy and avaricious to exploit and oppress the weak and impoverished. Like Nietzsche's concept of natural law, Gorky's concept of economic law is perhaps unjust and cruel, but it sustains those who adhere to it. Foma's crime is that he transgresses against this law: he is too kind to workers, he is generous with his money, and he reveals the corruption of his peers. From childhood on, he is unable to treat workers with the accustomed ruthlessness. Instead he makes gifts of grain to starving peasants and defends the rights of the oppressed. At the end of the novel, half-crazed and unable to control himself any longer, he lashes out against the merchants and their cruelty:

> Gushchin, do you help your nephews? Give them each at least a kopeck a day . . . you have stolen so much from them . . . Bobrov! Why did you slander your mistress? You had her convicted of stealing and thrown into prison. If you were sick of her, you could have given her to your son. . . . What does it matter, he has taken up with another of your mistresses. . . . You didn't know? Oh, you pig! . . . And you, Lup, why do you have a whorehouse, and why do you swindle your guests? . . . Who was it that you killed that time, Lup? (R, IV, 360)

Foma cannot tolerate the oppressiveness of this life, but without the support of strong values of his own he is forced to confront the void within himself. He sees the profound chaos lying beneath the apparent order of life. "A man is in a boat on a river," Foma paraphrases Schopenhauer and Nietzsche (BT, 36). "The boat may be strong, but it floats over an abyss. . . . It is sturdy, but if the man [in it] senses the dark abyss beneath him, . . . no boat can save him" (R, IV, 330–331). The falcon's and Foma's "madness of the brave" is not enough to turn rebellion to productive ends. A clear vision is needed.

Finally, Foma succumbs to the most ordinary insanity. His madness ironically does not reaffirm life, as does the divine madness of Nietzsche's tragic hero. *Foma Gordeev* ends with a sense of despair: the hero is confined to an insane asylum. Instead of being venerated as a seer, he is jeeringly called "the Prophet" (R, IV, 374). However, Gorky's novel ultimately expresses the feeling that people need a compelling dream of the good life if indeed the world is to change for the better. It is the goal of art to raise the desire for and even to sketch out that dream.

In Gorky's early works raw life force and the urge to rebel do not produce the positive social vision that would incite people to change their society. It is from his revaluaton of the populist utilitarian ethic of social duty that Gorky derives the needed social consciousness. Although the young writer is critical of the virtue of pity as it is traditionally practiced, he gropes for a vital—what he later would call "active"—compassion. In early stories, where he casts down meekness and pity as false goodness and lack of will, he also searches for a "true" social ethic. His vision always hinges on a revaluation of the virtue of pity. The two best examples of false virtue are Kirill Iaroslavtsev in "The Mistake" ("Oshibka," 1896) and Kain in "Kain and Artem." Iaroslavtsev dramatizes Preobrazhensky's popularized critique of altruism. In "The Mistake," he must decide whether he wants to visit and offer help to an old acquaintance suffering from a mental breakdown. He questions why he should want to help and whether he really "pities" this person. His self-doubt echoes Preobrazhensky's idea that "when we feel pity, we are fulfilling first of all our own emotional needs" (VP, 129). When someone has been wounded, we feel pain as if we ourselves had been hurt. This sensation motivates us to help the other person as if he were we. Iaroslavtsev asks whether he wants to visit Kravtsov merely to comfort himself: "Is it curiosity or pity, or a sense of duty? Madness is almost death. . . . It is remarkable that a person arouses attention . . . suddenly when he is near death . . . we pity him and talk about him. . . . As if death . . . brought us closer together . . . maybe, when we see another person dying, we remember that we have to die, and we pity ourselves in the other person" (R, I, 153). Pity, Iaroslavtsev concludes, is really only a form of egocentricity. Instead of helping the other person to recover, the person who pities feels sorry for himself.

To pity a sick or weak person is also to confirm our own sense of well-being. Preobrazhensky writes that the feeling of pity gives us pleasure "in the consciousness of our own strength." We are moved to help because doing so reaffirms our own sense of well-being. During his visit with Kravtsov, Iaroslavtsev wants to "cry for pity" as long as he knows that he is the healthier and stronger of the two (R, I, 167). However, this kind of pity is fickle. Preobrazhensky points out that when the sick person regains his health, he is often resented by the stronger person. "The opposite of pity," he remarks, "is . . . a profound antagonism toward another person's joy in willing and doing" (VP, 130). The two sentiments go hand in hand. In Gorky's story, Iaroslavtsev resents Kravtsov when he sees that his old classmate not only is not insane but, in fact, possesses a very powerful mind and spirit: "He was not sorry for Kravtsov and was even a bit angry with his exultant mood" (R, I, 168). Iaroslavtsev becomes irritated and ceases to feel for the reportedly sick man.

Although Gorky showed the essential "selfishness" of pity and altruism, he felt and would consistently argue that an active compassion for other people is the strongest bond to unite society. Thus, both in "The Mistake" and in "Kain and Artem" he started to think in terms of a revaluation of compassion. Whether this revaluation is possible and what its effect is remain to be seen. Our second example of a "good" person, Kain, is a more complex character than Iaroslavtsev. He is weak and in some ways contemptible, but not so impotent as the earlier character. Gorky shows why Kain is weak but appears to support him as a truly good person.

Kain's appearance and personality draw heavily on Max Nordau's vulgarization of Nietzsche, *Degeneration*. Nordau saw the idea of the slave as proof of Nietzsche's anti-Semitism. Stating Nietzsche's idea in a sociopolitical context, he upheld the concept of slave morality as "civilization" and democracy, and master morality as "barbarism," as physical oppression of the weak by the strong. Kain, thus, appears to be the slave type that Nietzsche describes metaphorically in *Beyond Good and Evil* and that Nordau interprets literally as a Jewish type in *Degeneration*: "the coward, the nervous, mean, . . . distrustful person with his disingenuous glance, the self-abusing human hound who allows himself to be abused, the begging flatterer, above all, the liar" (BGE, 205; Nordau, 422).[22] Kain is, indeed, cowardly and nervous. He is a self-abasing human hound: "when people mocked him, he only smiled guiltily, and sometimes even helped people laugh at him, as if paying his tormentors for the right to exist among them" (R, III, 128). He is distrustful, but he is neither vile nor mendacious. Above all, he is not vengeful, as the slave type is supposed to be. In fact, the narrator emphasizes his hero's virtues. He points out repeatedly that, although Kain is kind, capable, and intelligent, he has been insulted by fate. He is fearful and mistrustful because he has been robbed and beaten so many times.

Although miserably defenseless, Kain appears morally stronger than Iaroslavtsev because he acts on his moral sense: he does the good deed of saving a person's life. He is aware that he may receive no repayment and indeed more abuse from Artem, who like other hoodlums is a potential oppressor. All self-interest to the contrary, he helps Artem. Here Gorky shows a form of pity that is not just a foil for self-pity but is modestly effective, positive, life-affirming. It is important to note, however, that pity here remains a restrictive "taming" kind of virtue. It helps for a short while to curb Artem's violent urges, but it does not have the power to turn that energy toward some higher goal. We will find a stronger attempt to redefine pity as a creative virtue in the character of Mark Kravtsov in "The Mistake."

Gorky finds an uneasy balance between vitalist and utilitarian moral impulses in his archetype of the "creator." In the three stories "The Mistake," "The Reader" (1898), and "Man" ("Chelovek," 1904), Gorky first forges the vision of social change that will satisfy his urge to be a "prime mover" independent of patrons. It is significant that Gorky's interaction with Nietzsche intensifies in these works that are so central to the formation of his characteristic moral vision. He leaves aside his polemic with the popularized Nietzsche and engages in his own characteristic reading of the work that he admires most, *Thus Spoke Zarathustra*. Now he attempts to supplant Zarathustra's vision of the superman with his own vision of the creator. The creator-hero is an artist on a monumental scale: he conceives vital myth, creates values and attitudes, and inspires the masses to self-overcoming. His inner resources give him the energy needed to transform society. This energy is channeled into the utopian dream of creating a social order in which everyone will be equal and will treat each other with life-affirming love and pity.

The transition between the old morality and the new is made in "The Mistake" (1896). Here Gorky's dreamer rejects the passive, suffering mentality of late Populism and shapes a vision of the aggressive creator of the future. He presses for a different moral vision that combines compassion with aggressive, creative drive. Mark Kravtsov in "The Mistake" appears as a creator who has lived before his time and whose compelling dream falls on deaf ears. He sacrifices himself for a vision of a future society in which people will truly love each other and will actualize their own creative potential. He proselytizes a new morality of pity that differs from that criticized by Nietzsche: it is life-affirming and creative.

Kravtsov appears as a Russian incarnation of Nietzsche himself. His physical description resembles the well-known profile of Nietzsche:

> Kirill imagined Kravtsov's figure, not too tall, the dry, jagged, nervous face, with a black moustache that always trembled, and the almond-shaped, black eyes with their hot, searching look. The thick brows would jump frighteningly on the white, lined forehead, . . . now creeping up toward the coarse, bristly hair, now jumping suddenly down over the eyes. (R, I, 154)

Piercing eyes, thick brow, short hair, and a dark moustache can hardly be a chance resemblance. Moreover, Kravtsov's personality resembles Zarathustra's in several ways. Both are prophets searching for disciples to share their dreams of the future: Zarathustra's of future human consciousness and Kravtsov's of future society. Both envision man as creator and argue that those who realize their creative spirit will guide the way to a new and better world. The major difference is that Kravtsov is utopian in his thinking, whereas Zarathustra is decidedly antiutopian.[23]

Kravtsov offers a compelling revaluation of the idea of pity. He is single-mindedly devoted to a concept of pity that would inspire people to change the "garbage pit" in which they are living (R, I, 166). People can be "creators" and "bring alive the sands of the desert, by building sanctuaries of happiness" (R, I, 154). Despite its veneer of dynamism and creativity, this idea of "active" pity that Gorky produces has the same problem that Nietzsche sees in conventional pity: pity is a restrictive ethical virtue. It is not the basis on which to build a vital mythical system. It curbs and tames—even for Nietzsche, the supposed enemy of compassion, this effect is not bad—but ultimately it also denies aggressive, live-giving aspects of human nature. Unlike real love, pity cannot nurture life. Gorky's use of imagery belies a contemptuous, life-denying attitude. The world is now a "garbage pit" and a "desert" that has no redeeming features, no seed from which to grow the human society of the future. Hidden in Gorky's view is the ruinous contempt that undermined the old idea of pity. Kravtsov has only one goal toward which he suggests all people should strive, and, thus, he denies the differences in imaginative genius and vital energy that distinguish one individual from another. Finally, the goal itself—to build "sanctuaries of happiness"—suggests more a desire to shut out life and struggle and establish a utopian peace than to enrich existence.

Kravtsov's fearlessness and *amor fati* eventually lead him beyond the bounds of normalcy. He dreams so intensely of a utopian world that he is unable to live according to the rules and laws of this world. His dream, his reason for living eventually ruins him. People consider him insane, and like Foma Gordeev he is incarcerated in an asylum. Yet he has left the world inspired: such dreams will move future generations to great deeds.

The archetype of the dreamer bears out Gorky's conviction that higher vision is essential to lift people out of the mire of present life. However, this type lacks the energy to compel others to follow his example. He is branded as an outcast and a madman and suffers the same fate of frustration as visionary-protagonists in stories from the 1880s and early 1890s, such as the patient in Garshin's "The Red Flower" (1883) or Gromov in Chekhov's "Ward No. 6" (1892). In the end it is he who is destroyed while oppressive social conditions persist.

In "The Reader" Gorky calls directly for a new type of artist, the monumental formulator of human consciousness. This artist will be much more than the specialist in the realm of pure art, the Kantian who constructs a beautiful object that possesses "purposefulness without a purpose." He is a social leader who will use his creative power to transfigure human nature itself.

As he returns home late one evening from a literary gathering, a young writer encounters a shadowy, demonic personage. This stranger claims to have read all the writer's works, and he demands to know his purpose in writing. When the young man hesitates, the "reader" engages in a lengthy diatribe on the shortcomings of contemporary art. The reader himself closely resembles Zarathustra in tone, style of criticism, and philosophy

Revolutionary Romantics   193

of creativity. Both use emotionally laden exhortations mixed with more playful wit. In "Of Poets" and "Of the Way of the Creator," Zarathustra argues that ordinary artists typically write to satisfy personal ambition. Ambition, according to Zarathustra, is at best an ambiguous virtue: it does motivate a person to do well, but only for the ultimate goal of gaining public acclaim. "Alas, there is so much lusting for eminence!" Zarathustra says in "On the Way of the Creator." "There is so much convulsion of the ambitious! Show me that you are not one of the lustful or ambitious" (Z, 88–89). Gorky's reader claims similarly that the young writer writes only to earn the admiration of the public. Like Zarathustra, the reader argues that mere ambition too often replaces creativity's true motivation: a fresh, enlivening vision of the world. The reader expresses his thought with precisely the same word play as Zarathustra. Zarathustra juxtaposes the two words *Ehrgeiz* ("ambition") and *Ehre* ("honor"). Similarly, the reader sees a connection between *chestoliubie* ("ambition") and *chest'* ("honor"). The comparison in both languages highlights the negative meaning of ambition. Ambition is literally a "love of honor," but it is not honor itself. It is a poor replacement for the sense of personal integrity implied in *honor*. The truly creative spirit must be guided by an inner sense, not by the tastes and opinions of other people.

Following Zarathustra's lead, the reader criticizes contemporary writers for their vanity and dullness of spirit, their superficiality and staleness of thought. Zarathustra writes, "A little voluptuousness and a little tedium: that is all their best ideas have ever amounted to" (Z, 151). The reader echoes Zarathustra's exasperation at poets' fundamental lack of originality: "Everything is tedious, tedious people, tedious thoughts, tedious events ... when will people talk about the awakening of the spirit? ... Where is the call to profound creativity?" (R, III, 244).

The reader repeats Zarathustra's idea about the self-cultivation a person must perform to find deeper, world-creative energy. Both believe that the artist must loosen himself from the expectation of his readers. However, such freedom is constructive only if the writer perceives an overpowering, guiding force within. Zarathustra says, "Do you call yourself free? I want to hear your ruling idea, and not that you have escaped from a yoke!" (Z, 89). The reader likewise asks the young writer what great goals he strives toward. The younger man has no answer. Having asked this question, however, Gorky starts to mold his own idea of the artist as creator of social myth.

The state of freedom that the artist attains within unleashes the "chaos" requisite for true creation. Here Gorky deforms Nietzsche with respect to both the nature of the upheaval and the definition of "true creation." For Zarathustra, withering self-scrutiny and the destruction in oneself of fruitless ways of thinking are the first stages toward the personal goal of self-overcoming and the transformation of consciousness. Nietzsche urges each person, even the most ordinary reader, to nurture within him a sense of "great contempt" for complacency and comfort. He does not, at least in *Thus Spoke Zarathustra*, explore the broad social implications of self-transformation, but concentrates on the potentially fruitful results for the individual self. Gorky, in contrast, will imagine transfiguration by inculcating incendiary ideas from above into the "herd" as a whole.

In "The Reader" Gorky applies to a social situation what Nietzsche intends as an expression of a self-critical attitude. Nietzsche sees writing as a revelation of the writer's own soul. Whereas Nietzsche encourages self-critical independence, Gorky suggests that self-transformation will occur under the strict tutelage of the artist-leader. The readers' consciousness is the writer's artistic material. The writer, Gorky says, must compel his readers en masse to criticize themselves; he must make them suffer so that they will become conscious of their failings and thus be able to improve. The reader tells the young writer, "Do not be afraid to hurt a person: if you punish him because you cherish him, he will understand your punishment and will see that he deserved it. When that person is . . . ashamed of himself, be kind to him—and he will be regenerated" (R, III, 248–249). What Zarathustra views as an inner struggle, the reader sees as a social "education" of the reader-follower by the artist-leader.

With Zarathustra, Gorky's reader emphasizes the importance of "evil" in the creative process. The productive evil, for Nietzsche, is the destruction of outlived myth and the moral values it entails (Z, 139). Such evil, in Zarathustra's view, is essential to the ongoing process of creation that he associates with cultural vitality. Here, too, Gorky's reader continues his deformation of Nietzsche: he views evil as the necessary destruction of social myth that precedes the formation of new attitudes. The artist-leader, and not the people themselves, must be evil: he must encourage people to knock down and overturn. The true writer arouses in his readers: "sincere feelings with which, as with hammers, certain forms of life must be broken and destroyed in order to create other freer ones.... Anger, hatred, courage, shame, repulsion, and finally evil despair—those are the handles by which one can destroy everything on earth . . ." (R, III, 245–246). "Evil" feelings, the reader implies, are the stuff of radical social change: without them, there would be no upheaval for the ultimately creative cause of regenerating society. The role of the creator is to encourage people to protest and question, and then to clear the ground and build utopia.

The reader departs from Zarathustra in his ethical views. Like Gorky's other moral rebels, such as Mark Kravtsov and Foma Gordeev, he reaffirms the conventional values of compassion and love for other people. The artist-leader who will build the great utopia must feel warm compassion for humanity. However, it bears repeating that in Gorky's future-oriented vision the mythopoetic issues of fundamental destruction and creation dominate and push purely ethical considerations to the side. The place of pity in the process of social transformation remains problematic. Although Gorky insists it is a generative feeling, in his stories it typically involves a relationship of control, specifically the control of the artist-leader over his reader-adherents.

Toward the end of the story the reader voices Gorky's greatest dream. "Oh," the reader laments, "if only a stern and loving man with a flaming heart and a powerful all-embracing mind would appear!" (R, III, 247). Like his Populist mentors, Korolenko and Mikhailovsky, Gorky had always dreamed and written of a larger-than-life hero. For example, Danko in "The Old Woman Izergil'" ("Starukha Izergil'," 1895) cuts out his burning heart and holds it up as a torch to lead his people out of danger. Until he started to write "Man" in 1902, however, Gorky could not make a creator with a positive vision who, in Zarathustra's words was a "first motion," a "self-propelling wheel," a force that would compel the world to "revolve" around him. "Man" was Gorky's most passionate attempt to state his own "ruling idea." The irony is that this profession of faith fails to provide a truly vital myth of regeneration, because Gorky revives old types and values from another era without making them his own. The result is a sentimental, false-sounding sermon.

In this allegorical tale, Gorky's protagonist, Man, struggles with the personifications of the rational and psychological forces within his own character. Man faces despair: he feels that the virtues of love, faith, and friendship have degenerated into false values. He submits that his existence has no real purpose. Out of this despair arises a perception of new virtues and a clear life goal: Man is prepared to strive for social regeneration and to inspire people with love and respect for each other.

"Man" continues Gorky's intense appropriation of *Thus Spoke Zarathustra*. The hero, Man, is the embodiment of the Russian writer's archetype of the artist-leader. Unfortunately, this work, which was intended as Gorky's confession of faith, emerges as a bad imitation of its predecessor. Every action and every word invokes the blind, Dionysian powers within. As Zarathustra expresses the idea in "On Reading and Writing," the creator "writes in blood" (Z, 67). Gorky paraphrases this idea in a "kitschy," rococo style: "Man adorn[s] his lonely, proud path with the blood of his heart, and he creates from his burning blood the eternal flowers of poetry" (R [1919], IX, 4).

This figure embodies a creativity more fundamental than the artistry of the traditional poet: he shapes religious and moral value. Both Zarathustra and Man have strong, self-motivated "ruling ideas" that guide their efforts and to which they sacrifice their lives. Zarathustra's is the superman; Man's is "Thought" (*Mysl'*) itself. Thought, in this context, signifies Man's most fervent passion, his striving toward clarity and light; it has been interpreted as a Bazarovian faith in science. However, it bears a resemblance to the thinking of the men of the 1860s only in its ardor. This guiding idea departs from its Russian precursors in that it affirms the emotional as well as the cerebral. Man discovers the strength of "Thought" by destroying the old, false virtues of love, friendship, and faith. He discredits these virtues in a Zarathustrian way as barren, life-denying, hypocritical. He understands the "clever and base tricks of Love, its desire to dominate and possess, its wish to demean." He finds "in the rotten heart of Friendship a calculating caution, a cruel, empty curiosity, and the moldering blotches of envy." And finally, "in stagnant Faith" Man senses "the evil thirst for limitless power, striving to enslave all feelings" (5–6). Through his new virtue, Thought, his life goal becomes clear: he will strive to "illuminate the whole gloomy chaos of life" and to "create something new on the unshakable foundations ... of freedom, beauty and—respect for people!" (9) It is interesting that here Gorky makes no mention of pity. He has arrived at other values.

Decisive differences distinguish Gorky's Man from Zarathustra's creator. As in "The Reader," social regeneration supplants personal self-overcoming. Man believes that his own soul searching is only the first stage in the process of mass regeneration. This process will eventually generate the transfiguration of all society. "I am called," Man says, "to unbind the knots of ignorance and error which made frightened people into a bloody and repulsive herd of animals" (8–9). Here more than anywhere previously Gorky's artist-leader reveals his contemptuous priestly character: he sees people as they are in negative terms as a "repulsive herd," as animals that need to be trained and led. People hardly seem capable of self-scrutiny and self-cultivation. A dominative impulse denies the vitalist spontaneity expressed in his words. Gorky's moral consciousness shines through here in all its strange eclecticism. It interlaces a philosophical ascetic's *ideology* of affirmation and self-cultivation with a priestly *will* to inhibit, to dominate, and, in the end, to deny life-giving intuitive impulse. The effect is to create a type of leader we may call the "secular priest." Universal self-fulfillment is attempted ultimately not through self-motivation, self-creation, and self-knowledge but through acquiescence, obedience, service to the secular priest.

In his early work Gorky heroizes the rebellious "animal self" only then to punish, discredit and "tame" it. He achieves his goal by appeal to a traditional "reactive" virtue, pity for the other person. Incongruously, in resurrecting this virtue he invests pity with generative qualities. Kravtsov and the other ideal types speak of an active (not reactive) pity that inspires people to change their lives. Here is a problem: the same virtue that inhibits "evil," aggressive behavior against the weak, cannot also condone creative, aggressive behavior. Gorky has turned pity into something it is not. The result is a false moral tone. Gorky sublimates animal aggression and violence in his artist-leader type. This type sublimates raw, destructive urges as creative ones in his role as the welder of ideal social relations. But here again a purportedly productive moral outlook is belied by a will to manipulation and domination. The artist-leader may have "created" himself and discovered his fate within himself, but he has little faith in the ability of the masses of humanity to discipline, order, and channel their violent drives without ruining everything. The ironic result is that, like the teacher of self-determination in popular novels, he compels his following to realize their creative energies!

Gorky ultimately undermines his faith in "Man" with his contempt for "man" and his authoritarian approach to self-transformation. Just as in his letter to Chekhov he stated the fear that the artist could not be independent of patrons, so he ultimately believes that self-creation is not possible without guidelines imposed from outside. In the place of the traditional, divine regulative power now stands a human authority, the artist-leader.

"Man" was Gorky's most heartfelt attempt to synthesize Nietzschean moral rebellion with a socially oriented aesthetic theory (PSS, VI, 462). He wanted it to become the aesthetic credo of Russia's socially engaged literature. However, the story was too badly written and the creator-hero too authoritarian for most writers. It found little support among radical critics because of the hero's implicit elitism. One of Gorky's former mentors, Vladimir Korolenko, claimed that "Mr. Gorky's 'Man' . . . is really a Nietzschean man" because he "scorns the crowd."[24] With the failure of this programmatic piece, Gorky appeared to have failed in his own bid to be an artist-leader. In an important sense, he had not overcome the traditional position of artist as "valet to some morality" that he had earlier spurned. This failure probably contributed to his public shift away from his mentor, Nietzsche, who challenged the artist to be more than a "valet."

Another possible result of this disaster was Gorky's marked shift toward the relatively authoritarian Bolshevik party. If he could not be a "first motion," according to his own program, he was destined to serve someone who was. During his early career, Gorky had found little of interest in Marxist theory. In 1898, he had mentioned to Vladimir Posse that he disliked Marxism because it "belittled man."[25] However, shortly before 1905, he had started to support the Bolsheviks and urged wealthy admirers, such as S. T. Morozov, to do the same. Now, in 1905, Gorky himself capitulated to pressures from a leader apparently more convincing than he. In Lenin's 1905 essay "Party Organization and Party Literature," Gorky found a literary program more compelling than his failed "Man." Lenin exhorted writers to praise the heroic working class and to raise its political consciousness. He argued that individual artists were ineffectual "literary supermen."[26] Only through cooperation with the collective and the Party would the artist have a hand in forging the world of the future. Thus, partly following Lenin's lead, Gorky publicly rejected obviously "Nietzschean," that is, individualist, ideas and turned his efforts to writing publicistic works, such as the propagandistic novel *Mother*.

After the political unrest of 1905, Gorky became totally immersed in Bolshevik activities. In exile he worked to raise money for the Party. He published a great deal in the Bolshevik press. Most importantly, he helped to organize a school for workers on the island of Capri. During his exile, he came under the personal tutelage of Lenin, who liked him and tried to shape his literary efforts to serve the Bolshevik cause. In view of this strong support and his personal failure as artist-leader, Gorky may have found it desirable to conform in some measure to Bolshevik thinking.

In these years, the dream of the artist-leader seemed to have vanished. In actuality, it had not. Gorky, indeed, was a major leader and creator of social consciousness even though he was not a creator of new myth. Several of Gorky's Nietzschean works lived on as popular revolutionary literature, Korolenko's and others' criticisms notwithstanding. Both "The Song of the Falcon" and "Man" were read frequently at rallies and meetings. In 1919, banners carried into battle by Red Army soldiers bore the slogan, "To the madness of the brave we sing our song" (PSS, II, 590–591).

Gorky's open apprenticeship to Nietzsche had ended. The creator's regenerative energy, the "evil" rebelliousness, the *amor fati* were plowed under, but they were to reemerge after 1905 as the essential impetus for a broad "revolutionary romantic" revaluation of populist myth. The Russian people, as Gorky and other revolutionary romantics imagined them, were no longer the passive, suffering masses worshipped by the Populists. In Gorky's conception, the people had a strong will to self-determination: they were ready to commit crimes against their oppressors, and they were forcing on the intelligentsia their own vision, their own existential purpose. In the God-building movement that arose in these years, Gorky would continue to struggle with the two moral impulses in his character: the desire to believe in creative will and the doubt in its ultimate ability to create social utopia.

The Reappropriation of Populist Myth

Gorky had attempted to inculcate his revolutionary romantic vision into a variety of literary groups. He had a very short, frustrating relationship with the modernist writers around *Severnyi vestnik*. Over a longer period of time he had worked with Andreev, Kuprin, Bunin, and other writers in the *Sreda* circle but had failed to win their conversion.[27] His idea of the artist-leader found its most sympathetic audience in two young Marxist literary critics, Andreevich (Evgeny Andreevich Solovyov, 1863–1905) and Anatoly Lunacharsky. Like him, they had rejected populist thinking but were dissatisfied with the determinist aspects of Russian Marxism. It appeared to all of them to be hostile to moral and aesthetic issues. Partly through independent efforts and partly through their acquaintanceship with Gorky, they started to fill in what was lacking in their Marxist credo: a vibrant image of the working masses. This image assimilated diverse elements of the nineteenth-century Russian faith in the people, a Marxist belief in the world-historical role of the proletariat as the founder of future society, and the Nietzschean high estimation of human creativity.[28] It created from this material a mythic narrative that made mass revolution seem much more thinkable than had previous theory. It answered the strong religious need of its adherents by offering a way out of the bad present to a brilliant future. It promised more than the transformation of social structures and relationships: it gave hope for the transfiguration of human consciousness. Perhaps most importantly, it nurtured the future anxiety of socially oriented artists by providing a view of the future in which artistic genius would play an essential role.

The three "revolutionary romantics" who conceived the collectivist myth cannot be seen as a cohesive group; at most they are loosely linked through Gorky.[29] Many of their works from the period around 1905 stand in close relationship to each other both in textual allusion and in outlook. Critical essays of both Andreevich and Lunacharsky quote and embellish on themes from Gorky's work. These essays help to magnify the original text and present it as a source of heightened social and individual truth. Gorky's God-building works from 1908 and 1909 in turn reflect the impact of Lunacharsky's thinking. All three revolutionary romantics find in Nietzsche the needed psychological foundation for their dream of mass creative will.

Lunacharsky is well-known as Gorky's chief Bolshevik booster and image-maker. Andreevich filled much the same function, but in the period before 1905. Both men used Gorky's literary personality to color their own revolutionary dreams. Andreevich was drawn to Marxism sometime late in the 1890's. He had been grappling with Nietzsche's thought for longer, since at least 1893.[30] His acquaintance with Gorky began in 1899 when both worked on Posse's journal, *Zhizn'* (*Life*). Andreevich had written a great deal about the radicals of the 1860s and 1870s, but his first major work on contemporary literature was *A Book on Maksim Gorky and A. P. Chekhov* (1900), which had been commissioned by Gorky's publisher in order to advertise his work. It bears repeating that this book loomed large in the early effort to market Gorky's first published collection of stories and was important in the continuing process of popularizing Nietzsche.[31] In it Andreevich linked Marx and Nietzsche together in his discussion of Gorky's art. He saw in Gorky's tramp heroes the slowly awakening proletarian spirit that would change Russian life. His most important work, *An Essay in the Philosophy of Russian Literature* (1905), was devoted to establishing a concept of greater-than-human "selfhood" (*lichnost'*) that would bring social regeneration and personal fulfillment. Andreevich analyzes the history of *lichnost'* in Russian nineteenth-century literature and ends with speculation about its development in the present day. The book was strongly promoted by Gorky, who asked his partner, K. P. Piatnitsky, to pay Andreevich an advance for the book's completion. *An Essay* was finally published in Gorky's *Znanie* press.[32] The vision of the proletariat developed in this book anticipates Lunacharsky's and Gorky's later God-building myth, which they and a few other Bolsheviks developed when they were in exile in Italy after 1905. Andreevich died in 1905, too early to bring his thinking to full maturity. Had he lived, it is entirely possible that he might have participated in the God-building effort.

Anatoly Lunacharsky discovered Gorky somewhat later, writing about him first in 1903. Like Andreevich, he recognized Gorky as a prophet of things to come. The relationship between the critic and the writer has received a great deal of attention.[33] It has been argued that Gorky arrived at his final statement of the collectivist myth under Lunacharsky's influence; however, as R. Sesterhenn has recently argued, Gorky worked out his own social and aesthetic views well before Lunacharsky knew him.[34] It is true that, before 1905, Gorky focused on the archetype of a lone, greater-than-human artist who through his art would singlehandedly transform social relations. While that monumental creative spirit would remain central to the new myth, it would become "collectivized." In my view, all three major revolutionary romantics arrived independently at a certain attitude well before any myth took shape. It appears that in the pre-1905 period Gorky acted as the catalyst for a revision of the mythic image of the masses, while after 1905 the antielitist views of Lunacharsky (as well as other organizers of the Bolshevik Workers' School on the Italian island of Capri, A. A. Bogdanov and V. A. Bazarov) had an impact on Gorky.[35] In any case, Gorky had a much closer relationship with Lunacharsky than with his earlier critic and booster. Lunacharsky was a needed counterbalance to Lenin in the post-1905 period when Gorky was experiencing the harsh rupture from his Russian readership and the failure of his early artistic-social vision. Lenin was interested in nothing more than using art for political purposes, whereas Lunacharsky reversed the equation, seeing politics and revolution as expressions of deep aesthetic, form-giving power. Gorky and Lunacharsky cooperated in the Capri School, reading lectures on nineteenth-century Russian and European literature to a small group of Bolshevik workers in exile who were meant to become the proletarian elite. The two writers worked together on the collection of Marxist, antimodernist literary criticism, *Literary Decline* (*Literaturnyi raspad*, 2 vols., 1908–1909), and on the collection *Essays in the Philosophy of Collectivism* (*Ocherki filosofii kollektivizma*, 1908). They worked closely again in the early years after the Bolshevik revolution of 1917 to preserve existing cultural institutions and to establish new ones.

The myth of the self-creative working masses receives its first expression in Andreevich's 1905 work, *An Essay*, and is fully formed in works from the God-building period (1907–1911): in Lunacharsky's "The Tasks of Social Democratic Art" ("Zadachi sotsial-demokratichskogo khudozhestvennogo tvorchestva," 1907) and, his major philosophical work, *Religion and Socialism* (*Religiia i sotsializm*, 1908–1911), and in Gorky's "The Destruction of Personality" ("Razrushenie lichnosti," 1909) and *Confession* (*Ispoved'*, 1908). It is partly through their response to Nietzsche's challenge to traditional moral attitudes and his call to mythopoetry that the revolutionary romantics arrived at their own unique vision of the future and their view of themselves in it.

The new image of the collective is built on a conscious revaluation of the nineteenth-century populist myth of the peasant masses. The strong belief in the people as the bearer of cultural and social wholeness and of the moral virtues of compassion and self-denial had by the 1890s degenerated to a feeling of feckless pity before grinding poverty or, at best, a sense of anger at social stagnation. The discrediting of the myth was widespread. Chekhov exposed the peasantry as ignorant, bestial, mired in a life of squalor. Civic poets professed their sense of helplessness at the task of bearing the suffering of the people. Gorky was very harsh in his demythologizing of the peasant. Marxists were still more disparaging. The first Russian Marxist, Georgy Plekhanov, wrote in 1909 that the Populists were on the wrong track in their sympathy for peasants.[36] He argued that the Russian peasant could only blame himself for his sorry lot. By nature peasants were acquisitive, selfish, apathetic, and backward-looking. Real improvement of social conditions, in Plekhanov's view, would be initiated by the growing urban proletariat, not by the peasantry.

Andreevich and Lunacharsky discredited populist belief as part of an effort to establish themselves as critics of a new type. Andreevich had published a series of articles in the Marxist journal *Zhizn'* attacking populist positions. In *An Essay*, he embellished his view that the old ideal of the peasant commune had failed. The old virtues of "freedom in slavery" and "equality in poverty" no longer held (O, 418–421). Populist myth, so Andreevich argued, was the figment of the alienated, intellectual imagination. Lunacharsky dismissed populist art in his 1903 article on Gleb Uspensky. He wrote, "we aren't interested in sufferers, we are interested in protesters [protestanty], and if the peasantry is destined sometime again to stand at the center of public interest, it will have to win it back with a show of vital activity [zhiznedeiatel'nost']" (LSS8, VI, 289). In one of his major myth-building essays, "The Tasks of the Social-Democratic Art" (1907), Lunacharsky made it clear that the new image of the working masses was being formed on the ashes of the populist myth:

> The passive, long-suffering peasantry, the people as object needs, of course, "pitying artists," *pity* was exercised to the point of virtuosity by the great artists of pen and brush of Russia's last generation. But the *people as subject*, the people as creator of history, the proletariat, which is just becoming conscious of its great mission, of its [broad] reach . . . its right to happiness, such a people needs other spokesmen. Properly speaking peasantizing artists [muzhikovstvuiushchie khudozhniki] were not expressing the peasant himself but the intelligentsia's ardently hopeful faith in him[;] here is the source of the self-denial and asceticism which shines through their art. The artist of the proletariat has to join together with them and express their belligerent, egotistical, that is, the collectively egotistical mood of their class. (LSS8, VII, 160)

Lunacharsky uses his critique of the populist world view to define a different, more active and vibrant relationship between artist, critic, and the people. Another aspect of these efforts at self-definition should be mentioned: Lunacharsky and the other God-builders were intent on carving out an ideologically legitimate role for the arts in the Bolshevik-Marxist framework. Russian Marxist aesthetic views, as they had been expressed in the works of Lenin and Plekhanov, had been quite hostile to the fictive imagination. The revolutionary romantics wanted to justify artistic fantasy by claiming its link to the deep, invisible currents of social change. However, they inevitably ran into problems with this stance. By discounting populist myth as the fabrication of the alienated mind, they suggested the similarity of their own situation in relation to the proletariat. After all, their myth, like all products of the human mind, was a fabrication. Andreevich was clearer than the later God-builders in admitting that one cult of the people was replacing another; however, his self-irony did not stop him from weaving utopian dreams. By contrast, Lunacharsky asserted without hesitation that he and other Social-Democratic artists and critics had a connection to the blind forces of social change that afforded them a privileged view into the future.

Having discounted the moral substance and the credibility of the older myth of the people, the revolutionary romantics established themselves as the seers and the spokesmen of the people. Their link to the "truth" was Gorky, whom they saw as more than just a *samouchka*, a self-made writer: he was the embodiment of the dark masses become conscious of themselves. As Andreevich wrote, his tramp symbolized the "people's awakening but as yet undefined self-consciousness" (O, 520). It would be theorists and critics such as Andreevich and Lunacharsky who would shape this raw, recently self-conscious behemoth, magnify it, and give it purpose and direction. In so doing, they would also satisfy their strong sense of future anxiety: they would supersede strong predecessors and leave their mark on the national consciousness of the future.

A next stage in the mythopoetic process was to appropriate the collectivist "shell" of the older myth. Their hero was a massman, only now full of aggression and impatient with the present state of things. If the populist mass-man was feminized in his fictional image, then this reincarnation is childlike. His moral consciousness is neither priestly nor philosophical-ascetic. The animal self knows neither moral self-reflection nor restrictive forces of guilt or pity. He embodies a rough, primitive heroism much like that of Homer's Greeks. Andreevich compares the prototype of the mass hero, Gorky's tramp, with Nietzsche's superman: neither type "lies to himself," both are "naive and bold like a child or a genius" (MG, 29). This hero "stands up proudly for his right to unconditional spiritual freedom"; he is simple and direct in his opposition to "lie, hypocrisy, and compromise" (MG, 52).

It is important to note that the revolutionary romantic critics, unlike the early Gorky, underplay "old" virtues of compassion and kindness: those belong to the discredited Populist era. As Andreevich argues, the feeling of pity hampers the realization of real creative selfhood. A spirit of transgression is a necessary condition for change and experimentation (O, 28, 63). Thus, a gay destructiveness characterizes the revolutionary romantic proletarian mass-man. He is "evil" in much the same way as Preobrazhensky saw the superman as evil: in his personality, transgression is enveloped in an aura of violent but beautiful heroism. In "Dialogue on Art" (1905), Lunacharsky employs bold Nietzschean language to convey this mood:

> Life is struggle, it is a field of battle: we do not conceal that, we are glad of it because we see beyond the burdens of our labors, beyond . . . the rivers of blood, the victory of more grandiose, splendid, and humane forms of life. We want more light, more struggle, more energy, life and veracity toward ourselves and others: away with everything sickly, away with everything which thirsts for peace and quiet at any cost . . . away with decrepitude! We are not afraid of the hard truth, the cold mountain air or even of the "safe" but terrible and monstrous tedium of everyday. (DI, 160)

Perhaps the key quality of the new hero is what Andreevich called *proletarian individualism* and Lunacharsky *collective egotism*.[37] This characteristic raises him above the ordinary, isolated, weak individual and gives him the anarchic energy to destroy and create on a colossal scale. He is both "I" and "we" become one: in him is contained what Nietzsche might call the "little reason" (Z, 61), the ego, as well as a vaster "Self," a deep, unconscious but vital community of individual self with the mass of humanity. Andreevich says that "proletarian individualism" combines "full freedom and full independence of the personal [*intimnyi*] side of human nature, that is, the area of faith and artistic creativity, with full subordination to the interests of peaceful cooperative production, to the findings of exact science, of social justice" (O, 534). Andreevich sees the harmonic balance of individual self and social mass-self as the condition for broad cultural flowering.

Lunacharsky and Gorky are more concerned than Andreevich with the epistemological implications of the new concept of selfhood, that is, the role of the new self in imposing meaning upon existence. They go to considerable effort to put collective man in a "divine" position as assigner of meaning and value. Lunacharsky distinguishes proletarian selfhood as "militant" and "collectively egotistical," active, aggressive, and monumentally creative. In his review of Gorky's *Summerfolk* (1905), he envisions the mass-hero not so much as a fighter against outlived social institutions but as a monumental destroyer of myth and belief, and as a bridge-builder, a forger of new world visions. The mass-man's struggle is not in the streets but in the imaginative world. Lunacharsky sees him "manfully going forward along the tragic path of knowledge of reality, along the grinding path of struggle with [actuality], breaking the sharp marble corners around him which scratch his breast, casting bridges over abysses" (LSS8, II, 9). Collective egotism empowers the new man to conceive "illusions," that is, a living myth that shapes and gives purpose to existence. Referring directly to the voluntarism of "On the Way of the Creator," Lunacharsky writes:

> man is free to create his own illusions and dreams if only they lead him forward along the path of creative conquests, toward the growth of his powers, [and] regal happiness [derived from] supremacy over nature. Even if [man's] dream cannot be realized, even if he lacks the ability to achieve his ideal, at least it is good that he has dared and has pressed forward. Take away this illusion, and, if man is strong, he will create a new and still more splendid illusion. And perhaps, what awaits him will be more splendid than any dream. (LSS8, II, 10)

The highest dream, Lunacharsky says, is the "miraculous human dream," the whole "life of humanity." Later, in *Religion and Socialism*, he would reiterate the point, again with reference to Nietzsche, that it is man's goal in life to "give meaning to the world." Now, he defines this task as the collective "subordination of the world to the spirit in its concrete form as human society" (RiS, 46).

In his answer to a poll on religious belief taken in *Mercure de France* in 1907, Gorky expressed a similar thought that human beings create "gods" out of a religious need for higher purpose.[38] Here God and the traditional dualist system are displaced by collective man as the master-creator of a monist utopian world. Humanity through its collective selfhood has taken its rightful position away from the old God as the value-giving force.[39] Thus, the mythic superhuman power that penetrates the human order is the world-creative proletariat.

The final stage in myth-building was the narrative "predicate" for the greater-than-human "subject." The sacred time here is the very near future. The degenerate order is the hobbled, petit-bourgeois individualism of existing capitalist society. In the God-building narrative, the helpless "I" becomes regenerated through union with the all-creative "we." The story typically proceeds in a Dionysian cycle. The blind masses possess an intense but undirected thirst for life. They strike out against the social forces binding them and develop self-consciousness and eloquence by producing from their midst a great individual leader. The leader gradually develops his own individual consciousness and takes on a divine countenance in the popular imagination. In his incarnation as a god, he becomes isolated from the masses and their nurturing life force; he oppresses them, but is himself consequently mortally weakened. Eventually in his place appear thousands of small, feckless, isolated selves: this is the stage at which society now finds itself. The isolated self eventually regains true selfhood (*lichnost'*) only in union with the superhuman life force of the massive whole of humanity. Here "I" and "we," singular and plural, are miraculously merged. In the process of coming together, tremendous world-shaping energy is released. Like all utopian thinkers, the revolutionary romantics dreamed of stopping the progress of time once they had reached the desired future state. Thus, as they envisioned it, the Dionysian cycle would halt at the very point of renewal. The result is a utopian social order that allows the perfect balance between self and masses. All three revolutionary romantics see Russia at the brink of a national uprising and reunion of self and collective. The sacred time is at hand.

This general picture is first outlined in Andreevich's *An Essay*. Here we sense most of all what Nietzsche, and later Gorky, had seen as the precondition to new consciousness: self-doubt and self-contempt. Andreevich's book expresses a deep, oppressive sense of cultural inferiority. Contemporary Russian high culture, in his view, is a mere "translation" of Western achievements. Its result is a ridiculous, petty form of individualism: two intellectuals comparing themselves to each other (here Andreevich borrows an image from Turgenev) is as foolish as comparing two birch trees (O, 28). He also blames capitalism, especially capitalism in its rough Russian form, for squandering national intellectual wealth (O, 431). Through the energy of his despair, he fabricates a utopian time when all people will be gods and everyone will be united yet able to be individually fulfilled.

The process of liberation and development of real selfhood happens through malaise and struggle, through transgression of existing social boundaries. With Gorky, Andreevich asserts that this kind of great "crime" is necessary for great regeneration (O, 28). Thus, he urges the "free ferment of social forces, of class contradictions" (O, 34).

Andreevich envisions a coming sacred time in which the superhuman force of the working class will forge a supremely productive era of proletarian individualism: "if not today then tomorrow a proletarian individualism will appear on the stage instead of the petit-bourgeois, metaphysical, oppositionist individualism of our time" (O, 534). The valuative basis for producing higher collective selfhood is utopian Marxism, which Andreevich calls the "religion of the proletariat" (O, 497). Here for the first time in the Russian context Marxism is turned from theory into a living mythopoetic system. Andreevich anticipated by three years Lunacharsky's heretical claim that socialism was the religion of the future. The final mythic realization of collective selfhood is less well-realized in Andreevich's work than in Lunacharsky's or Gorky's. However, the direction of his thought seems clear. Had he not died prematurely, he might easily have come to similar conclusions.

Like Andreevich, Lunacharsky sees the sacred time of personal and social transfiguration as the future, even the very near future: there is an urgency in his writing, particularly around 1905, that suggests that social transformation might just be upon them. As early as 1905 he wrote that the proletariat's "splendid illusion" would soon bear fruit in an even more splendid existence. The future—and here Lunacharsky shows just how close his attitude is to that of a religious mystic when he quotes I Corinthians, 13:12—appears to us now "'as in a mirror,'" but then we will "'know it face to face'" (LSS8, II, 10). In "The Realm of the Unclear" ("V mire neiasnogo," 1906), he sees the collective form of selfhood as a godly state of being that brings "salvation from death." The key event in his, and subsequently Gorky's, version of the myth was the "transferral of the center of gravity from oneself, from one's physical 'I' to the great 'we' of creative, fighting, progressive humanity" (VMN, 71). The result will be the maximization of a sense of life's fullness and the release of world-transfiguring energy.

In *Religion and Socialism*, Lunacharsky examines the latter, productive stage of this mythic transformation.[40] The small self, in Lunacharsky's view, becomes merged with the greater self through the vital feeling of enthusiasm. Lunacharsky's notion of "enthusiasm" seems distantly comparable to Viacheslav Ivanov's "ecstasy," in that both convey the most intense possible feeling of "life." However, Ivanov's *bogoborets* carries on a struggle within his psyche, while Lunacharsky's individual is to be merged with the larger social whole. Moreover, Ivanov's godseeker stands beyond his small ego, literally in "ex-stasy," when he sacrifices his "small reason" to his god. Lunacharsky's new man, in contrast, remains within himself, aware at once of being himself and a part of the greater whole of the people. He, in unison with the people, *is* the god, that is, the creator of illusions, of grand existential goals. The ultimate result of this sustained, intense religious passion is the establishment of socialist institutions that promote the search for happiness, wholeness, fulfillment, progress in technical and scientific knowledge, and, thus, the greatest maximization of human life.

Of all the revolutionary romantics, Gorky most fully dramatized the myth of collective selfhood in works written during his years of exile, between 1906 and 1913. "The Destruction of Personality" (1909) gives an abstract explication of Gorky's idea of cultural and social transformation. Gorky diagnoses the malaise of selfhood as the result of total isolation from the collective. The people, both historically and at present, are the wellspring of raw life energy. The relation of self to nation and the respective creative abilities of each, as Gorky imagines them, seem analogous to the relationship between the Apollonian and the

Dionysian in Nietzsche's thought. In isolation from the people, Gorky argues, the individual can do nothing and create nothing. His intellectual, form-giving powers turn in on themselves and dwell on their own emptiness. Contemplation of death becomes the chief theme of this self-referential kind of art.

True creativity happens only when there is a strong psychic bond between the artist and his national creative heritage. His work springs from the myths created intuitively, involuntarily by the masses. In the nineteenth century, Gorky claims, the mass of the people became fractionalized as "thousands of Manfreds," each singing about his own spiritual sickness (SS30, XXIII, 36). However, now, he says, the conditions are right for the formation of a new potent social unity: the oppressiveness of capitalism is spurring the proletariat to coalesce and act with one will. In this new force Gorky sees the blind creative power necessary to weave myth and to bring forth heroes and gods. This process, it is implied, may follow the historical pattern Gorky outlines at the start of the essay. Here he shows what Ophelia Schutte has called "regressive-progressive" thinking, which Nietzsche uses in creating his Dionysian myth: both men look to the deep past for signposts to the future.[41] In primitive society the idea of a greater-than-human hero arises when part of a community perishes. Each surviving member involuntarily invests in this memory-figure his own best acts. The hero challenges human fate and, in so doing, ennobles and fulfills all humanity (SS30, XXIII, 29).

The emergence of the primitive rebel archetype in the popular imagination releases deep creative energy. He becomes the focus of broad cultural activity. Now the artistic individual and the community have a mutually enriching relationship. The artist takes material from popular myth but gives the myth its finest expression. Gorky sees the best example of this process in the period of the German Reformation: "In this period of social storms selfhood (*lichnost'*) becomes a focal point for thousands of wills, that have chosen it as their representative organ, and it arises before us in the wonderful light of beauty and strength, in the bright flame of the yearnings of its nation. . ." (34). He points to Faust as a hero first created by a whole people, the product of thousands of individual wills, and only much later perfected by the genius of one artist, Goethe. Gorky is clearly alert to the signs of a similar process of aesthetic and social revolt, liberation, and creative release in the newly emerging proletarian collective of his own time.

In its cyclicity, Gorky's theoretical construct reveals its Dionysian roots. Decline and death alternate with rebirth. In new versions of the myth, the relationship between hero and community, indeed the very community itself, gradually becomes deformed and then disintegrates. The hero separates himself from the community, viewing himself as a semidivine power unto himself. In this stage, he loses first his vital creativity and only much later his power. Like Dionysius in his late stage, he becomes a tyrant and oppresses the people both physically and ideologically. He creates a single god in his own image, one that denies the people their essential value-assigning energy. In the final death stage the hero becomes everyman: the colossal, rebellious hero and the myth-building people are altogether lost, replaced by thousands of petty pseudoheroes. Now, Gorky suggests, the collective is ripe for rebirth.

It is curious that, while intimating that Russia is about to enter a God-building period, Gorky does not explore the possible results implied by his own theory: the forceful reversion of the Russian people to a more primitive state and their suppression by a terrible dictator who would create a single god in his own image. Here, it is possible to speculate, is a direct literary precursor to Stalinism and the "cult of personality." However, Gorky, like the other revolutionary romantics and like Nietzsche himself, thirsted most for the initial liberating storm. They so yearned for the fight and the release of life-giving energy that they ignored the ultimate consequences.

In his God-building novel, *Confession*, Gorky dramatizes the initial thrust of popular feeling that will release mythopoetic energy and create self-consciousness and direction in the collective hero. Gorky's protagonist, Matvei, is an orphan who, like his author, goes through a long string of jobs, wanders the length and breadth of his country, and encounters all different kinds of people. His wandering turns into a quest for existential meaning and justification. He seeks a spiritual mentor, but all he finds are empty, arrogant, would-be "priests." The world is filled with petty individual selves. By chance he meets another wanderer,

Iegudiil, and discovers in him a Lunacharskian enthusiasm. Iegudiil resembles Zarathustra, only in the guise of a Russian sectarian. He has played all the traditional roles of Russian holy men, but his views are too heretical to be contained by any of their dogmas. He has been an Orthodox priest and a monk and has found the dogma and the physical, personal regime of both positions too constraining. Like his Nietzschean predecessor, Iegudiil is gay and irreverent and cannot contain his overflowing passion for life within any one dogma: like Zarathustra, he speaks as if he were "drunk with joy" (PSS, IX, 341).

Through Iegudiil, Matvei learns to search within for his god and to have faith in his own feeling of intoxication with life. An overabundance of inner energy in him and in all people will eventually coalesce in the form of a new hero. Iegudiil sees the broad masses of humanity as this creative force. However, the people are just breaking out of a long period of subjugation. Society's leaders have manipulated faith in such a way as to make its object seem determined a priori. It is thus used to oppress and bind the masses. The leaders, in order to maintain their power over the masses, have supported a view of the world that shows the masses as docile and impotent. They have transposed the people's monumental creative energy to some mythic time in the past. Ideals have been objectified and the principle of creativity made to appear in a higher realm beyond the human psyche. Thus, the idea of human creative genius has been discredited, and religious ideals have become a means to control and pacify the very people who first conceived them.

Iegudiil hails the "whole working people of the earth" as the creator of a new god, one that will cast down fear and oppression and return to the people their natural, explosive creativity. He says: "the will of the people is awakening, a great, forcibly disunited [power] is [now] coalescing, already many people are seeking ways to fuse all earthly forces into one[,] from this force will be formed, bright and splendid, the all-embracing god of the earth!" (PSS, IX, 342).

The mythic process of merging "small reason" with greater "Self" is completed as Matvei joins a community of workers like himself. He goes to work at their factory. Gradually his sense of enthusiasm overflows and merges with the others': "The eyes [ochi] of other people flare up, from them shines the newly awakened human soul, and my vision also is broadened and sharpened. . . . You take strength from all the hearts opened before you and with this strength you unite them into one heart" (384). Matvei starts to speak during demonstrations in front of huge crowds and is buoyed by their support and good will. He comes to feel that he as speaker is turning into the embodiment of their will. He *is* the new hero arising. Yet he is not the only one to gain strength. Everyone in the collective is bolstered by the great energy of the whole. The new consciousness emerges completely at a mass demonstration during which a young girl is healed through mass faith: now finally, "I" has become "we" while retaining a full consciousness of personal selfhood.

The myth of the masses as creator may be seen as a creative deformation of several sources. Here, the source itself is rejected while certain aspects are appropriated to fit the needs of the new idea. George L. Kline mentions Feuerbach's anthropology of religion as an important influence.[42] Feuerbach's impact is directly felt in the speculation that the people created God and then became alienated from and oppressed by their own creation. Other immediate influences are Marx, Nietzsche, and the Russian Populists. Nietzsche's role is unique in that he is an avowedly antisocialist, antiutopian thinker whose thought is appropriated for a socialist myth.

All three revolutionary romantics were avid admirers of Nietzsche's thought. Although they rejected Nietzsche's social views, they deeply loved him as an antidote to what they saw as the ruinous self-negation of Populism and the lack of emotional depth in Marxism. Andreevich was one of the first younger intellectuals, along with Shestov, to devote an article to Nietzsche.[43] In *An Essay*, he singled out Nietzsche, along with Gorky and Marx, as an influence in orienting intellectuals toward the future (O, 423). Lunacharsky praised Nietzsche as a vital thinker in his 1902 article, "The Russian Faust."[44] He particularly loved the "healthy" egoism of the superman and the creative impulse inherent in the idea of the will to power. Although after 1905 Lunacharsky and Gorky publicly pigeonholed Nietzsche as a bourgeois philosopher, their main goal was to discredit "modernist" and popular cults of Nietzsche. In so doing, they implied that there was another, better reading of the German philosopher to be made. The revolutionary romantics' mature response to Nietzsche is their myth of the collective. Here they have deformed his thought in such a way that characteristic "Nietzschean" views and sentiments are no longer really recognizable as "Nietzsche": they have made his thought their own.

The pattern of deformation used by the revolutionary romantics implies a certain mode of valuation. Their assimilation of Nietzsche's thought follows a generally Russian pattern in its distaste for his skepticism and liking for his mythopoetic pathos. They employ Nietzschean irony to undermine outlived populist myth and its valuations. Having established their own myth, they devalue philosophical skepticism as "cynicism," that is, an undesirable aspect of a bourgeois mentality.[45] Thus Nietzsche is simplified, made bombastic, and deprived of the essential balance in his thought between mythopoetry and irony.

Nietzsche's effort to fabricate myth involves the sublimation of violent, normally extroverted drives, that is, the channelling of that energy into oneself to higher cultural purpose. His prose is filled with a compelling, almost sensual yearning. The revolutionary romantics appropriate from Nietzsche a process of sublimation that eventually leads to a fusion of personal energy with the rebellious will of the entire community. Raimund Sesterhenn has ventured the opinion that Nietzsche's vision of the future had a collectivist God-building component.[46] However, Nietzsche's late mythbuilding efforts do not seem directed toward the making of a new collective. The "I–thou" relationship within the self and the struggle between "master" and "slave" impulses within the mind's imaginative life are typically of greater importance to Nietzsche than the relationship of self-conscious individual to the collective in society. When he does discuss social relations, his topic is usually the interaction between ruler and ruled, not between equals in a mass collective. It should be noted, however, that the primitive Dionysian collective of ancient Greece holds a fascination for the early Nietzsche. Later, it is true, Zarathustra does hold up ancient peoples as a true value-giving force (Z, 75). Nonetheless, these images do not figure strongly in Nietzsche's own Dionysian formulations for the future. The community imagined by Andreevich, Lunacharsky, and Gorky resembles more the primitive community that Nietzsche sees in the Dionysian Greeks. The difference between the two is that the revolutionary romantics have some limited notion of balancing individual consciousness and Apollonian creativity with the Dionysian collective.

Underlying the revolutionary romantic myth we find an aesthetic vision close in some ways to Nietzsche's. Nietzsche distinguishes between three kinds of creativity. In *Birth of Tragedy* he speaks almost exclusively of *Kunst*, that is, craft, art, shaping power. In *Thus Spoke Zarathustra*, *Kunst* is narrowly used as "practice" or "manner," or art understood pejoratively as artfulness or deception (Z, 193–94, 225, 268–69, 281). Here Nietzsche most commonly replaces *Kunst* with *Schaffen*, which has the broader and more active connotation of making, building, fabricating (Z, 55, 88–91, 102). He uses the term *der Schaffende* to refer to his creator type. The more rarely used Schillerian word *Schöpfung* is reserved for the deep, mythopoetic, evaluative creativity of the deep Self (Z, 101, 139, 146; see also, BT, 38). Although in *Thus Spoke Zarathustra* Nietzsche uses *Schaffen* far more frequently than *Schöpfung*, *Schöpfung* has perhaps the greater weight. Like Nietzsche, the revolutionary romantics, and particularly Lunacharsky and Gorky, distinguish between *iskusstvo* (art, craft) and *tvorchestvo* (value-giving creative drive). Here the comparison ends. If Nietzsche makes fun of contemporary art (*Kunst*), he treats high culture (*Schaffen*) as the greatest of human achievements. By contrast, Lunacharsky in "Dialogue on Art" and elsewhere values deep creativity over art as such. Gorky in "On Cynicism" ("O tsinizme," 1908) devalues all high culture and its artistic forms (SS30, XXIV, 6). In "Destruction of Personality" he belittles the classic great works of art and their authors. Although both represent value-giving creativity, *Schöpfung* and *tvorchestvo* are treated in very different ways by Nietzsche and the revolutionary romantics. *Schöpfung* is an inner psychic drive, while *tvorchestvo* is a will exerted collectively by the masses of humanity—no single human being possesses it. Lunacharsky in his review of *Summerfolk* hails the general human drive to shape reality and assign meaning. In *Religion and Socialism*, it is this colossal creative will of the masses that interests him: it alone can motivate social change. The artist and his work are merely adjuncts to the earth-shaking will of the collective. Gorky agrees with this position in "Destruction of Personality" when he states: "Art (*iskusstvo*) is in the power of the individual, only the collective is capable of creation (*tvorchestvo*)" (SS30, XXIV, 34). While Nietzsche sees Apollonian *Kunst* as the finest result of the deeper Dionysian drive, Gorky and Lunacharsky clearly value the life-giving surge of collective will and find something comparatively insubstantial and weak in individual works of art. On this point the revolutionary romantics appear closer to their Romantic forebears, Belinsky and Grigorev, who argued that great art should create national archetypes and express the national will.

The revolutionary romantics use Nietzsche to deform and appropriate other modes of thought. For example, although all of them considered themselves Marxists, or at least very close to Marxism, all of them felt keenly its emotional and philosophical insufficiency. It will be remembered that Gorky had criticized Marxism earlier because he felt it "belittled" man. Lunacharsky felt strongly the criticism of Marxism levelled at it by ideological opponents, the modernists and idealists: "the enemies of Marxism would like very much to discount it now and forever more as a 'dry dogma,' to discount it as something dead . . . incapable of life and development."[47] In 1919, he would justify Godbuilding by saying that "scientific Marxism" was not capable of reaching the simple people. Picturing it as a religion made it more accessible.[48] The themes which Nietzsche and Marx have in common have been studied by Kline.[49] However, the creative function of this similarity-in-opposition in revolutionary romantic thinking is not made clear. "Reconciliation" seems perhaps too peaceable a description of the actual process of appropriation. Since Nietzsche and Marx were popularly perceived as inimical, it seems more accurate to see their relationship as a hostile but fruitful deformation in which each type of thought was "violated," that is, shaken from its accepted interpretation, and used in the interests of a significant and vital revaluation. Thus, the revolutionary romantics, relying on Nietzsche's voluntarism, pointed out the insufficiency of Russian Marxist thought. At the same time, to readers from generally anti-Nietzschean radical circles, they successfully disguised their indebtedness to the German philosopher. They even added to the radicals' vulgarization of Nietzsche as the decadent philosopher of a dying class. In this way, these people with their overwhelming sense of future anxiety managed to set two precursors against each other and to cast themselves as original valuators for the future. In the fabrication of collectivist myth, they certainly touched a vital Russian chord that was destined to reverberate both before and after the Revolution.

Probably the deepest influence on the new myth was the native populist tradition. Because it was so important, it was the most harshly discounted and distorted. Here Nietzsche's attack on the social ethic of self-denial and compassion was used to discredit populist myth and to deprive it of all valuative power. Then the tool of skepticism was itself thrown away. The mass myth was later resurrected with a combination of both Marxist and Nietzschean virtues: the future consciousness of both, the Marxist faith in the working masses, and the Nietzschean emphasis on the signifying activity of human will. The most basic aspect of Nietzsche's influence is to be found in the shift from "virtues" of self-negation, resignation, and denial of personal will and passion, to affirmation of irrational energies as they are channeled into social action. The fusion of personal and collective energies is active, ecstatic, and ultimately self-affirming because it brings a heightened sense of being.

Living myth establishes and preserves moral codes and indicates "right" behavioral patterns. The values established by the new myth long outlasted the myth as it was first expressed between 1905 and 1911. "Bad" and "wrong" were defined as the capitalist elite presently in power, the whole existing socioeconomic structure, its emphasis on crass accumulation of material wealth, and the dualist earth-negating forms of faith engendered by it. "Good" and "right" were reaffirmation of primal life force, the sweeping, greater-than-human energy of the collective, the balance of individual self-consciousness with the deeper, nourishing blind will of the masses. Vast present destruction is condoned for the sake of massive future construction.

The question arises as to whether this myth represents real revaluation or merely another version of herd morality. The moral-aesthetic consciousness underlying the revolutionary romantic effort is problematic and difficult. While the revolutionary romantics are intent upon fomenting fresh creativity and asserting the monumental creative drive of the masses, they are at a loss to let it demonstrate itself. The revolutionary romantic myth shares with its populist predecessor a radical "otherworldliness." Both Lunacharsky and Gorky wish to tear down the value structures of the present, which are seen as decadent. Nothing of the present should be salvaged. High art with its moribund forms must give way to the brute, mythopoetic force of mass consciousness. The refined self-reflection of high culture and the contrived ratiocination of individual self-consciousness must give way to mass "enthusiasm." In theory there is a revaluation, but in their art and criticism none of the revolutionary romantics succeeds in realizing their dream. For example, at the end of *Confession,* Gorky's hero Matvei attends a kind of faith healing demonstration in which a cripple regains the ability to walk. The feeling which grips and unites everyone is pity (*zhalost'*). Although this emotion has a certain healing power, it does not manifest mythopoetic energy. Gorky has merely put the masses in place of the old Christ. At most, this scene is a sentimental reenactment of an incomparably more powerful New Testament episode. Despite Gorky's unconvincing reassertion of a morality of pity, it is possible to point to a real revaluation of populist values. Art and particularly deep creative energy are not conceived as inimical to social feeling as they were in the populist code. Indeed, the revolutionary romantics saw this aesthetic drive as the source for the imaginative conceptualization of a new society. Nature and rural tradition are no longer the basis for a future utopia; rather, human artifice is to conquer nature for the benefit of humanity. Another aspect of the revaluation is the attempt to affirm both the validity of self within the context of the mass and the vitality of irrational values." Changes in outlook serve to disguise the elements of herd mentality that survive in the new myth. The right of the self to dissent, to rebel, and to take a stance different from that of the collective is denied: the mass will is "right." The self who opposes the mass will is either degenerate or oppressive, depending upon the extent of its power. The only legitimate selfhood is that which rides along with and gives profile to the surging mass will. The potential here for new oppression is considerable. Indeed, in the 1930s a myth that was meant to liberate both the self and the masses would be revived and used to restrain and constrict.

The myth of the people, like everything to do with Godbuilding, was roundly rejected by Lenin as heresy. Lunacharsky was severely reprimanded but was not dissuaded from his myth. He continued to help run the workers' school when it reopened in Bologna in 1910, and he published the second volume of *Religion and Socialism* in 1911. Even in the Soviet period, he persisted in believing in Nietzsche's universal value precisely in the terms set forth in the myth: "in Nietzsche's work one comes across separate pages and chapters which are acceptable in general for any class that affirms life, struggle, development."⁵⁰ Despite his enthusiasm for collective struggle, after the Revolution Lunacharsky shifted his political sights considerably. A. L. Tait has shown that, during the earliest years of the Revolution, Lunacharsky in his historical dramas was siding with leaders, even oppressive leaders, against the masses. Tait sees here an unexpected "authoritarian" streak.⁵¹ This discussion has shown that perhaps this development was not so unexpected. Lunacharsky's God-building work is inspired with a concept of future society he feels is bound to come true. When it does not happen spontaneously, he, like Gorky long before him, resorts to an archetype of the coercive, domineering leader to make it come true.

Lenin made peace with his protégé Gorky only late in 1909, a year after the publication of the novel, *Confession*. He wrote that he had first believed Gorky had willingly sided with Lunacharsky and Bogdanov. Now, however, Lenin had changed his mind after learning that the writer had been pulled "unwittingly" into this renegade group.⁵² Despite these political pressures, the myth of deep human creativity held its allure for Gorky. From 1898 on, it had been a sustaining belief, no matter how it was twisted and distorted. Lenin would not be able to talk him out of it, even in 1913 when the subject arose yet again. Now Gorky, who had returned to Russia that year after the amnesty, attacked his rivals—the philosophical idealists and the mystical symbolists—in his article "More on Karamazovism" ("Eshche o karamazovshchine"). He wrote: "You have no God, you haven't created it. Gods are not found, they are created."⁵³ When Lenin saw these words, he exploded. His letter to Gorky brings out the essential difference between his own simpleminded, materialist view and those of more discerning, philosophical, and literary minds whom he wished to subjugate. Lunacharsky and Gorky, as well as their God-building colleague Bogdanov, insisted on the independent, motivating role played by subjective consciousness in evaluation and judgment of phenomena. Lenin, in contrast, stubbornly held to a simplistic and old-fashioned view that judgment, interpretation, opinion is produced by a "correlation of social forces, by the objective correlation of classes."[54] Subjective, that is, irrational or voluntarist, forces have no validity in and of themselves in Lenin's world view.

As in 1905, Gorky seemed again to be in a position of retreat from an unsuccessful "ruling idea." However, just as he did not give in before, so he did not give in now; he merely changed his tactics. Now he affirmed his own biographical connections to the world-creative energy of the masses. In the first volume of his autobiography, *Childhood* (*Detstvo*, 1913), written in the aftermath of the Capri affair, Gorky implicitly established himself as a true embodiment of creative *lichnost'*. *Childhood* shows Gorky's family, particularly his grandmother and grandfather, as archetypes of God-building energy. The grandmother joins in the collective energy of the whole people, indeed, the whole of nature, while the grandfather has a self-seeking, petit-bourgeois mentality. Both characters are portrayed as practicing Christians. However, Gorky sees the God to which each prays as the involuntary fabrication of that individual and the mentality of his or her class. For example, Grandfather Kashirin is tightfisted, strict, unforgiving. His God is the same: "In his stories about God's invincible strength [Grandfather] always made a special point of emphasizing His cruelty: some people sinned and were drowned, others sinned and were burnt, and their towns razed to the ground. God punished with famine and pestilence and He was always a sword over the land, a scourge to sinners" (Ch, 106). Grandfather's God is like a usurer, exacting and greedy. "God's a miser," Grandfather remarks. "[He] gives you minutes in return for years, and without any interest" (Ch, 172). This God appears to demand strict adherence to dogma and ritual. One must pray in the "correct" way, repeating the right words.

Grandmother's God, by contrast, is joyous, kind, and forgiving, much as she is: "Her God was with her all day, and she even talked about him to animals. It was plain that it was easy for everything to submit to this God: people, dogs, birds, bees, even herbs. He bestowed his kindness on all earthly creatures without distinction, and was close to all things" (Ch, 101). This God celebrates everything on earth and welcomes human creativity.

Grandmother is forever finding new words to praise God. The effect is a living, personal faith that also draws a person to behave in a moral way. It is through Grandmother, and not Grandfather, that the young boy Aleksei receives his moral education. The child sees that his grandfather "shows off" before God (Ch, 155). By contrast, the beautiful words with which Grandmother speaks of God and nature and the gentleness with which she treats everyone, animals and people alike, attract Aleksei and bring him to behave in a similarly gentle manner: "Grandmother's God I could understand, and he didn't terrify me, yet it was impossible to tell a lie in his presence—that would have been shameful" (Ch, 102).

It is interesting that Grandmother's God is really androgynous: this God is as much the "Blessed Virgin," the "Golden Sun," or the "Dearest heart of Heaven" as a male figure (Ch, 100). This bisexuality is reminiscent of Dionysus, who appears in the guise of either sex. Such a god affirms all life and is himself whole, life-giving, and nurturing. Grandmother's God, unlike Grandfather's, is much fuller than any one dogma. Gorky clearly sides with his grandmother, making her the chief character in the book. Thus, he reaffirms an old claim to mythic stature: as young boy, he is exposed to and suffused with the world-creative energy of the people in the figure of his grandmother. Here is the origin of his own dynamic, liberating will.

With this work Gorky achieved his full literary maturity. Now, when he had withdrawn from politics and, through *Confession* and *Childhood*, regained his Russian readership, the earlier moral eclecticism—the conflict between personal belief and social-political ideological constraint—quieted and mellowed. In *Childhood*, Gorky found his most original and fitting expression of his creative myth. It is curious that in an autobiography, a book in which he creates his own past, he has "overcome" his Russian and Western mentors and established his ideological and stylistic independence. Here he writes with a true stylistic richness and moral integrity that he matched in only a few other works.

The myth of the world-creative people was important as part of an overall effort of one faction of Bolsheviks to introduce voluntarist concepts into radical revolutionary thinking. To be convinced of the revolutionary romantics' central importance in enriching and popularizing the larger Bolshevik cause, we need only compare their vibrant image of the people with Plekhanov's canonical but dry definition of the proletarian as a "producer who possesses no means of production."[55] Although the myth was rebuffed by political leadership and appeared to have no relevance to practical politics, the idea of the regeneration of society willed by the masses took on a life of its own. Although the present study is limited to the analysis of Nietzsche's influence upon prerevolutionary literature, it should be noted that this aspect of Nietzsche's reception reverberated strongly in the Soviet period. Although the organizers of the Capri School were reprimanded, and some even expelled from the party, they were summoned in the years after the October Revolution of 1917 to help organize and administer Soviet cultural and educational institutions. The impact of the God-building myth on early Soviet culture calls for study.[56] The resurgence of the myth in the late 1920s also deserves attention: here, we may speculate, is a living myth coopted as propaganda for Stalinist reconstruction.[57] Finally, it might be argued that the concept of *lichnost'* as the convergence of the individual's small reason and the collective Self for the release of deep energy was a possible antecedent to the socialist realist "positive hero."[58]

The God-building myth took root in the soil of the revolutionary movement. Revolutionary romanticism in its various forms provided needed verve to the Russian Marxist cause but was ultimately subordinated to more pressing political and ideological concerns. The literary and critical work of revolutionary romantics helped to popularize Marxism, to conceptualize a Marxist aesthetic theory, and to incite revolutionary fervor. The confrontation with Nietzsche's philosophy instigated important changes in attitude toward the masses. His critique of egalitarianism and the herd morality of pity spurred radicals to examine their own values and to develop a more vivacious and energetic ethos. Nietzsche's mythopoetic drive and his emphasis on human creativity were incorporated in the revolutionary romantics' vision of the future. Although radicals eventually disowned their German mentor, they absorbed vital aspects of his philosophy.

7

Conclusion

OUR CONSIDERATION of Nietzsche's reception in early-twentieth-century Russian literature has revealed a cultural dynamic that distinguishes this epoch from those that precede and follow it. It has been possible to move away from a kind of history that reviews literary historical artifacts and to characterize the period in terms of its inner literary-philosophical relationships, its living social and cultural dialogues, and its characteristic patterns of reading and interpretation. By taking this approach we find a multileveled literary culture with a remarkable social breadth and artistic vigor. Interaction between popular, middlebrow, and esoteric modes of discourse spurred vital change and indeed resulted in the production of some of the great critical and artistic works of Russia's early twentieth century. Through consideration of the ways in which writers interpreted and appropriated Nietzsche and other important philosophical precursors, we have been able to trace the ideological movement toward literary renaissance. The point of departure in this period was the automatized treatment of ideas and ideological debate in the 1890s. For example, the once-flourishing novel-of-ideas was in the process of becoming stereotypical, as we saw in the novels of Boborykin. Stale versions of this genre's dialogues, debates, and philosophically motivated action figured in the work of emerging writers such as Merezhkovsky and Gorky. The style of appropriation of precursors used in these texts was often vulgarizing: it ignored the singularity of the precursor's outlook. Philosophical material was employed to make some judgment about new intellectual trends, whether positive or negative.

This automatization process set the context for innovations in reading and interpretation that soon arose. Writers perceived the stereotypical nature of the prevalent reading and soon started to polemicize with it. We have observed this phenomenon in the careers of major writers such as Gorky and Merezhkovsky and even Belyi, as well as among middlebrow writers. It should be repeated that this process did not occur on the lowest literary level of the best-selling, popular novel. Here stereotypical "interpretations" were borrowed indiscriminately to "educate" as well as titillate culturally uninformed or semi-informed readers. In *Sanin*, Artsybashev blindly copied ideas and formulations first made by the vulgarizer, Nordau. Verbitskaia in *Keys of Happiness* borrowed wholesale from *Sanin*. The excitement and freshness of such books clearly lay not in the quality of aesthetic or philosophical interpretation but in their incorporation of fashionable ideas in an easily grasped adventure plot that involved the partially educated reader in what for him was a new and plausible story of self-discovery and self-determination.

Writers who pretended to originality revised and often repudiated this stereotypical reading with the result that they developed their own style and identity as a writer. In their polemic with vulgarization they reached backward, appropriated, and recast as their own the mythic visions of their great Russian precursors. Thus, Andreev argued with Boborykin's image of the Nietzschean "new man" and, in his search for a counterimage, reached back through Nietzsche to a new perception of Dostoevsky. Kuprin and Ropshin polemicized with Nietzsche's thought in its vulgarized form and, in looking for an alternative, also rediscovered Dostoevsky. In the 1890s Merezhkovsky and Gorky both helped to instigate the popular cult of *individualizm* for which Nietzsche became the chief ideologue. Later both retreated from their early position and polemicized with the popular Nietzscheanism with which they had been widely associated. In so doing they too reached backward into the cultural past. The result in each case was a profoundly stated mythic revision.

The question still stands, Did this ferment produce a real revolution of moral consciousness? The answer is certainly yes if we allow that revolution is a new expression of old questions that in turn opens up fresh insight. What remains now is to define its essential qualities and the role played in it by the discovery of Nietzsche's thought.

The culture of the early twentieth century is frequently called "apocalyptic." Certainly the belles lettres treated in this study show a radical denial of the present and recent past and a strong concern with the future. However, the prophetic vision usually associated with this culture is only one expression of the future anxiety that is so prevalent in this period. The frequency of radical narrative endings—the death, ruin, and self-destruction that many protagonists choose—create a powerful sense of foreboding. More importantly, however, these solutions must be seen as part of a widespread effort to create a mythic narrative of successful cultural and spiritual change. Although the result is not what writers first envisioned, a kind of composite, future-oriented vision does emerge from the texts treated here. The total departure from all previous human experience that writers first expected gives way to other more fruitful conceptualizations of change that interweave in complex ways with the past. This futurist imagination rests on a "progressive-regressive" mode of thinking. Writers' solutions to their anxiety about the future involve the discreditation of precursors from the immediate past and the revival of the distant past.

The resulting visions of the future are unexpectedly primitive. If the Populist mentality contained much that was "monastic" (ascetic, self-denying) and "feminine" (suffering, tender, compassionate), then the new literary sensibility is "worldly" and at times "childlike," that is, impulsive, energetic, direct, naive, and crude. Images of new beginnings—of chaos, conceptions, and childhood—are found everywhere. Ropshin invokes primitive, social anarchy. Verbitskaia popularizes the naive heroism of Homeric Greece. Ivanov and Blok imagine renewal in the setting of primal spiritual darkness. Ivanov speaks of unleashing creative drive in terms of conception. Belyi everywhere sees the child as the symbol of transfigured consciousness.

Perhaps the clearest primitivist images are found in the work of the two great "sign makers" of the age, Merezhkovsky and Gorky. Gorky imagines utopia as a primitive mass society. He conjures up a Dionysian communality. Merezhkovsky searches throughout the deep historical past, in novels and in literary criticism. In the Russian historical context he traverses backward across Populist and *raznochinets* culture to reopen to the literary imagination Petrine Russian culture and its greatest literary genius, Aleksandr Pushkin. The Petrine imagery is reassumed by Belyi in *Petersburg*. It is curious that the anticlimactic ending to Belyi's novel recovers only the "near" past of a populist precursor, Tolstoi. In the context of the "progressive-regressive" mentality of the turn of the century, this shallow reversion constitutes a shattering admission of the failure of the creative imagination, of defeat. Belyi here has not only not secured his own myth of resurrection but has taken down with him the constructs of Merezhkovsky and Ivanov. It is curious that when Belyi does arrive at his own myth in his third novel, *Kotik Letaev*, he uses his own canonical primitivist image, the child. He probes beyond conscious, human existence to prenatal, preconscious being. In retracing and recovering the origins of his human consciousness, he experiences a real if very private new wholeness of spirit.

Another stereotypic quality of this age is the so-called individualist ethos of its writers. Writers certainly look to the human imagination, will, and energy as the source of renewal. Early on they see themselves as higher individuals and as new "meta-artists" whose goal is to do more than create beautiful artifice: they intend to envision a new society and culture and, most importantly, a new, whole human psyche. Their final purpose then is the transfiguration of human consciousness. Their individualism is not of the usual kind: they do not consider self-realization and the exercise of personal will the right of every person. With a remarkable uniformity that appears to presage a later political "cult of personality," these writers imagine the worthy individual as a single social leader who herds the masses toward social and cultural change. Merezhkovsky looks to great past political leaders such as Emperor Julian and Peter the Great. Gorky heroizes the greater-than-human "Man," the artist-leader who uses as his artistic material human social consciousness. Verbitskaia popularizes this type as the revolutionary, Jan. The young Belyi imagines a Christ Pantocrator who will rule the peoples with an iron rod. It is of great importance that all these writers at a later stage revise their autocratic-individualist archetypes as too tyrannical, oppressive, and destructive of that most treasured human attribute, spontaneous creative genius. The most fruitful outgrowth of this brand of individualism is their later investment of true creative will in the self searching for interaction with a valued other self—whether the human collective or the daimonic spirit within.

Finally, we must return to the generalization we questioned at the outset, the idea that Nietzschean adherents sacrificed ethical values for aesthetic ones. Certainly a shift in emphasis from ethos to mythos is prevalent in all levels of the response to Nietzsche. Established norms of good and right judgment lose value in the face of a strong desire to break through to new consciousness. Traditional moral codes are challenged and broken. Conventional moral judgment is perceived as inimical to exploration, discovery, and creative release. However, the debate about the role and meaning of moral judgment remains at the center of the literary imagination, even in the morally anarchic thinking of Blok or Ropshin.

In a discussion of the seeming aestheticism of the period, we must take into account the view of art held by these writers. Their aestheticism cannot be understood as a belief in art for art's sake if we consider that all of them put great stock in art as an epistemological vehicle to carry them and their readers to a new way of knowing and acting in the world. In their mature work, artifact is valued lower than the blind creative energy that motivates artistic and meta-artistic activity. Human artifice (*iskusstvo*) is treated as a relatively weak representation of essential creative drive (*tvorchestvo*). For example, Merezhkovsky regards art as an allegory for historical forces of change. Gorky considers spontaneous creativity, not the finished work, the true transformative force. Belyi, in his chosen artistic role as "amanuensis" to transcendent power, values art only insofar as it hints at unearthly, higher being.

In his autobiography, Nietzsche challenged all future readers with the thought that "Ultimately, nobody can get more out of things, including books, than he already knows" (EH, 261). He questioned whether there is such a thing as influence and whether people learn from their experience. Certainly most

Russian readers read Nietzsche in the same vulgarizing way as they had grown accustomed to reading their own romantic writers. And certainly even younger, more innovative writers found in his philosophy a sensibility that to varying degrees reenforced their own. Although the revolution of moral consciousness was about the rereading of Russian traditions, Russian values, and Russian myths, the experience of reading Nietzsche cast those traditions in a new light. It did make a difference. Both as critic of morality and as seeker of myth, Nietzsche was a crucial catalyst in the regeneration of the Russian impulse to moral rebellion.

Key to Abbreviations

Citations of Nietzsche's work are given in the text according to the following key:

BT   *The Birth of Tragedy*, trans. Walter Kaufmann (New York: Vintage, 1967).
GS   *The Gay Science*, trans. W. Kaufmann (New York: Vintage, 1974).
Z   *Thus Spoke Zarathustra*, trans. R. J. Hollingdale (Harmondsworth: Penguin, 1975).
BGE *Beyond Good and Evil*, trans. W. Kaufmann (New York: Vintage, 1966).
GM   *On the Genealogy of Morals*, trans. W. Kaufmann (New York: Vintage, 1969).
TI   *Twilight of the Idols*, trans. R. J. Hollingdale (Harmondsworth: Penguin, 1975).
A   *The Anti-Christ*, trans. R. J. Hollingdale (Harmondsworth: Penguin, 1975).
EH   *Ecce Homo*, trans. W. Kaufmann (New York: Vintage, 1969).
WP   *The Will to Power*, trans. W. Kaufmann and R. J. Hollingdale (New York: Vintage, 1974).

Citations from major works of Russian authors are given in the text according to the following key. Keys are given in the order in which the works are discussed.

NKM Nikolai K. Mikhailovskii, *Literaturnye vospominaniia i sovremennaia smuta* (St. Petersburg: 1900) II.
VP   Vasilii P. Preobrazhenskii, "Kritika morali al'truizma," *Voprosy filosofii i psikhologii*, 15 (1892), 115–160.

232 Abbreviations

P   Petr D. Boborykin, *Pereval*, in: *Sobranie romanov, povestei i rasskazov v 12-i tomakh* (St. Petersburg: 1897), VII.

N   ———, *Nakip'* (St. Petersburg: 1900).

Zh   ———, "Zhestokie," *Russkaia mysl'*, 1901. The number of the journal precedes the page number.

SP   Leonid N. Andreev, "Rasskaz o Sergee Petroviche," *Sobranie sochinenii v 8-i tomakh* (St. Petersburg: 1908), II.

D   Aleksandr Kuprin, "Poedinok," *Sochineniia v 2-kh tomakh* (Moscow: Khudozhestvennaia literatura, 1981), 68–219. Citations are take from *The Duel*, trans. A. R. MacAndrew (New York: Signet, 1961).

KB   V. Ropshin, *Kon' blednyi* (Nice: M. A. Tumanov, 1912).

VS   Mikhail Artsybashev, *Sanin* (Letchworth: Bradda, 1972).

L   Anatolii Kamenskii, *Liudi* (St. Petersburg: 1910).

KS   Anastasia Verbitskaia, *Kliuchi schast'ia* (Moscow: Kushnerev, 1910–1913).

LTD   Dmitrii S. Merezhkovskii, "L. Tolstoi i Dostoevskii," *Mir iskusstva*, 1–12, 13–24 (1900).

J   ———, *Smert' bogov: Iulian otstupnik* (St. Petersburg: M. V. Pirozhkov, 1906).

LV   ———, *Voskresshie bogi: Leonardo da Vinci* (St. Petersburg: M. V. Pirozhkov, 1906).

PA   ———, *Antikhrist: Petr i Aleksei* (St. Petersburg: M. V. Pirozhkov, 1906).

ML   ———, *M. Iu. Lermontov* (1911; rpt. Letchworth: Prideaux, 1979).

ASP   ———, *Pushkin* (1906; rpt. Letchworth: Prideaux, 1971).

SS   Viacheslav Ivanov, *Sobranie sochinenii* (Brussels: Foyer Chrétien Oriental, 1971–).

SS8   Aleksandr Blok, *Sobranie sochinenii v 8-i tomakh* (Moscow: GIKhL, 1960–1963).

SII   Andrei Belyi, "Simfoniia. 2-aia dramaticheskaia," *Chetyre simfonii* (Munich: W. Fink, 1971).

SIII   ———, "Vozvrat. 3-ia simfoniia," *Chetyre simfonii*.

SD   ———, *Serebrianyi golub'* (1922; rpt. Munich: W. Fink, 1967). Citations are taken from *Silver Dove*, trans. G. Reavey (New York: Grove, 1974).

P   ———, *Petersburg* (1916). Citations are taken from *Petersburg*, trans. R. A. Maguire, J. E. Malmstad (Bloomington: Indiana University Press, 1978).

R   Maksim Gor'kii, *Rasskazy* (St. Petersburg: Znanie, 1903).

SS30   ———, *Sobranie sochinenii v 30-i tomakh* (Moscow: GIKhL, 1949–1956).

PSS   ———, *Polnoe sobranie sochinenii* (Mowcow: Nauka, 1968–1972).

Abbreviations   233

Ch ———, *My Childhood*, trans. R. Wilks (Harmondsworth: Penguin, 1980).
MG Andreevich (Evgenii Andreevich Solov'ev), *Kniga o Maksime Gor'kom i A. P. Chekhove* (St. Petersburg: 1900).
O ———, *Opyt filosofii russkoi literatury* (St. Petersburg: Znanie, 1905).
LSS8 Anatolii Lunacharskii, *Sobranie sochinenii v 8-i tomakh* (Moscow: Khud. lit., 1963–1969).
DI ———, "Dialog ob iskusstve," *Otkliki zhizni* (St. Petersburg: O. N. Popova, 1906).
VMN ———, "V mire neiasnogo," *Otkliki zhizni* (St. Petersburg: O. N. Popova, 1906).
RiS ———, *Religiia i sotsializm* (St. Petersburg: Shipovnik, 1908).

Notes

Chapter 1

1. See, for example, S. A. Vengerov, *Russkaia literatura XX veka* (Moscow: 1914; rpt. Munich: W. Fink, 1972), 26. Nikolai Berdiaev, *Smysl tvorchestva: Opyt opravdaniia cheloveka* (1916; rpt. Paris: YMCA, 1985), 297. V. L'vov-Rogachevskii, *Ocherki po istorii noveishei russkoi literatury (1881–1919)* (Moscow: V.C.S.P.O., 1920), chapters 1 and 2.
2. Two works that stress Nietzsche's philosophy of creativity and see it as exerting an antiethical influence in the Russian sphere are George L. Kline, "'Nietzschean Marxism' in Russia," *Demythologizing Marxism: A Series of Studies of Marxism* (The Hague: M. Nijhoff, 1969), 125–153, esp. p. 167; Bernice G. Rosenthal, "Nietzsche in Russia: The Case of Merezhkovsky," *Slavic Review*, 3 (1974), 429–452, esp. p. 436–438; V. V. Dudkin, K. M. Azadovskii, "Problema 'Dostoevskii-Nitsshe'," *Literaturnoe nasledstvo* 86 (1973), 678–688. See, also, Carol Anschuetz, "Bely's *Petersburg* and the End of the Russian Novel," *The Russian Novel from Pushkin to Pasternak*, ed. J. Garrard (New Haven: Yale University Press, 1983), 126.
3. See, for example, a recent history of the period: A. G. Sokolov, *Istoriia russkoi literatury kontsa XIX–nachala XX veka* (Moscow: Vysshaia shkola, 1979), 68–71, 152–160. See also M. L. Mirza-Avakian, "F. Nitsshe i russkii modernizm," *Vestnik erevanskogo universiteta*, 3 (1972), 92–103. See S. S. Averintsev, "Poeziia Viacheslava Ivanova," *Voprosy Literatury*, 8 (1975), 145–192, esp. on p. 151–152; B. V. Mikhailovskii, *Tvorchestvo M. Gor'kogo i mirovaia literatura* (Moscow: Nauka, 1965), 36–38; N. E. Krutikova, *V nachale veka: Gor'kii i simvolisty* (Kiev: Naukova dumka, 1978).

It must be noted that the real groundwork for the study of Nietzsche's reception in Russia has been done beyond the borders of the

Soviet Union. For an early sketch of the problem, see L. Szilard-Mihalne, "Nietzsche in Russland," *Deutsche Studien* 12 (1974), 159–163. Large, ground-breaking efforts include Richard D. Davies, "Nietzsche in Russia, 1892–1917: A Preliminary Bibliography," *Germano-Slavica*, 2 (1976), 107–146; 3 (1977), 201–220. This bibliography is reprinted with some changes in *Nietzsche in Russia*, ed. B. G. Rosenthal (Princeton: Princeton University Press, 1986). Two recent dissertations on the topic are Ann M. Lane, "Nietzsche in Russian Thought, 1890–1917," Ph.D. dissertation, University of Wisconsin, 1976. Edith W. Clowes, "A Philosophy 'For All and None': The Early Reception of Friedrich Nietzsche's Thought in Russian Literature, 1892–1912," Ph.D. dissertation, Yale University, 1981.
4. Lionel Trilling, "The Sense of the Past," *Influx: Essays on Literary Influence*, ed. Ronald Primeau (Port Washington, N.Y.: National University Publications, 1977), 29.
5. Harold Bloom, *Anxiety of Influence* (Oxford: Oxford University Press, 1975), 7.
6. The term *transaction* comes from Louise Rosenblatt, "Toward a Transactional Theory of Reading," *Influx*, 121–136.
7. V. M. Zhirmunskii, *Bairon i Pushkin* (Leningrad: 1924; rpt., Leningrad: Nauka, 1978), 17.
8. Bloom, *A Map of Misreading* (New York: Oxford, 1975), 3.
9. Hans Robert Jauss, "Literaturgeschichte als Provokation der Literaturwissenschaft," *Literaturgeschichte als Provokation* (Frankfurt: Suhrkamp, 1970), 175–185.
10. Isaiah Berlin, "Birth of the Russian Intelligentsia," *Russian Thinkers* (Harmondsworth: Penguin, 1979), 125.
11. M. Iu. Lermontov, *Geroi nashego vremeni* (Moscow: Khudozhestvennaia literatura, 1985), 426.
12. Alfred Kelly, *The Descent of Darwin: The Popularization of Darwinism in Germany, 1860–1914* (Chapel Hill: University of North Carolina Press, 1981), 52.
13. David S. Thatcher, *Nietzsche in England, 1890–1914: The Growth of a Reputation* (Toronto: University of Toronto, 1970), 23.
14. Iurii Tynianov, "O literaturnoi evoliutsii," *Texte der russischen Formalisten*, vol. 1 (Munich: W. Fink, 1969), 454.
15. Nordau had a similar effect at least on Nietzsche's earliest reception in England. See Thatcher, *Nietzsche in England*, 27.
16. In the English-speaking world this recognition is due to Walter Kaufmann. See his *Nietzsche: Philosopher, Psychologist, Antichrist* (New York: Vintage, 1968), 3–18.
17. Two recent counterexamples are Richard Freeborn, *The Russian Revolutionary Novel* (Cambridge: Cambridge University Press,

Notes   237

1982), 39–64; Georges Nivat, *Vers la fin du mythe russe* (Lausanne: L'Age d'Homme, 1982), 150–154, 181–183.
18. I take the term *revolutionary romantic* for this particular type of socially committed writer from E. B. Tager, "Revoliutsionnyi romantizm Gor'kogo," *Russkaia literatura kontsa XIX–nachala XX veka*, vol. 1 (Moscow: Nauka, 1968), 213–243. Their social-aesthetic orientation is of great significance as a predecessor to the politically sanctioned literature of the Stalin era.
19. Iu. Tynianov, "Dostoevskii i Gogol': k teorii parodii," *Texte der russischen Formalisten*, 302.
20. John Burt Foster, *Heirs to Dionysus: A Nietzschean Current in Literary Modernism* (Princeton: Princeton University Press, 1981), 23–37.
21. Bloom, *A Map of Misreading*, 35.
22. Quoted in Anatolii Lunacharskii, "Budushchee religii," *Obrazovanie* 10 (1907), 7.
23. Mircea Eliade, *Myth and Reality* (New York: Harper, 1963), 8.

Chapter 2

1. Arthur Schopenhauer, *Essays and Aphorisms*, trans. R. J. Hollingdale (Harmondsworth: Penguin, 1981), 49.
2. George Brandes, *Friedrich Nietzsche* (London: Heinemann, 1914), 69. Friedrich Nietzsche, *Werke*, ed. K. Schlechta (Frankfurt am Main: Ullstein, 1984), vol. 4, 1272.
3. See C. A. Miller, "Nietzsche's 'Discovery' of Dostoevsky," *Nietzsche Studien*, 2 (1973), 202–257.
4. See GM, 116, where Nietzsche writes of his antecedent: "the *ascetic priest* provided until the most modern times the repulsive and gloomy caterpillar form in which alone the philosopher could live and creep about."
5. Ophelia Schutte, *Beyond Nihilism* (Chicago: University of Chicago Press, 1984), 8.
6. Ibid., 15–16, 124.
7. Walter Kaufmann, *Nietzsche: Philosopher, Psychologist, Antichrist* (New York: Vintage, 1968), 110–113.
8. For a clear summary of this view see Bernd Magnus, *Nietzsche's Existential Imperative* (Bloomington: Indiana University Press, 1978), 25–32.
9. The point should be brought out that Nietzsche as reader of Russian literature represents one of the first major examples of Russian influence upon European letters. See, for example, C. A. Miller, "Nietzsche's 'Discovery' of Dostoevsky," *Nietzsche Studien*, 2

(1973), 202–257. Miller sees some influence of Dostoevsky's idea of the weak heart on Nietzsche's idea of slave morality. Another example can be found in the impact of Tolstoi's and Dostoevsky's Christian ideals on Nietzsche's late reconsideration of Christ in *The Anti-Christ*. Even when Nietzsche disagrees heartily with the ascetic spirituality of Tolstoi or the "decadent," "sublime," "sick," and "childlike" Christ of Dostoevsky (A, 142–143), it is with the deepest admiration for both writers. He shares a great deal with each. In *The Anti-Christ* he arrives at an almost exultant rediscovery of the earthly Christ of the Gospel, stripped of the paraphernalia attributed to him by St. Paul and hundreds of years of theology. This Christ figure is possessed of a consciousness of being blessed. His morality is very similar to Tolstoi's idea of nonresistance to evil (A, 145). Like Dostoevsky's Christian idea, this Christ's "kingdom of God" is "an experience within a heart" (A, 147). As with both Russians, Nietzsche's Christ bears out his state of heart through earthly practice, through living and dying according to his own sense of blessedness, through *loving* (A, 148). Nietzsche finds in Christ his own highest value: "Only we, we *emancipated* spirits, possess the prerequisite for understanding something nineteen centuries have misunderstood—that integrity becomes instinct and passion which makes war on the 'holy lie' even more than any other lie" (A, 148).

10. See P. Annenkov, *Literaturnye vospominaniia* (Moscow-Leningrad: Academia, 1928), 558–563.

11. N. K. Mikhailovskii, *Literaturnye vospominaniia i sovremennaia smuta* (St. Petersburg: Vol'f, 1900), vol. 2, 398. V. A. Posse, *Moi zhiznennyi put': dorevoliutsionnyi period (1864–1917 gg.)* (Moscow-Leningrad: Zemlia i fabrika, 1929), 106. Stirner's philosophy was eclipsed in the decades of the 1860s and 1870s by a variety of other socialist and anarchist doctrines. With the discovery of Nietzsche, Stirner's philosophy enjoyed renewed popularity. Mikhailovsky, writing in 1894, called Stirner a "forerunner" of Nietzsche. He summarized Stirner's philosophy of egotism as the primacy of self-will: "I alone exist . . . and I, only I am the bearer of all moral value." Posse, a Marxist journalist who "discovered" Gorky and aided his speedy rise to fame, remembered placing Stirner on a plane with Nietzsche. In *The Course of My Life*, Posse wrote, "I found in Stirner an ingenious anticipation of the revolutionary and liberating significance of the general strike. I found in him a daring pronouncement of the right to crime, to that secret order with which we can win freedom of speech, freedom of assembly and all the other freedoms that are so assiduously limited by the most liberal legislation."

12. For a good contrastive treatment of Nietzsche and the Russian nihilists, see Arthur C. Danto, *Nietzsche as Philosopher* (New York:

Macmillan Publishing Co., 1970), 29-31. Danto calls the Russians' scientific outlook a new faith that replaced demoted religious faith.
13. Ellen Chances makes a similar point when she shows the ambivalent attitude of Russian authors to these characters. She discusses the superfluous man archetype in terms of its nonconformity and shows the strength of the impulse to conformity in nineteenth-century novel writing. See *Conformity's Children: An Approach to the Superfluous Man in Russian Literature* (Columbus: Slavica, 1978).
14. Mythic archetypes representing humility, tenderness, sorrowful joy are deeply embedded in the Russian tradition of *kenosis*. For a discussion of this heritage, see G. P. Fedotov, *The Russian Religious Mind*, vol. 1 (Cambridge: Harvard University Press, 1966), 94-130.
15. Donald Fanger, "The Peasant in Literature," *The Peasant in Nineteenth-Century Russia*, ed. W. S. Vucinich (Stanford: Stanford University Press, 1968), 231-262.
16. Andrei Belyi, *Vospominaniia o A. A. Bloke* (Munich: Fink, 1969), 28.
17. Some prominent intellectuals of the younger generation, such as the well-known Idealist (and former Marxist) thinker Sergei Bulgakov, felt the same way. See his "Ivan Karamazov (v romane Dostoevskogo 'Brat'ia Karamazovy') kak filosofskii tip," *Voprosy filosofii i psikhologii*, 61 (Jan.-Feb. 1902), 826-863.
18. Andrei Belyi, "Merezhkovskii," *Lug zelenyi* (Moscow: Al'tsiona, 1910), 139.

Chapter 3

1. George Brandes, *Friedrich Nietzsche*, 88-91.
2. Ibid., 98.
3. See "Vagnerianskii vopros: muzykal'naia problema," trans. O. O. R., *Artist*, 40 (1894), 61-75.
4. "Mysli i paradoksy Fridrikha Nitsshe," ed. A. Reingol'dt, *Novosti*, 209, 252, 256 (1891).
5. Marianna Tax Choldin, *A Fence Around the Empire: The Censorship of Foreign Books in Nineteenth Century Russia*, Ph.D. dissertation, University of Chicago, 1979, 40, 44, 77. Published as a book under the same title: (Durham: Duke University Press, 1985).
6. Quoted from L. I. Polianskaia, "Obzor fonda tsentral'nogo komiteta tsenzury inostrannoi," *Arkhivnoe delo*, 1 (1938), 88.
7. The best bibliography of Nietzsche's reception in Russia is Richard D. Davies, "Nietzsche in Russia, 1892-1917: A Preliminary Bibliography," *Germano-Slavica*, 2 (1976), 107-146; 3 (1977), 201-220. This bibliography reappears in shortened form in *Nietzsche in Rus-*

sia, ed. B. G. Rosenthal (Princeton: Princeton University Press, 1986), 355-392.
8. Daniel Balmuth, *Censorship in Russia, 1865-1905* (Washington, D.C.: University Press of America, 1979), 109, 116.
9. Arkhiv A. M. Gor'kogo, I. M. L. I., Vladimir Posse to A. M. Gor'kii, St. Petersburg, Jan. 13, 1899.
10. Otdel rukopisei, Gos. publ. biblioteka im. Saltykova-Shchedrina, f. 124, no. 2780, D. S. Merezhkovskii to M. E. Prozor, July 8-21, 1904.
11. Arkhiv A. M. Gor'kogo, E. P. Peshkova to A. M. Gor'kii, Nizhnii Novgorod, Oct. 15, 1899.
12. P. P. Pertsov, *Literaturnye vospominaniia* (Moscow-Leningrad: Akademiia, 1933), 7.
13. Posse, *Moi zhiznennyi put'* (Moscow-Leningrad: Zemlia i fabrika, 1929), 105.
14. Liubov' Gurevich, "Istoriia 'Severnogo vestnika'," *Russkaia literatura XX veka (1890-1910)*, ed. S. A. Vengerov (Moscow: Mir, 1914), 255.
15. See Dmitrij Tschizewskij, "Hegel in Russland," *Hegel bei den Slaven* (Darmstadt: Wiss. Buchgesellschaft, 1961), 145-396. First published in Russian in Paris, 1939. Also see Wsewolod Setschkareff, *Schellings Einfluss in der russischen Literatur der 20er und 30er Jahre des XIX. Jahrhunderts* (Leipzig: 1939; rept. Nendeln: Kraus, 1968).
16. See Bernice Glatzer Rosenthal, "Nietzsche in Russia: The Case of Merezhkovskii," *Slavic Review*, 3 (1974), 429-452; Ann M. Lane, *Nietzsche in Russia, 1892-1917*, Ph.D. dissertation, University of Wisconsin, 1976, 418-486.
17. O. Deshart, "Vvedenie," in Viacheslav Ivanov, *Sobranie sochinenii* (Brussels: Foyer Oriental Chrétien, 1971), vol. 1, 16-17.
18. See, for example, remarks on the lay reader in Jeffrey Brooks, *When Russia Learned to Read: Literacy and Popular Literature, 1861-1917* (Princeton: Princeton University Press, 1985), 147-148.
19. George L. Kline has found other examples of censorship of citations from Nietzsche in critical texts. In Lev Shestov's *Good in the Teaching of Count Tolstoi and Fr. Nietzsche* [*Dobro v uchenii gr. Tolstogo i Fr. Nitshe*, 1903], Kline reports, Shestov quotes Nietzsche in German, probably in an effort to evade the censors. In a selection from *Genealogy of Morals*, (GM, 47), Nietzsche writes: "[the resentful] give me to understand that they are not merely better than the mighty, the lords of the earth whose spittle they have to lick (*not from fear, not at all from fear: but because God has commanded them to obey the authorities*)—that they are not merely better but are also 'better off'. . . ." In Shestov's text, the italicized phrase, "but

because God has commanded them to obey the authorities," was omitted. Courtesy of George L. Kline and Bernice G. Rosenthal.
20. Fridrikh Nitsshe, *Tak govoril Zaratustra*, trans. V. Izraztsov (St. Petersburg: 1913), 19.
21. Polianskaia, "Obzor fonda tsentral'nogo komiteta tsenzury inostrannoi," 88.
22. Max Nordau, *Entartung* (Berlin: Carl Dunker, 1895), 322.
23. Ibid., 318.
24. See B. I. Esin, "Russkaia legal'naia pressa kontsa XIX–nachala XX veka," *Iz istorii russkoi zhurnalistiki kontsa XIX–nachala XX veka*, ed. B. I. Esin (Moscow: Izdatel'stvo Moskovskogo universita, 1973), 3–66. See, also, B. I. Esin, *Russkaia zhurnalistika 70–80 godov XX veka* (Moscow: Izdatel'stvo Moskovskogo universita, 1963), 116.
25. V. Evgen'ev-Maksimov, D. Maksimov, *Iz proshlogo russkoi zhurnalistiki* (Leningrad: 1930), 97.
26. M. Bohachevsky-Chomiak, B. G. Rosenthal, "Introduction," *A Revolution of the Spirit: Crisis of Value in Russia, 1890–1918* (Newtonville, Mass.: Oriental Research Partners, 1982), 19.
27. Fridrikh Nittsshe, *Tak govoril Zarathustra*, trans. Nani (St. Petersburg: M. M. Stasiulevich, 1899), vii.
28. See, for example, Fridrikh Nitsshe, *Tak govoril Zarathustra*, trans. A. N. Achkasov (Moscow: D. P. Efimov, 1906). Achkasov gives a great deal of historical information on Zoroaster, textual history, stylistic commentary, and interpretation of key concepts.
29. Nikolai Grot, "Nravstvennye idealy nashego vremeni: Fridrikh Nitsshe i Lev Tolstoi," *Voprosy filosofii i psikhologii*, 1 (1893), 148.
30. Ivan Bichalets, "Chelovek-Lopukh i Chelovek-Zver'," *Kievskoe slovo*, 1873 (April 3, 1893), 1.
31. Grot, "Nravstvennye idealy nashego vremeni," 147.
32. F. I. Bulgakov, "Iz obshchestvennoi i literaturnoi khroniki zapada," *Vestnik inostrannoi literatury*, 5 (1893), 206–207.
33. V. Chuiko, "Obshchestvennye idealy Fridrikha Nitsshe, *Nabliudatel'*, 2 (1893), 234, 247.
34. Nestor Kotliarevskii, "Vospominaniia a Vasilii Petroviche Preobrazhenskom," *Voprosy filosofii i psikhologii*, 4 (Sept. 1900), 532.
35. Andreevich, "Ocherki tekushchei russkoi literatury: O Nitche," *Zhizn'*, 4 (1901), 286.
36. Andrei Belyi, *Na rubezhe dvukh stoletii* (Moscow-Leningrad: Zemlia i fabrika, 1930), 13.
37. Andreevich, "Ocherki tekushchei russkoi literatury," 287.
38. L. Shestov, *Dobro v uchenii gr. Tolstogo i F. Nitsshe: filosofiia i propoved'* (St. Petersburg: Stasiulevich, 1900), 100–101, 187.
39. Andreevich, "Ocherki tekushchei russkoi literatury," 291.

40. E. V. Tarle, "Nitssheanstvo i ego otnoshenie k politicheskim i sotsial'nym teoriiam evropeiskogo obshchestva," *Vestnik evropy*, 8 (1901), 729.
41. Shestov, *Dobro v uchenii*, 177–178.
42. See, for example, Volzhskii, *Iz mira literaturnykh iskanii* (St. Petersburg: D. E. Zhukovskii, 1906), 140; Nevedomskii, "Vmesto predisloviia," intro. to Anri Likhtenberzhe, *Filosofiia Nittsshe* (St. Petersburg: O. N. Popova, 1901), cxx: here Gorky is called a "self-made Nietzschean" (*nittsseanets-samorodok*); P. Orlovskii, *Iz istorii noveishei russkoi literatury* (Moscow: Zveno, 1910), 5.
43. For more on Balmont's response to Nietzsche, see E. W. Clowes, "The Nietzschean Image of the Poet in Some Early Works of Konstantin Bal'mont and Valerij Brjusov," *Slavic and East European Journal* (Summer 1983), 68–80.
44. E. Anichkov, "Bal'mont," *Russkaia literatura XX veka*, ed. S. Vengerov (Moscow: Mir, 1914), vol. 1, 86. "Ia zhizn', ia solntse, krasota,/ Ia vremia skazkoi zacharuiu./ Ia v strasti zvezdy sozdaiu,/ Ia ves' vesna, kogda kogo liubliu./ Ia svetlyi bog, kodga tseluiu" (86). See, also, Ellis, "Konstantin Bal'mont," *Russkie simvolisty* (Moscow: 1910; rpt. Letchworth: Bradda, 1972), 54.
45. Anichkov, "Bal'mont," 90.
46. Iu. Aleksandrovich, *Posle Chekhova: Ocherki molodoi literatury poslednego desiatiletiia, 1898–1908* (Moscow: Obshchestvennaia pol'za, 1908), 61–66, 177–178.
47. N. K. Mikhailovskii, "O g. Maksime Gor'kom i ego geroiakh," *Kriticheskie stat'i o proizvedeniiakh Maksima Gor'kogo* (St. Petersburg: 1901), 53–105; M. Gel'rot, "Nitsshe i Gor'kii: Element nitssheanstva v tvorchestve Gor'kogo," *Russkoe bogatstvo*, 5 (1903), 25–68.
48. Andreevich, *Kniga o Maksime Gor'kom i A. P. Chekhove* (St. Petersburg: A. E. Kolpinskii, 1900), 28–29.
49. M. P. Nevedomskii, "Vmesto predisloviia," iii.
50. N. Minskii, "Fr. Nitsshe," *Mir iskusstva*, 19–20 (1900), 144.
51. V. Solov'ev, "Ideia sverkhcheloveka," *Sobranie sochinenii* (St. Petersburg: Obshchestvennaia pol'za, 1903), vol. 8, 312.
52. Ibid., 310.
53. L. Tolstoi, *Polnoe sobranie sochinenii* (Moscow: Gosizdat, 1935), vol. 54, 77.
54. Ibid., vol. 30, 172–173.
55. Ibid., vol. 34, 309.
56. Ibid., vol. 54, 9.
57. Ibid., vol. 57, 176.
58. For example, Belyi would forge a restrictive, otherworldly moral view, appropriating Solovyov as an example. See Chapter 5. One of Tolstoi's disciples, Lev Semenov, was strongly affected by Tolstoi's

antivitalism and antirelativism. In his memoirs, he recalls that Russian youth relied on Nietzsche to justify the most aberrant and inhuman acts. See L. D. Semenov, "Zapiski," *Trudy po russkoi i slavianskoi filologii,* vol. 28 (Tartu: 1977), 114–115.
59. Petr Boborykin, 'O nitssheanstve," *Voprosy filosofii i psikhologii,* 54 (1900), 540.
60. It is interesting that children of Moscow merchants often did receive a classical education in this period. Examples are Briusov and Konstantin Alekseev-Stanislavsky. See *O Stanislavskom: Sbornik vospominanii, 1863–1936,* ed. L. Ia. Gurevich (Moscow: Vserossiiskoe teatral'noe obshchestvo, 1948), 49–50; K. Mochul'skii, *Valerii Briusov* (Paris, YMCA, 1962), 20.
61. See, for example, Vladimir Solov'ev, *The Justification of the Good* (London: 1918), 114.
62. Minskii, "Fridrikh Nitsshe," 141.
63. A. B., "Kriticheskie zametki: 'Zhestokie,' roman g. Boborykina," *Mir bozhii,* 8 (1901), 1.
64. P. Boborykin, "O nitssheanstve," *Voprosy filosofii i psikhologii,* 4 (Sept. 1900), 546.
65. Mikhailovskii, "Literatura i zhizn'," *Russkoe bogatstvo,* 2 (1900), 150, 152.
66. Ibid., 148.
67. Andrei Belyi, *Nachalo veka* (Moscow-Leningrad: Gosizdat, 1933; rpt. Chicago: Russian Language Specialties, 1966), 460–461. James Billington, *The Icon and the Axe* (New York: Vintage, 1970), 484. Suzanne Massie, *The Land of the Firebird: The Beauty of Old Russia* (New York: Simon & Schuster, 1980), 384–406.
68. *Literaturnoe nasledstvo* (Moscow: Nauka, 1976) vol. 85, 286.
69. Boborykin, "O nitssheanstve," 543.
70. Ibid., 546.
71. Ibid., 543.
72. N. Kotliarevskii, "Vospominaniia o Vasilii Petroviche Preobrazhenskom," *Voprosy filosofii i psikhologii,* 4 (1900), 532.
73. For example, Prince D. S. Mirsky calls Artsybashev's *Sanin* the "Bible" of post-1905 Russian youth. See Mirsky, *Contemporary Russian Literature, 1881–1925* (London: George R. Routledge, 1926; rpt. New York: Kraus Reprint Co., 1972), 139–140. See, also, Richard Stites, *The Women's Liberation Movement in Russia: Feminism, Nihilism, and Bolshevism, 1860–1930* (Princeton: Princeton University Press, 1978), 185–188. Stites discusses the uproar created by *Sanin* and compares it to that around Chernyshevsky's *What Is to Be Done* in the 1860s. Mirsky also notes that Verbitskaia's novel, *Keys of Happiness,* was at the top of the list of books most in demand at public libraries. See Mirsky, p. 147. For numbers of copies

sold, see Jeffrey Brooks, *When Russia Learned to Read: Literacy and Popular Literature, 1861–1917* (Princeton: Princeton University Press, 1985), 154. Discussed in Chapter 4.

Chapter 4

1. For analysis of the more ascetic mythos of self-transformation in radical literature, see Katerina Clark, *The Soviet Novel: History as Ritual*, 2d ed. (Chicago: University of Chicago Press, 1985), 46–67.
2. M. L. Loe, "Maksim Gor'kii and the *Sreda* Circle: 1899–1905," *Slavic Review*, 1 (Spring 1985), 49–66.
3. See *Literaturnyi raspad*, 2 vols. (St. Petersburg: EOS, 1908–1909).
4. Jutta Scherrer, *Die Petersburger Religiös-Philosophischen Vereinigungen: Die Entwicklung des religiösen Selbstverständnisses ihrer Intelligencija-Mitglieder (1901–1917)* (Berlin-Wiesbaden: O. Harrassowitz, 1973), 182–183.
5. Quoted from L. Iezuitova, *Tvorchestvo Leonida Andreeva, 1892–1906* (Leningrad: Izdatel'stvo Leningradskogo universiteta, 1976), 92.
6. Fedor Dostoevskii, *The Devils*, trans. David Magarshack (London: Penguin, 1969), 126.
7. Fedor Dostoevskii, "Brat'ia Karamazovy," *Polnoe sobranie sochinenii* (Leningrad: Nauka, 1976), vol. 14, 215.
8. The older generation was likely to blame Nietzsche. Younger critics blamed writers for arriving at a harmful, faulty reading of the philosopher. See, for example, E. Anichkov, "Doloi Nittshe," *Novaia zhizn'* 9 (1912), 126.
9. Andreev, for example, confused Dostoevsky and Nietzsche more than once. See *Literaturnoe nasledstvo* (Moscow: Nauka, 1965), vol. 72, 88. For a treatment of middlebrow fiction in English literature in the 1920s, see Q. D. Leavis, *Fiction and the Reading Public* (London: Chatto and Windus, 1932), 46–47. Leavis also defines middlebrow writing as admiring and imitative of high-brow art. She also notes middlebrow authors' lack of aesthetic discrimination.
10. See, for example, Iu. Aleksandrovich, *Posle Chekhova: Ocherk molodoi literatury poslednege desiatiletiia, 1898–1908* (Moscow: Obshchestvennaia pol'za, 1908), 42. F. Beliavskii, "Gor'kaia pravda," *Slovo*, 157 (May 22, 1905), 5. Another book that aroused widespread discussion in the literary press both in Russia and abroad, Artsybashev's *Sanin*, is discussed in the next section. See, for example, Arskii, "Motivy Solntsa i Tela v sovremennoi belletristike," *Voprosy pola*, 2 (1908), 28–30; *Sud'ba 'Sanina' v Germanii*, trans. V. I. Rotenstern (St. Petersburg: 1909), 82–83; S. A. Vengerov, "Etapy neoromanticheskogo dvizheniia," *Russkaia literatura XX veka* (Moscow: Mir, 1914), 22.

11. Richard Stites, *The Women's Liberation Movement in Russia* (Princeton: Princeton University Press, 1978), 159–160, 168. Jeffrey Brooks, *When Russia Learned to Read* (Princeton: Princeton University Press, 1985), 153–165.
12. Tan, "Sanin v iubke," *Utro Rossii* (Dec. 31, 1909), 3.
13. Brooks, *When Russia Learned to Read*, 154.
14. K. Chukovskii, "Ideinaia pornografiia," *Rech'*, 304 (Dec. 11, 1908), 2.
15. For a discussion of lowbrow fiction and its readers in England, see Q. D. Leavis, *Fiction and the Reading Public*, 48–64. Leavis notes the demand among the lowbrow readership for satisfaction of religious feeling, especially for "terrific vitality set to turn the machinery of morality" (64). See also Leo Lowenthal, "The Reception of Dostoevski's Work in Germany: 1880–1920," *The Arts in Society*, ed. Robert N. Wilson (Englewood Cliffs, N.J.: Prentice-Hall, 1964), 122–147. Lowenthal characterizes the German middle-class public as possessing a veneer of "cultural pretention." He finds them morally and politically apathetic, mentally lazy, inwardly directed, and in search of some semireligious comfort.
16. E. Anichkov, "Doloi Nitsshe," *Novaia zhizn'* 9 (1912), 133–134.
17. M. Nevedomskii, "Vmesto predisloviia," foreword to Anri Likhtenberzhe, *Filosofiia Nittshe* (St. Petersburg: O. Popova, 1901), ii.
18. N. K. Mikhailovskii, *Poslednie sochineniia* (St. Petersburg: Russkoe bogatstvo, 1905), vol. 1, 77.
19. V. I. Lenin, "Partiinaia organizatsiia i partiinaia literatura," *Sochineniia* (Moscow: GIPL, 1952), vol. 10, 27.
20. N. Minskii, "Filosofiia toski i zhazhda voli," *Kriticheskie stat'i o proizvedeniiakh Maksima Gor'kogo* (Kiev: A. G. Aleksandrov, 1901), 21.
21. *Leksika russkogo literaturnogo iazyka XIX-nachala XX veka*, ed. F. P. Filin (Moscow: Nauka, 1981), 226.
22. The Marxist historian E. V. Tarle tantalizingly suggested as early as 1901 that the popular cult of Nietzscheanism may have helped its followers to break through social-moral inhibitions. This general corrosion of social mores made it possible for radical political and social theories of all kinds to be put into practice. See Tarle, "Nitssheanstvo i ego otnoshenie k politicheskim i sotsial'nym teoriiam evropeiskogo obshchestva," *Vestnik evropy*, 8 (1901), 704–750, esp. 730.

Chapter 5

1. D. S. Merezhkovsky, *Polnoe sobranie sochinenii* (St. Petersburg: Vol'f, 1911), vol. 12, 257. Hereafter: *PSS* (1911).

2. A. Belyi, "Fridrikh Nitsshe," *Arabeski* (Moscow: 1911; rpt. Munich: W. Fink, 1969), 90.
3. S. Vengerov, *Russkaia literatura XX veka* (Moscow: Mir, 1914), 292.
4. Otdel rukopisei, Publichnaia biblioteka im. Saltykov-Shchedrina, fond K. Vladimirova, no. 150, Zapisnye knizhki, no. 379.
5. See, for example, "Poetu," "Poroi, kak obraz Prometeia," "I khochu, no ne v silakh liubit' ia liudei," and "Naprasno ia khotel otdat' vsiu zhizn' narodu." *Polnoe sobranie sochinenii* (Moscow: Sytin, 1914), vol. 22, 5–12. Hereafter: *PSS* (1914).
6. Vengerov, *Russkaia literatura XX veka*, 291.
7. See, D. S. Merezhkovskii, "Misticheskoe dvizhenie nashego veka: Otryvok," *Trud: Vestnik literatury i nauk*, vol. 18, 4 (1893), 33–40.
8. Bernice G. Rosenthal, *Dmitry Sergeevich Merezhkovsky and the Silver Age* (The Hague: M. Nijhoff, 1975), 18. For other analyses of Merezhkovsky and Nietzsche, see B. G. Rosenthal, "Nietzsche in Russia: The Case of Merezhkovskii," *Slavic Review*, 3 (1974), 429–452; Edith W. Clowes, "The Integration of Nietzsche's Ideas of History, Time, and 'Higher Nature' in the Early Historical Novels of Dmitry Merezhkovsky," *Germano-Slavica* 3, no. 6 (Fall 1981), 401–416; B. G. Rosenthal, "Stages of Nietzscheanism: Merezhkovsky's Intellectual Evolution," *Nietzsche in Russia* (Princeton: Princeton University Press, 1986), 69–94.
9. Valerii Briusov, *Dnevniki, 1890–1910* (Moscow: Sabashnikov 1927), 53.
10. Merezhkovskii, *PSS* (1914), vol. 18, 181.
11. Ibid., 214–217.
12. Rosenthal, "Nietzsche in Russia," 446. Rosenthal goes further in her most recent work, "Stages of Nietzscheanism" (see n. 8). Here she focuses on Merezhkovsky's effort to synthesize in his neo-Christianity the "pagan," Nietzschean love of the earth with Christian heavenly truth.
13. Ibid., "Nietzsche in Russia," 433.
14. D. S. Merezhkovskii, "Spokoistvie," *Severenyi vestnik* 2 (1877), 238.
15. *PSS* (1911), vol. 12, 257.
16. *PSS* (1914), vol. 13, 69–70.
17. Ibid., 12.
18. Ibid., 69–70.
19. Rosenthal, "Nietzsche in Russia," 446.
20. Merezhkovskii, *PSS* (1914), vol. 13, 32.
21. Ibid., 77. Italics removed.
22. Rosenthal, *Merezhkovsky and the Silver Age*, 100.
23. A. Belyi, "Merezhkovskii," 150.

24. N. Berdiaev, "O novom religioznom soznanii," *Sub specie aeternitatis* (St. Petersburg: M. V. Pirozhkov, 1907), 341.
25. A. Belyi, "Merezhkovskii," 150.
26. Avril Pyman, "Aleksandr Blok and the Merezhkovskijs," *Aleksandr Blok Centennial Conference*, ed. W. N. Vickery (Columbus: Slavica, 1984), 246.
27. See, for example, Sergei Bulgakov, "Ivan Karamazov (v romane 'Brat'ia Karamazovy') kak filosofskii tip," *Voprosy filosofii i psikhologii* 61 (1902), 826–863. E. N. Trubetskoi, *Filosofiia Nitsshe: Kriticheskii ocherk* (Moscow: I. N. Kushnerev, 1904).
28. Fedor Stepun, *Mystische Weltschau* (Munich: Carl Hanser, 1964), 202.
29. Ibid., 253.
30. Olga Deshart, "Vvedenie," in Viacheslav Ivanov, *Sobranie sochinenii* (Brussels: Foyer Oriental Chrietien, 1971), vol. 1, 34.
31. Ibid.
32. V. I. Ivanov, "Ellinskaia religiia stradaiuschego boga," *Novyi put'*, 5 (1904), 35.
33. For example, Oleg Maslenikov, *The Frenzied Poets* (Berkeley: University of California Press, 1952), 7. Other examples are given in Chapter 1, n. 2.
34. Ivanov's critical articles stand in very close relation to his poems as a kind of exegesis. Both are devoted to revealing the nature of Dionysus. Frequently in the course of critical argument he quotes poems from his first two collections to illustrate a point. This practice has the beneficial effect of clarifying otherwise very difficult poetry.
35. Avril Pyman, *The Life of Aleksandr Blok* (Oxford: Oxford University Press, 1979) vol. 1, 229.
36. Jutta Scherrer, *Die Petersburger Religiös-Philosophischen Vereinigungen* (Berlin-Wiesbaden: O. Harrassowitz, 1973), 159–167; see, also, Martha Bohachevsky-Chomiak, Bernice G. Rosenthal, eds., *A Revolution of the Spirit* (Newtonville, Mass.: Oriental Research Partners, 1982), 191–193.
37. See Bernice G. Rosenthal, "Theater as Church: The Vision of the Mystical Anarchists," *Russian History* 4 (1977), 122–141.
38. Quoted from K. Mochulsky, *Andrei Bely: His Life and Works*, trans. N. Szalavitz (Ann Arbor: Ardis, 1977), 87. Belyi probably got the expression from Blok, who called himself the "unresurrected Christ" in a poem from 1907 to his wife, Liubov: "Without regretting what was,/I have understood your loftiness:/ Yes. You are native Galilee/To me—the unresurrected Christ" (O tom, chto bylo, ne zhaleia,/Tvoiu ia ponial vysotu:/Da. Ty—rodnaia Galileia/ Mne— nevoskresshemu Khristu" (SS8, vol. 8, 187).

39. Quoted from Pyman, *Life of Aleksandr Blok*, 172.
40. Ibid., 172.
41. Ibid., 174.
42. Ibid., 228.
43. Ibid., 229.
44. Blok, *Zapisnye knizhki* (Moscow-Leningrad: GIKhL, 1965), 72–74, 84, 86.
45. Pyman, *Life of Aleksandr Blok*, 230.
46. Mochulsky, *Andrei Bely*, 57.
47. Ibid., 178. Blok first performed *Snow Mask* during just such a meeting.
48. Blok, *Zapisnye knizhki*, 84.
49. Ibid., 86.
50. I wish to thank Timothy Westphalen for his careful work in tracing Christological motifs in *Snezhnaia maska:* "Imagistic Centers in Aleksandr Blok's 'Snezhnaja maska'," unpublished honors essay, Knox College, Galesburg, Illinois, spring 1982.
51. *Literaturnoe nasledstvo*, vol. 92, 3 (1982), 299. For a different view of mystical anarchism, see Bernice Glatzer Rosenthal, "The Transmutation of the Symbolist Ethos: Mystical Anarchism and the Revolution of 1905," *Slavic Review* 4 (December, 1977), 608–629.
52. A. Belyi, "Na perevale No. 7: Shtempelevannaia kalosha," *Vesy*, 5 (1907), 52.
53. Belyi, Review of "Tsvetnik Or," *Vesy*, 6 (1907), 68.
54. Earlier in 1910 in his lecture "The Testaments of Symbolism" ("Zavety simvolizma"), Ivanov had characterized Symbolist art as a kind of Dionysian-ascetic practice, an "inner feat of the individual self" in which personal will was sacrificed to the god within (SSII, 602–603).
55. Magnus Ljunggren, *The Dream of Rebirth: A Study of Andrei Belyi's Novel* Peterburg (Stockholm: Almquist and Wiksell, 1982), 18. A. Belyi, *Vospominaniia o A. A. Bloke* (Munich: Fink, 1969), 24.
56. A. Belyi, *Vospominaniia ob Aleksandre Bloke* (Letchworth: Bradda, 1964), 14.
57. Ibid., 39.
58. A. Belyi, *Na rubezhe dvukh stoletii* (Moscow-Leningrad: Zemlia i fabrika, 1930), 465.
59. Ibid., 466.
60. Ibid., 468.
61. Belyi, *Vospominaniia* (Fink), 20.
62. A. Belyi, "Nastoiashchee i budushchee russkoi literatury," *Lug zelenyi* (Moscow: Al'tsiona, 1907), 81.
63. Belyi, "Fridrikh Nittsshe," *Arabeski* (Munich: W. Fink, 1969), 90.
64. Belyi, *Vospominaniia* (Letchworth), 101.

65. Ljunggren, *The Dream of Rebirth*, 77.
66. Belyi, *Na rubezhe*, 13.
67. Belyi, *Vospominaniia* (Letchworth), 101, 159.
68. Belyi, "Nastoiashchee," 61.
69. Belyi, *Na rubezhe*, 402–403.
70. Belyi, "Nastoiashchee," 85.
71. Belyi, "Merezhkovskii," 139.
72. Belyi, *Vospominaniia* (Letchworth), 112.
73. Ibid., 14, 101.
74. Ljunggren, *The Dream of Rebirth*, 77.
75. Belyi, *Vospominaniia* (Letchworth), 113.
76. Ibid.
77. Vladimir Alexandrov, *Andrei Bely: The Major Symbolist Fiction* (Cambridge: Harvard University Press, 1985), 40.
78. Ibid., 51.
79. For a treatment of Nietzschean motifs in *Petersburg*, see Virginia Bennett, "Echoes of Friedrich Nietzsche's *The Birth of Tragedy* in Andrej Belyj's *Petersburg*," *Germano-Slavica*, 4 (Fall 1980), 243–259.
80. Here Belyi echoes Merezhkovsky, who observed in 1908 that nineteenth-century anarchistic individualists, such as Bakunin, Stirner, Nietzsche, Dostoevsky, and Tolstoi, would perceive the new religion first. See Merezhkovskii, PSS (1914), vol. 13, 12.
81. Alexandrov, *Andrei Bely*, 143.
82. Carol Anschuetz, "Bely's *Petersburg* and the End of the Russian Novel," *The Russian Novel from Pushkin to Pasternak*, ed. J. Garrard (New Haven: Yale University Press, 1983), 126.
83. Belyi, "Fridrikh Nittsshe," 84.
84. Scherrer, *Die Petersburger Religiös-Philosophischen Vereinigungen*, 57.
85. Alexandrov, *Andrei Bely*, 128.
86. Ibid., 25.
87. For a parallel phenomenon in western European modernism, see Foster's treatment of Mann's *Doktor Faustus* in *Heirs to Dionysus* (Princeton: Princeton University Press, 1981). Foster discusses Mann's ambivalence to the Dionysian and his ultimate demonization of it. Foster shows, however, that Mann considers the liaison between Dionysian creativity and political tyranny to be a skewed reading of Nietzsche (340).

Chapter 6

1. Anton Chekhov, *Selected Letters* (Berkeley: University of California Press, 1975), 382.
2. K. Bal'mont, *Izbrannoe* (Moscow: Khud. lit., 1980), 444.

3. M. Nevedomskii, "Vmesto predisloviia," in Henri Lichtenberger, *Filosofiia Nittsshe* (St. Petersburg: O. Popova, 1901), cxx. The Russian expression is "nash 'nittssheanets-samorodok'."
4. I. Aleksandrovich, *Posle Chekhova* (Moscow: Obshchestvennaia pol'za, 1908), 178.
5. N. K. Mikhailovskii, "O g. Maksime Gor'kom i ego geroiakh," *Kriticheskie stat'i o proizvedeniiakh Maksima Gor'kogo* (Kiev: A. G. Aleksandrov, 1901), 96.
6. Vladimir Posse, *Moi zhiznennyi put'* (Moscow-Leningrad: Zemlia i fabrika, 1929), 151.
7. G. M. Tumanov, *Kharakteristiki i vospominaniia*, (Tiflis: Trud, 1905), vol. 2, 48.
8. See, for example, Gor'kii to F. D. Batiushkov, October, 1898, SS30, vol. 28, 33; Gor'kii to K. P. Piatnitskii, December, 1901, *Arkhiv A. M. Gor'kogo*, vol. 4 (Moscow: Khud. lit., 1954), 58; Gor'kii to L. N. Andreev, *Literaturnoe nasledstvo*, vol. 72 (Moscow: Nauka, 1965), 88.
9. B. Y. Forman, "The Early Prose of Maksim Gorky, 1892–1899," Ph.D. dissertation, Harvard University, 1983. See esp. pp. 539–582.
10. Ibid., 569–571.
11. N. S. Dorovatovskii, "Pis'ma Maksima Gor'kogo k S. P. Dorovatovskomu," *Pechat' i revoliutsiia*, 2 (1928), 68–88.
12. W. L. Phelps, "Gorki," *Essays on Russian Novelists* (New York: Macmillan Publishing Co., 1911), 219.
13. Arkhiv A. M. Gor'kogo, IMLI, Elizabeth Förster-Nietzsche to A. M. Gor'kii, Weimar, March 12, 1906.
14. See Mary Louise Loe, "Gorky and Nietzsche: The Quest for a Russian Superman," *Nietzsche in Russia*, ed. B. G. Rosenthal (Princeton: Princeton University Press, 1986), 251–274. Loe sees Gorky's Nietzschean views as a point of friction between him and Lenin and later Stalin. Gorky's conflict between voluntarism and social utilitarianism also corresponds to the conflict between "spontaneity" and "consciousness" that Katerina Clark sees in the Socialist Realist novel. See Clark, *The Soviet Novel: History as Ritual* (Chicago: University of Chicago Press, 1981), 15–24.
15. Arkhiv A. M. Gor'kogo, IMLI, A. M. Gor'kii to A. L. Volynskii, Nizhnii Novgorod, December 1897. Also, A. M. Gor'kii to L. A. Nikiforova, March–April 1910.
16. P. P. Pertsov, *Literaturnye vospominaniia* (Moscow-Leningrad: Akademiia, 1933), 30–31.
17. B. Y. Forman, "The Early Prose of Maksim Gorky," 100–104, 183–192.
18. Max Nordau, *Entartung* (Berlin: Carl Dunker, 1895), 326.
19. Ibid., 322.
20. *Literaturnoe nasledstvo*, vol. 72, 122.

21. See B. Y. Forman, "Nietzsche and Gorky in the 1890's: The Case for an Early Influence," *Western Philosophical Systems in Russian Literature*, ed. A. M. Mlikotin (Los Angeles: University of Southern California Press, 1979), 153–164.
22. Nordau, *Entartung*, 422.
23. See n. 45.
24. Zhurnalist (Korolenko), "O sbornikakh tovarishchestva 'Znaniia' za 1903 g.," *Russkoe bogatstvo*, 8 (1904), 132.
25. Posse, *Moi zhiznennyi put'*, 126.
26. Vladimir Lenin, "Partiinaia organizatsiia i partiinaia literatura," *Sochineniia* (Moscow: GIPL, 1952), vol. 10, 27.
27. See Mary Louise Loe, "Maksim Gor'kii and the *Sreda* Circle: 1899–1905," *Slavic Review*, 44, 1 (Spring, 1985), 49–66.
28. See George L. Kline, "'Nietzschean Marxism' in Russia," *Demythologizing Marxism: A Series of Studies in Marxism*, ed. F. J. Adelman (The Hague: M. Nijhoff, 1969), 166–183; George L. Kline, "The 'God-Builders': Gorky and Lunacharsky," *Religious and Anti-Religious Thought in Russia* (Chicago: University of Chicago Press, 1968), 103–126; J. C. McClelland, "Bogostroitel'stvo," *The Modern Encyclopedia of Russian and Soviet History*, ed. J. L. Wieczynski (Gulf Breeze, FL: Academic International Press, 1977), 42–45; Raimund Sesterhenn, *Das Bogostroitel'stvo bei Gor'kij und Lunacarskij bis 1909* (Munich: Otto Sagner, 1982).
29. I take the term *revolutionary romantic* from E. B. Tager, "Revoliutsionnyi romantizm Gor'kogo," *Russkaia literatura kontsa XIX-nachala XXv. 90-e gody* (Moscow: Nauka, 1968), 213–243.
30. A. M. Lane, "Nietzsche in Russia," Ph.D. dissertation, Wisconsin, 1976, 502–503.
31. N. S. Dorovatovskii, "Pis'ma Maksima Gor'kogo k S.P. Dorovatovskomu," *Pechat' i revoliutsiia*, 2 (1928), 72.
32. See K. D. Muratova, "Soputniki (V. Veresaev i M. Gor'kii)," *M. Gor'kii i ego sovremenniki* (Leningrad: Nauka, 1968), 58.
33. Two useful discussions are N. A. Trifonov, "A. V. Lunacharskii i M. Gor'kii (k istorii literaturnykh i lichnykh otnoshenii do Oktiabria)," *M. Gor'kii i ego sovremenniki*, ed. K. D. Muratova (Leningrad: Nauka, 1968), 110–157; N. A. Trifonov, "Soratniki (Lunacharskii i Gor'kii posle Oktiabria)," *Russkaia literatura*, 1 (1968), 23–48.
34. Sesterhenn, *Das Bogostroitel'stvo*, 161.
35. These people will not be treated here although, as Kline has shown, they entertained their own forms of Nietzschean Marxism. They did not, however, contribute greatly to the myth under discussion.
36. G. Plekhanov, "Pervye shagi sotsial-demokraticheskogo dvizheniia v Rossii" (1909), *Sochineniia* (Moscow: Gosizdat, 1927), 176–197.
37. In "Voprosy morali i M. Meterlink," Lunacharsky calls it "macro-

psychic individualism." See *Etiudy* (Moscow-Peterburg: Gosizdat, 1922), 256. I wish to thank George L. Kline for this insight.
38. Quoted in Lunacharskii, "Budushchee religii," *Obrazovanie*, 10 (1907), 5–7.
39. Sesterhenn, *Das Bogostroitel'stvo*, 44.
40. See Sesterhenn, *Das Bogostroitel'stvo*, 60–69, for a fuller discussion of Lunacharsky's theory as presented in these works.
41. O. Schutte, *Nietzsche Without Masks* (Chicago: University of Chicago Press, 1984), 8.
42. Kline, *Religious and Anti-Religious Thought*, 103–104.
43. Andreevich, "Ocherki tekushchei russkoi literatury: O Nitche," *Zhizn'*, 4 (1901), 286–321. See chapter 3, nts. 4 and 6.
44. Lunacharskii, "Russkii Faust," *Voprosy filosofii i psikhologii*, 3 (1902), 783–795.
45. Gor'kii, "O tsinizme," *Literaturnyi raspad: kriticheskii sbornik* (St. Petersburg: 1908), vol. 1.
46. Sesterhenn, *Das Bogostroitel'stvo*, 101–108.
47. See *Literaturnyi raspad* (St. Petersburg: EOS, 1909), vol. 2, 89.
48. Trifonov, "A. V. Lunacharsky i M. Gor'kii," 132.
49. According to Kline, these include a general historicism (in *Religious and Anti-Religious Thought*, Kline sees the superman as "man's historical self-transcendence" [107]); a strong orientation toward the future; a justification of present social destruction for future construction; and an approbation of individual creativity.
50. Trifonov, "A. V. Lunacharskii i M. Gor'kii," 114.
51. A. L. Tait, "The Literary Biography of A. V. Lunacharsky: Problems and Perspectives," unpublished paper, read at ICSEES Conference, Washington, D.C., November 3, 1985.
52. B. Meilakh, "Iz temy: Lenin i Gor'kii," *Voprosy literatury i estetiki* (Leningrad: Sovetskii pisatel', 1958), 121.
53. Quoted in V. I. Lenin, *Polnoe sobranie sochinenii* (Moscow: Politicheskaia literatura, 1970), vol. 48, 226.
54. Ibid.
55. G. Plekhanov, "Proletariat i krest'ianstvo" (1903), *Sochineniia* (Moscow: Gosizdat, 1923), vol. 12, 286.
56. Sesterhenn, *Das Bogostroitel'stvo*, 118. See also Katerina Clark. *The Soviet Novel*, 147–155. It strikes me that E. Zamiatin's *We* might be read as a dystopian response to God-building.
57. The revolutionary masses lose the autonomy and life-giving, value-giving power given in the original revolutionary-romantic myth as it is harnessed and sacrificed to the Party. In 1925 Lunacharsky reprinted his articles from around 1905 in *Kriticheskie etiudy* (Leningrad: 1925). Included here are "Zadachi sotsial-demokratiche-

skogo khudozhestvennogo tvorchestva" and articles from *Literaturnyi raspad*. In his foreword, Lunacharsky helped in the process of reappropriaton by the Party by revoking the articles' God-building ideology as "mistaken" and by characterizing the "strict judgment of the Party" as "true in many ways." Importantly, he sees the connection that would make the myth appealing in the context of collectivization and industrialization: the "idea of the rebuilding of the world" [perestroika mira]. This time, however, the Party provides guidance and the masses only the raw physical power.

In addition, Gorky reinvoked the God-building era in an article from 1927, "Desiat' let" (SS30, XXIV). With more consistency than Lunacharsky, he kept to his God-building belief in the human "ability to create miracles." In the late 1920s, he saw his belief justified by the previous decade of achievements of Soviet society. A letter from 1929 to the emigré radical, Ekaterina Kuskova, shows that Gorky still warmly believed in the essence of his voluntarist myth: "What is important for me [in Soviet life] is the rapid all-round development of personality, the birth of a new man of culture, the workman in a sugar-refining factory reading Shelley in the original. . . . Such men do not . . . need the petty accursed truth in the midst of which they are struggling. They need the truth they create for themselves." (Quoted from Richard Hare, *Maxim Gorky: Romantic Realist and Conservative Revolutionary* [London: Oxford University Press, 1962], 122–123.)

58. For example, Lunacharsky, in his review of Gorky's *Dachniki*, employs the term *positive* [polozhitel'nyi] to describe Gorky's Nietzschean-Marxist heroes. See LSS8, II, 29.

Selected Bibliography

Achkasov, A. *Arcybashevskii "Sanin" i okolo polovogo voprosa.* Moscow: Kn. mag. A. D. Drutmana, 1908.
Aleksandrovich, Iurii. *Posle Chekhova: Ocherki molodoi literatury poslednego desiatiletiia, 1898–1908.* Moscow: Obshchestvennaia pol'za, 1908.
Alexandrov, Vladimir. *Andrei Belyi: The Major Symbolist Fiction.* Cambridge: Harvard University Press, 1985.
Andreas-Salome, Lou. "Fridrikh Nitsshe v svoikh proizvedeniiax," *Severnyi vestnik,* 3 (1896), 273–295; 4 (1896), 253–272; 5 (1896), 225–239.
———. *Nietzsche in Seinen Werken.* Vienna: C. Konegen, 1894.
Andreev, Leonid N. "Rasskaz o Sergee Petroviche," *Sobranie sochinenii v 8-i tomakh.* St. Petersburg: 1908, vol. 2.
Andreevich (E. A. Solovyov). *Kniga o Maksime Gor'kom i A. P. Chekhove.* St. Petersburg: A. E. Kolpinskii, 1900.
———. *Ocherki po istorii russkoi literatury XIX veka.* St. Petersburg: N. P. Karbasnikov, 1902.
———. *Opyt filosofii russkoi literatury.* St. Petersburg: Znanie, 1905.
Anichkov, E. "Doloi Nitsshe," *Novaia zhizn',* 9 (1912), 114–139.
Annenkov, P. V. *Literaturnye vospominaniia.* Moscow-Leningrad: Academia, 1928.
Anon. "Sverkhchelovek vremen vozrozhdeniia," *Knizhki nedeli,* 6 (1900), 208–211.
Anschuetz, Carol. "Bely's *Petersburg* and the End of the Russian Novel," *The Russian Novel from Pushkin to Pasternak.* Ed. by J. Garrard. New Haven: Yale University Press, 1983, 125–153.
———. "Ivanov and Bely's *Petersburg,*" *Vyacheslav Ivanov: Poet, Critic and Philosopher.* Ed. by R. L. Jackson and L. Nelson, Jr. New Haven: Yale Center for International and Area Studies, 1986, 209–219.
Anton Chekhov's Life and Thought: Selected Letters and Commen-

tary. Trans. by M. H. Heim; trans. and ed. by S. Karlinsky. Berkeley: University of California Press, 1975.

Arskii (N. Ia. Abramovich). "Motivy Solntsa i Tela v sovremennoi belletristike (O nichsheanstve v 'Sanine')." *Voprosy pola*, 2 (1908), 28–30; 3 (1908), 27–31.

Artsybashev, Mikhail. *Sanin*. Letchworth: Bradda, 1972.

Astaf'ev, P. E. "Genezis nravstvennogo ideala dekadenta," *Voprosy filosofii i psikhologii*, 16 (1893), 56–75.

Averintsev, S. "Poeziia Viacheslava Ivanova," *Voprosy literatury*, 8 (1975), 145–192.

Azadovskii, K. M., V. V. Dudkin. "Problema 'Dostoevskii-Nitsshe'," *Literaturnoe nasledstvo*, 86 (1973), 678–688.

B., A. (A. I. Bogdanovich). "Kriticheskie zametki (Petr i Aleksei)," *Mir bozhii*, 3 (1904), 7–10.

Bal'mont, K. *Izbrannoe*. Moscow: Khudozhestvennaia literatura, 1980.

Balmuth, Daniel. *Censorship in Russia, 1865–1905*. Washington, D.C.: University Press of America, 1979.

Basargin, A. (A. I. Vvedenskii). "Kriticheskie zametki: Kesarevo i bozhie," *Moskovskie vedomosti*, 241 (September 3, 1905), 3–4; 248 (September 10, 1905), 3–4.

Batiushkov, F. "Komediia ili tragediia individualizma," *Novosti*, 104 (April 16, 1900), 2–3.

———. "V mire bosiakov (M. Gor'kii: *Ocherki i rasskazy*)," *Kosmopolis*, 11 (1898), 95–120.

Bedford, Charles Harold. *The Seeker: D. S. Merezhkovsky*. Lawrence: University of Kansas Press, 1975.

Belen'kii, E. I. "Zametki ob aforizmakh M. Gor'kogo," *Uchenye zapiski omskogo ped. in-ta*, vol. 15. Omsk: 1961.

Beliavskii, F. "Gor'kaia pravda," *Slovo*, 157 (May 22, 1905), 5.

Belyi, Andrei. *Arabeski*. Moscow: 1911; rpt. Munich: W. Fink, 1969.

———. "Fr. Nitsshe," *Vesy*, 7 (1908), 45–50; 8 (1908), 55–65; 9 (1908), 30–39.

———. *Lug zelenyi*. Moscow: Al'tsiona, 1910.

———. *Na rubezhe dvukh stoletii*. Moscow-Leningrad: 1930; rpt., Letchworth: Bradda, 1966.

———. *Nachalo veka*. Leningrad: 1933; rpt. Chicago: Russian Language Specialties, 1966.

———. *Peterburg*. 1916; *Petersburg*, trans. R. A. Maguire, J. E. Malmstad. Bloomington: Indiana University Press, 1978.

———. *Serebrianyi golub'*. Munich: W. Fink, 1967. *Silver Dove*, trans. G. Reavey. New York: Grove Press, 1974.

———. "Simfoniia: 2-aia dramaticheskaia," *Chetyre simfonii*. Munich: W. Fink, 1971.

———. *Vospominaniia o A. A. Bloke*, intro. G. Donchin. Letchworth: Bradda, 1964.
———. *Vospominaniia o A. A. Bloke*. Moscow-Berlin: 1922–1923; rpt. Munich: Fink, 1969.
Bennett, Virginia. "Echoes of Friedrich Nietzsche's *The Birth of Tragedy* in Andrej Belyj's *Peterburg*," *Germano-Slavica*, 4 (Fall 1980), 243–259.
Berdiaev, N. A. *Dukhovnyi krizis intelligentsii*. St. Petersburg: Obshchestvennaiia pol'za, 1910.
———. *The Meaning of the Creative Act*. New York: Harper, 1955.
———. *Smysl tvorchestva: Onyt opravdaniia cheloveka*. 1916; rpt. Paris: YMCA, 1985.
———. *Sub specie aeternitatis*. St. Petersburg: M. V. Pirozhkov, 1907.
Berg, L. *Sverkhchelovek v sovremennoi literature: Glava k istorii umstvennogo razvitiia XIX veka*, trans. L. Gorbunova. Moscow: I. N. Kushnerev, 1905.
Berlin, Isaiah. *Russian Thinkers*. Harmondsworth: Penguin, 1979.
Bichalets, Ivan. "Chelovek-Lopukh i Chelovek-Zver'," *Kievskoe slovo* 1873 (April 3, 1893), 1.
Billington, J. H. *The Icon and the Axe*. New York: Vintage, 1970.
———. *Mikhailovskii and Russian Populism*. Oxford: Clarendon, 1958.
Blok, Aleksandr. *Sobranie sochinenii v 8-i tomakh*. Moscow: GIKhL, 1960–1963.
Bloom, Harold. *The Anxiety of Influence*. New York: Oxford University Press, 1973.
———. *A Map of Misreading*. New York: Oxford University Press, 1975.
Boborykin, Petr D. *Pereval*, in *Sobranie romanov, povestei i rasskazov v 12-i tomakh*. St. Petersburg: A. F. Marks 1897, vol. 7.
———. *Nakip'*. St. Petersburg: 1900.
———. "O nitssheanstve," *Voprosy filosofii i psikhologii*, 4 (September 1900), 539–547.
———. "Zhestokie," *Russkaia mysl'*, 1901.
Bogdanov, A. A. *Novyi mir*. Moscow: Dorovatovskii i Charushnikov, 1905.
Brandes, Georg. "Fridrikh Nitsshe: Aristokraticheskii radikalizm," *Russkaia mysl'* 11 (1900), 103–153; 12 (1900), 143–161.
———. *Friedrich Nietzsche*, trans. by A. G. Chater. London: Heinemann, 1914.
———. "Maksim Gor'kii" (1901), *Sobranie sochinenii*, vol. 19. St. Petersburg: n.d., 285–299.
Bridgewater, Patrick. *Nietzsche in Anglosaxony: A Study of Nietzsche's Impact on English and American Literature*. Leicester: Leicester University Press, 1972.

Briusov, V. Ia. *Dnevniki, 1890–1910*. Moscow: Sabashnikov, 1927.
Brooks, Jeffrey. *When Russia Learned to Read: Literacy and Popular Literature, 1861–1917*. Princeton: Princeton University Press, 1985.
Bulgakov, F. I. "Iz obshchestvennoi i literaturnoi khroniki zapada," *Vestnik inostrannoi literatury*, 5 (1893), 197–224.
Bulgakov, Sergei. "Ivan Karamazov (v romane Dostoevskogo 'Brat'ia Karamazovy') kak filosofskii tip," *Voprosy filosofii i psikhologii*, 61 (1902), 826–863.
Chances, Ellen. *Conformity's Children: An Approach to the Superfluous Man in Russian Literature*. Columbus: Slavica, 1978.
Choldin, Marianna Tax. *A Fence Around the Empire: The Censorship of Foreign Books in Nineteenth Century Russia*. Durham: Duke University Press, 1985.
Chuiko, V. V. "Obshchestvennye idealy Fridrikha Nitsshe," *Nabliudatel'*, 2 (1893), 231–247.
Chukovskii, K. "Ideinaia pornografiia," *Rech'*, 304 (December 11, 1908), 2.
Cioran, Samuel D. *The Apocalyptic Symbolism of Andrej Belyj*. The Hague: Mouton, 1972.
Clark, Katerina. *The Soviet Novel: History as Ritual*. Chicago: University of Chicago Press, 1985.
Clowes, Edith W. *A Philosophy "For All and None": The Early Reception of Friedrich Nietzsche's Thought in Russian Literature, 1892–1912*. Ph.D. dissertation, Yale University, 1981.
———. "The Integration of Nietzsche's Ideas of History, Time, and 'Higher Nature' in the Early Historical Novels of Dmitry Merezhkovsky," *Germano-Slavica* 3, no. 6 (Fall, 1981), 401–416.
———. "The Nietzschean Image of the Poet in Some Early Works of Konstantin Bal'mont and Valerii Brjusov," *Slavic and East European Journal* (Summer, 1983), 68–80.
Danto, Arthur. *Nietzsche as Philosopher*. New York: Macmillan Publishing Co., 1965.
Davies, Richard D. "Nietzsche in Russia, 1892–1917: A Preliminary Bibliography," *Germano-Slavica*, 2 (1976), 107–146; 3 (1977), 201–220.
Donchin, Georgette. *The Influence of French Symbolism on Russian Poetry*. The Hague: Mouton, 1958.
Dorovatovskii, N. S. "Pis'ma Maksima Gor'kogo k S. P. Dorovatovskomu," *Pechat' i revoliutsiia*, 2 (1928), 68–88.
Dostoevsky, F. M. *The Devils*. Trans. by D. Magarshack. London: Penguin, 1969.
———. *Polnoe sobranie sochinenii*. Leningrad: Nauka, 1972–.

Ellis (Lev Kobilinskii). "Konstantin Bal'mont," *Russki simvolisty*. Moscow: 1910; rpt. Letchworth: Bradda, 1972, 51–121.
Engel'gardt, N. "*Poklonenie zlu* (Po povodu romana g. Merezhkovskogo 'Otverzhennyi')." *Knizhki nedeli*, 12 (1895), 140–172.
Esin, B. I., ed. *Iz istorii russkoi zhurnalistiki kontsa XIX–nachala XX v.* Moscow: Izd. Moskovskogo universiteta, 1973.
———. *Russkaia zhurnalistka 70–80ykh godov 19. veka*. Moscow: Izd. Moskovskogo universiteta, 1963.
Evgen'ev-Maksimov, V., D. Maksimov. *Iz proshlogo russkoi zhurnalistiki*. Leningrad: 1930.
Fanger, Donald. "The Peasant in Literature," in *The Peasant in Nineteenth-Century Russia*. Ed. W. S. Vucinich. Stanford: Stanford University Press, 1968, 231–262.
Fedotov, G. P. *The Russian Religious Mind*. Vol. 1. Cambridge: Harvard University Press, 1966.
Felitsyn, S. "Komnatnyi Zaratustra," *Izvestiia knizhnykh magazinov T-va M. O. Vol'f*, 1 (1910), 17–18.
Forman, Betty Y. *The Early Prose of Maksim Gorky, 1892–1899*. Ph.D. dissertation, Harvard University, 1983.
———. "Nietzsche and Gorky in the 1890's: The Case for an Early Influence," *Western Philosophical Systems in Russian Literature*. Ed. Anthony M. Mlikotin. Los Angeles: University of Southern California Press, 1979), 153–164.
Foster, John Burt. *Heirs to Dionysus*. Princeton: Princeton University Press, 1981.
Freeborn, Richard. *The Russian Revolutionary Novel*. Cambridge: Cambridge University Press, 1982.
G—— v, G. (G. A. Grossman). "'Sanin' i nemetskaia kritika," *Russkie vedomosti*, 3 (January 4, 1909), 4.
Gautama. *Koe-chto o nitssheantsakh*. St. Petersburg: N. N. Klobukov, 1902.
Gel'rot, M. "Nitsshe i Gor'kii: Elementy nitssheanstva v tvorchestve Gor'kogo," *Russkoe bogatstvo*, 5 (1903), 25–68.
Gerasimov, N. I. *Nitssheanstvo*. Moscow: I. N. Kushnerev, 1901.
Gippius, Z. N. *Dmitrii Merezhkovskii*. Paris: YMCA, 1951.
Glinskii, B. "Bolezn' ili reklama? Literaturnyi molodezh'," *Istoricheskii vestnik*, 2 (1896), 636–648; 6 (1896), 932–936.
Golovin, K. F. *Russkii roman i russkoe obshchestvo*. St. Petersburg: A. F. Marks, 1904.
Gor'kii, Maksim. *My Childhood* trans. R. Wilks. Harmondsworth: Penguin, 1980.
———. *Polnoe sobranie sochinenii*. Moscow: Nauka, 1968–1972.
———. *Rasskazy*. St. Petersburg: Znanie, 1903.

260 Bibliography

———. *Sobranie sochinenii v 30-i tomakh.* Moscow: GIKhL, 1949–1956.
Gornfel'd, A. G. "Eroticheskaia belletristika," *Knigi i liudi: literaturnye besedy,* vol. 1. St. Petersburg: Zhizn', 1908, 22–31.
Grot, N. Ia. "Nravstvennye idealy nashego vremeni: Fridrikh Nitsshe i Lev Tolstoi," *Voprosy o filosofii i psikhologii,* 16 (January 1893), 129–154.
Hahn, Beverly. *Chekhov: A Study of the Major Stories and Plays.* Cambridge: Cambridge University Press, 1977.
Hare, Richard. *Maxim Gorky: Romantic Realist and Conservative Revolutionary.* London: Oxford University Press, 1962.
Hingley, Ronald. *Russia: Writers and Society in the Nineteenth Century,* 2d ed. London: Weidenfeld and Nicolson, 1977.
Iezuitova, L. A. *Tvorchestvo Leonida Andreeva: 1892–1906.* Leningrad: Izd. Leningradskogo universiteta, 1976.
Ivanov, V. I. "Nitsshe i Dionis," *Po zvezdam.* St. Petersburg: Ory, 1909; rpt. Letchworth: Bradda, 1971, 1–20.
———. *Po zvezdam,* 1909; rpt. Letchworth: Bradda, 1971.
———. *Sobranie sochinenii.* Brussels: Foyer Chrétien Oriental, 1971– .
Ivanov-Razumnik, R. *Russkaia literatura XX veka: 1890–1915 gg.* Petrograd: Kolos, 1920.
———. *Istoriia russkoi obshchestvennoi mysli: Individualizm i meshchanstvo v russkoi literature i zhizni XIX v.* St. Petersburg: M. M. Stasiulevich, 1907.
Jauss, Hans Robert. *Literaturgeschichte als Provokation.* Frankfurt: Suhrkamp, 1970.
Kamenskii, Anatolii. *Liudi.* St. Petersburg: Progress, 1910.
Katalog rassmotrennykh inostrannoiu tsenzuroiu sochinenii zapreshchennykh i dozvolennykh s iskliucheniiami, s 1-go iiulia 1871 g. po 1-e ianvaria 1897 g. St. Petersburg: Tipografiia ministerstva vnutrennikh del, 1898.
Kaufmann, Walter. *Nietzsche: Philosopher, Psychologist, Antichrist.* New York: Vintage, 1968.
Kaun, Alexander. *Maxim Gorky and His Russia.* New York: Benjamin Blom, 1931.
Kelly, Alfred. *The Descent of Darwin: The Popularization of Darwinism in Germany, 1860–1914.* Chapel Hill: University of North Carolina Press, 1981.
Kline, George L. "Nietzschean Marxism in Russia," *Boston College Studies in Philosophy,* 2 (1968), 166–183.
———. "The Nietzschean Marxism of Stanislav Volsky," *Western Philosophical Systems in Russian Literature,* ed. Anthony M. Mlikotin. Los Angeles: University of Southern California Press, 1979, 177–195.

———. *Religious and Anti-Religious Thought in Russia*. Chicago: University of Chicago Press, 1968.
Knapp, Shoshana. "Herbert Spencer in Čexov's 'Skučnaja istorija' and 'Duel'": The Love of Science and the Science of Love," *SEEJ*, 29, 3 (Fall 1985), 279–296.
Kogan, P. "Nashi literaturnye kumiry: Nitsshe," *Russkoe slovo*, 206 (September 5, 1908), 2.
Koltonovskaia, E. A. "Nasledniki Sanina," *Kriticheskie etiudi*. St. Petersburg: Prosveshchenie, 1912, 69–83.
———. "Problema pola i ee osveshchenie u neorealistov," *Obrazovanie*, 1 (1908), 114–130.
Kostka, Edmund. "Maksim Gorky: Russian Writer with a Western Bent," *Rivista di letterature moderne e comparate*, 23 (1970), 5–20.
Kotliarevskii, N. "Vospominaniia o Vasilii Petroviche Preobrazhenskom," *Voprosy filosofii i psikhologii*, 4 (September 1900), 501–538.
Krainii, A. (Z. Gippius). *Literaturnyi dnevnik*. St. Petersburg: M. V. Pirozhkov, 1908.
Kriticheskie stat'i o proizvedeniiakh Maksima Gor'kogo. Kiev: A. G. Aleksandrov, 1901.
Krutikova, N. E. *V nachale veka: Gor'kii i simvolisty*. Kiev: Naukovo dumka, 1978.
Kuprin, Aleksandr. "Poedinok," *Sochineniia v 2-kh tomakh*. Moscow: Khudozhestvennaia literatura, 1981, 68–219. *The Duel*, trans. A. R. MacAndrew. New York: Signet, 1961.
Lane, Ann Marie. *Nietzsche in Russian Thought 1890–1917*. Ph.D. dissertation, University of Wisconsin, 1976.
Leavis, Q. D. *Fiction and the Reading Public*. London: Chatto and Windus, 1932.
Leksika russkogo literaturnogo iazyka XIX–nachala XX veka. Ed. F. P. Filin, Moscow: Nauka, 1981.
Lengyel, Bela. *Gorky es Nietzsche*. Budapest: Akadèmiai Kiadù, 1979.
Lenin, V. I. *Sochineniia*, vol. 10. Moscow: Gosudarstvennoe izdatel'stvo politicheskoi literatury, 1952.
Letopis' zhizni i tvorchestva A. M. Gor'kogo. Moscow: Akademiia nauk, 1958–1960.
Likhtenberzhe, G. "Fridrikh Nitsshe: Etiud," *Obrazovanie*, 10 (1899), 17–34.
Lichtenberger, Henri. *La philosophie de Nietzsche*. Paris: Alcan, 1898.
Literaturno-esteticheskie kontseptsii v Rossii kontsa XIX–nachala XX v. Ed. B. A. Bialik. Moscow: Nauka, 1975.
Literaturnyi raspad: Kriticheskii sbornik, vol. 1. St. Petersburg: T-vo izdatel'skoe biuro, 1908; vol. 2, St. Petersburg: 1909.

Ljunggren, Magnus. *The Dream of Rebirth: A Study of Andrei Belyi's Novel Peterburg.* Stockholm: Almquist and Wiksell, 1982.
Loe, Mary Louise. "Maksim Gor'kii and the *Sreda* Circle: 1899–1905," *Slavic Review,* 1 (Spring 1985), 49–66.
Lopatin, L. "Bol'naia iskrennost'. (Zametka po povodu stat'i V. Preobrazhenskogo 'Fridrikh Nitsshe: Kritika morali al'truizma.)," *Voprosy filosofii i psikhologii,* 16 (1895), 109–114.
Lowenthal, Leo. "The Reception of Dostoevski's Work in Germany, 1880–1920," *The Arts in Society.* Ed. by Robert N. Wilson. Englewood Cliffs: Prentice Hall, 1964, 122–147.
Lunacharskii, A. V. "Budushchee religii," *Obrazovanie,* 10 (1907), 1–23; 11 (1907), 31–67.
———. *Kriticheskie etiudy.* Leningrad: Knizhnyi sektor Gubono, 1925.
———. *Otkliki zhizni.* St. Petersburg: O. N. Popova, 1906.
———. *Religiia i sotsializm.* St. Petersburg: Shipovnik, 1908.
———. "Russkii faust," *Voprosy filosofii i psikhologii,* 3)1902), 783–795.
———. *Sobranie sochinenii v 8-i tomakh.* Moscow: Khudozhestvennaia literatura, 1963–1969.
L'vov-Rogachevskii, V. *Ocherki po istorii noveishei russkoi literatury (1881–1919).* Moscow: V.C.S.P.O., 1920.
Magnus, Bernd. *Nietzsche's Existential Imperative.* Bloomington: Indiana University Press, 1978.
Makarov, A. A. *Legenda o nitssheanstve A. M. Gor'kogo kak burzhuaznaia reaktsiia na rasprostranenie filosofii marksizma v Rossii.* Candidate diss., Moskovskii gosudarstvennyi universitet, 1972.
Massie, Suzanne. *The Land of the Firebird: The Beauty of Old Russia.* New York: Simon & Schuster, 1980.
Mathewson, Rufus W., Jr. *The Positive Hero in Russian Literature,* 2d ed. Stanford: Stanford University Press, 1975.
Meilakh, B. "Iz temy: Lenin i Gor'kii," *Voprosy literatury i estetiki.* Leningrad: Sovetskii pisatel', 1958, 106–125.
Merezhkovskii, D. S. *Antikhrist: Petr i Aleksei.* St. Petersburg: M. V. Pirozhkov, 1906.
———. "L. Tolstoi i Dostoevskii," *Mir iskusstva,* 1–12, 13–24 (1900).
———. *M. Iu. Lermontov.* 1911; rpt. Letchworth: Prideaux, 1979.
———. "Misticheskoe dvizhenie nashego veka: Otryvok," *Trud: Vestnik literatury i nauk.* 18, 4 (1893), 33–40.
———. *Pushkin.* 1906; rpt. Letchworth: Prideaux, 1971.
———. *Smert' bogov: Iulian otstupnik.* St. Petersburg: M. V. Pirozhkov, 1906.
———. "Spokoistvie," *Severnyi vestnik,* 2 (1897), 238.
———. *Voskresshie bogi: Leonardo da Vinci.* St. Petersburg: M. V. Pirozhkov, 1906.

Mikhailovskii, B. V. *Tvorchestvo M. Gor'kogo i mirovaia literatura, 1892–1916*. Moscow: Nauka, 1965.

Mikhailovskii, N. K. "Literatura i zhizn'" (Review of Englegardt's *Progress, kak evoliutsiia zhestokosti*; Boborykin's *Nakip'*; L. Shestov's *Dobro v uchenii gr Tolstogo i F. Nitsshe*), *Russkoe bogatstvo*, 2 (1900), 139–167.

———. "Literatura i zhizn': O Fr. Nitsshe," *Russkoe bogatstvo*, 11 (1894), 111–131; 12 (1894), 84–110.

———. *Literaturnye vospominaniia i sovremennaia smuta*. vol. 2. St. Petersburg: 1900.

———. *Poslednie sochineniia*. St. Petersburg: Russkoe bogatstvo, 1905.

Miller, C. A. "Nietzsche's 'Discovery' of Dostoevsky," *Nietzsche-Studien*, 2 (1973), 203–257.

Minskii, Nikolai. "Filosofiia toski i zhazhda voli," *Kriticheskie stat'i o proizvedeniiakh Maksima Gor'kogo*. Kiev: A. G. Aleksandrov, 1901.

———. "Fridrikh Nitche," *Mir iskusstva*, 19–20 (1900), 139–147.

———. *Pri svete sovesti*, 2d ed. St. Petersburg: Iu. N. Erlikh, 1897.

Mirsky, Prince D. S. *Contemporary Russian Literature, 1881–1925*. London: Routledge, 1926; rpt. New York: Kraus Reprint Co., 1972.

Mirza-Avakian, M. L. "F. Nitsshe i russkii modernizm," *Vestnik erevanskogo universiteta: Obshchestvennye nauki*, 3, 18 (1972), 92–103.

Mochulsky, Konstantin. *Andrei Bely: His Life and Works*. Trans. by N. Szalavitz. Ann Arbor: Ardis, 1977.

The Modern Encyclopedia of Russian and Soviet History. Ed. J. L. Wieczynski. Gulf Breeze, Fla.: Academic International Press, 1976–1987.

Muratova, K. D., ed. *Istoriia russkoi literatury kontsa XIX–nachala XX veka: Bibliograficheskii ukazatel'*. Moscow-Leningrad: Akademiia nauk, 1963.

———. *M. Gor'kii i ego sovremenniki*. Leningrad: Nauka, 1968.

———. "Maksim Gor'kii i Leonid Andreev," *Literaturnoe nasledstvo*, vol. 72. Moscow: ANSSSR, 1965, 9–60.

Nalimov, A. P. "Nitsheanstvo u nashix belletristov," *Interesnye romany, povesti i rasskazy luchshikh pisatelei*. St. Petersburg: 1905, 94–99.

Nevedomskii, M. "Vmesto predisloviia," intro. to Anri Likhtenberzhe, *Filosofiia Nittsshe*. St. Petersburg: O. N. Popova, 1901, i–cxliv.

Nietzsche, Friedrich. *The Anti-Christ*, trans. R. J. Hollingdale. Harmondsworth: Penguin, 1975.

———. *Beyond Good and Evil*, trans. W. Kaufmann. New York: Vintage, 1966.

———. *The Birth of Tragedy*, trans. Walter Kaufmann. New York: Vintage, 1967.
———. *Ecce Homo*, trans. W. Kaufmann. New York: Vintage, 1969.
———. *The Gay Science*, trans. W. Kaufmann. New York: Vintage, 1974.
———. *On the Genealogy of Morals*, trans. W. Kaufmann. New York: Vintage, 1969.
———. *Thus Spoke Zarathustra*, trans. R. J. Hollingdale. Harmondsworth: Penguin, 1975.
———. *Twilight of the Idols*, trans. R. J. Hollingdale. Harmondsworth: Penguin, 1975.
———. *The Will to Power*, trans. W. Kaufmann and R. J. Hollingdale. New York: Vintage, 1974.
Nietzsche in Russia. Ed. B. G. Rosenthal. Princeton: Princeton University Press, 1986.
Nitsshe, Fridrikh. *Tak govoril Zaratustra*, trans. A. N. Achkasov. Moscow: D. P. Efimov, 1906.
———. *Tak govoril Zaratustra*, trans. V. Izraztsov. St. Petersburg: 1913.
Nittsshe, Fridrikh. *Tak govoril Zaratustra*, trans. Nani. St. Petersburg: Stasiulevich, 1899.
Nivat, Georges. *Vers la fin du mythe russe*. Lausanne: L'Age d'Homme, 1982.
Nordau, Max. *Entartung*. Berlin: Carl Dunker, 1895.
———. *Vyrozhdenie: Psikhopaticheskie iavleniia v oblasti sovremennoi literatury i iskusstva*, 2d ed. St. Petersburg: P. P. Soikin, 1896.
Obolenskii, L. E. *Maksim Gor'kii i prichiny ego uspekha*. St. Petersburg: 1903.
Oduev, S. F. *Tropami Zaratustry: Viliianie nitssheanstva na nemetskoi burzhuaznoi filosofii*. Moscow: Mysl', 1977.
Orlov, Vl. N. *Pereput'ia*. Moscow: Khudozhestvennaia literatura, 1976.
Pertsov, P. P. *Literaturnye vospominaniia*. Moscow: Akademiia, 1933.
Phelps, W. L. *Essays on Russian Novelists*. New York: Macmillan Publishing Co., 1911.
Plekhanov, Georgii. *Izbrannye filosofskie proizvedeniia*, vol. 3. Moscow: Gosudarstvennoe izdatel'stvo politicheskoi literatury, 1957.
———. *Literaturnoe nasledie Plekhanova*, vol. 7. Moscow: Gosudarstvennoe sotsial-ekonomicheskoe izdatel'stvo, 1939.
———. *Sochineniia*. Moscow: Gosudarstvennoe izdatel'stvo, 1923.
Polianskaia, L. I. "Obzor fonda tsentral'nogo komiteta tsenzury inostrannoi," *Arkhivnoe delo*, 1 (1938), 88.
Posse, Vladimir. *Moi zhiznennyi put'*. Leningrad: Zemlia i fabrika, 1929.
Preobrazhenskii, V. P. "Fridrikh Nitsshe: Kritika morali al'truizma," *Voprosy filosofii i psixologii*, 15 (1892), 115–160.

Primeau, Ronald, ed. *Influx: Essays on Literary Influence.* Port Washington, N.Y.: National University Publications, 1977.
Pyman, Avril. "Aleksandr Blok and the Merezhkovskijs," *Aleksandr Blok Centennial Conference.* Ed. by W. N. Vickery. Columbus: Slavica, 1984, 237–270.
———. *The Life of Aleksandr Blok.* 2 vols. Oxford: Oxford University Press, 1979.
Reingol'dt, A. "Bol'noi filosof," *Ezhemesiachnye sochineniia,* 8 (1900), 253–258.
———. ed. "Mysli i paradoksy Fridrikha Nitsshe," *Novosti,* 209 (1891).
A Revolution of the Spirit: Crisis of Value in Russia, 1890–1918. Ed. M. Bohachevsky-Chomiak and B. G. Rosenthal. Newtonville, Mass.: Oriental Research Partners, 1982.
Ropshin, V. *Kon'blednyi.* Nice: M. A. Tumanov, 1912.
Rosenthal, Bernice Glatzer. *Dmitri Sergeevich Merezhkovsky: The Development of the Revolutionary Mentality.* The Hague: M. Nijhoff, 1975.
———. "Nietzsche in Russia: The Case of Merezhkovsky," *Slavic Review,* 3 (1974), 429–452.
———. "Theater as Church: The Vision of the Mystical Anarchists," *Russian History,* 4 (1977), 122–141.
———. "The Transmutation of the Symbolist Ethos: Mystical Anarchism and the Revolution of 1905," *Slavic Review,* 4 (1977), 608–629.
Russkaia literatura kontsa XIX–nachala XX v. Ed. B. A. Bialik. 3 vols. Moscow: Nauka, 1968–1972.
Savodnik, V. F. "Nitssheanets sorokovykh godov: Maks Stirner i ego filosofiia egoizma," *Voprosy filosofii i psikhologii* (September–October 1901), 560–614.
Scherrer, Jutta. *Die Petersburger Religios-Philosophischen Vereinigungen: Die Entwicklung des religiösen Selbstverstandnisses ihrer Intelligencija-Mitglieder (1901–1917).* Berlin-Wiesbaden: O. Harrassowitz, 1973.
Schopenhauer, Arthur. *Essays and Aphorisms,* trans. R. J. Hollingdale. Harmondsworth: Penguin, 1981.
Schutte, Ophelia. *Beyond Nihilism: Nietzsche without Masks.* Chicago: University of Chicago Press, 1984.
Sesterhenn, Raimund. *Das Bogostroitel'stvo bei Gor'kij und Lunacharskij, bis 1909.* Munich: Otto Sagner, 1982.
Setschkareff, Wsewolod. *Schellings Einfluss in der russischen Literatur der 20er und 30er Jahre des XIX. Jahrhunderts.* Leipzig: 1939; rpt. Nendeln: Kraus, 1968.
Shestov, Lev. *Dobro v uchenii gr. Tolstogo i F. Nitshe (Filosofiia i propoved').* St. Petersburg: Stasiulevich, 1900.

———. *Dostoevsky, Tolstoy and Nietzsche*, trans. Bernard Martin. Columbus: Ohio State University Press, 1969.
Sokolov, A. K. *Istoriia russkoi literatury kontsa XIX–nachala XX veka.* Moscow: Vysshala shkola, 1979.
Solov'ev, Vladimir. *Sobranie sochinenii.* St. Petersburg: Obshchestvennaia pol'za, 1902–1907.
———. *The Justification of the Good*, trans. N. A. Duddington. London: Constable and Co., Ltd., 1918.
Spengler, Ute. *D. S. Merezhkovskii als Literaturkritiker: Versuch einer religiosen Begrundung der Kunst.* Luzen: C. J. Bucher, 1972.
Stammler, Heinrich. "Dmitri Merezkovskii: 1865–1965," *Welt der Slaven*, 12 (1967), 142–152.
———. "Julianus Apostate Redivivus: Dmitri Merezhkovsky: Predecessors and Successors," *Welt der Slaven*, 11 (1966), 180–204.
Stepun, Fedor. *Mystische Weltschau.* Munich: Carl Hanser, 1964.
Stites, Richard. *The Women's Liberation Movement in Russia.* Princeton: Princeton University Press, 1978.
Sud'ba 'Sanina' v Germanii. Ed. V. I. Rotenstern. St. Petersburg: V. I. Rotenstern, 1909.
Szilard-Mihalne, L. "Nietzsche in Russland," *Deutsche Studien*, 23 (1974), 159–163.
Tager, E. B. "Revoliutsionnyi romantizm Gor'kogo," *Russkaia literatura kontsa XIX nachala XX veka, 90 e gody*, vol. 1. Moscow: Nauka, 1968, 213–243.
Tait, A. L. "The Literary Biography of A. V. Lunacharsky: Problems and Perspectives," unpublished paper, read at ICSEES Conference, Washington, D.C., November 3, 1985.
Tan (Vladimir Bogoraz). "Sanin v iubke," *Utro rossii* (December 31, 1909), 3.
Tarle, E. V. "Nitssheanstvo i ego otnoshenie k politicheskim i sotsial'nym teoriiam evropeiskogo obshchestva," *Vestnik evropy*, 8 (1901), 704–750.
Thatcher, David S. *Nietzsche in England 1890–1914: The Growth of a Reputation.* Toronto: University of Toronto Press, 1970.
Trotsky, Leon. *Literature and Revolution.* New York: Russell and Russell, 1957.
Trubetskoi, E. N. *Filosofiia Nitsshe: Kriticheskii ocherk.* Moscow: I. N. Kushnerev, 1904.
Tschiževskij, Dmitrij. *Hegel bei den Slaven.* Darmstadt: Wissenschaftliche Buchgesellschaft, 1961.
Tumanov, G. M. *Kharakteristiki i vospominaniia*, vol. 2. Tiflis: Trud, 1905.
Tynianov, Iu. "O literaturnoi evoliutsii," *Texte der russischen Formalisten*, vol. 1. Munich: W. Fink, 1969.

Vengerov, S. A. *Russkaia literatura XX veka*. Moscow: Mir, 1914.
Verbitskaia, Anastasia. *Kliuchi schast'ia*. Moscow: Kushnerev, 1910–1913.
Volynskii, A. L. (A. L. Flekser). "Literaturnye zametki: Apollon i Dionis," *Severnyi vestnik*, 11 (1896), 232–255.
Volzhskii (A. S. Glinka). *Iz mira literaturnykh iskanii*. St. Petersburg: D. E. Zhukovskii, 1906.
West, James. *Russian Symbolism: A Study of Vyacheslav Ivanov and the Russian Symbolist Aesthetic*. London: Methuen, 1970.
Westphalen, Timothy. "Imagistic Centers in Aleksandr Blok's 'Snezhnaia maska,'" B.A. honors essay, Knox College, Galesburg, Illinois, 1982.
Wolfe, Bertram. *The Bridge and the Abyss: The Troubled Friendship of Maksim Gorky and V. I. Lenin*. New York: Frederick A. Praeger, 1967.
Zernov, Nicolas. *The Russian Religious Renaissance*. New York: Harper & Row, 1963.
Zhirmunskii, V. M. *Bairon i Pushkin*. Leningrad, 1924; rpt. Leningrad: Nauka, 1978.
Zhurnalist (V. Korolenko). "O sbornikakh tovarishchestva 'Znaniia' za 1903 g.," *Russkoe bogatstvo*, 8 (1904), 129–149.

Index

Aestheticism, 41, 57, 133, 229. See also Moral consciousness, and aesthetic values
Aleksandr II, Tsar, 44
Aleksandr III, Tsar, 45
Aleksandrovich, Iury, 64, 176
Alexandrov, Vladimir, 159, 164, 170
Altruism. See Pity; Compassion
Amor fati, 25, 36, 92, 192, 199
Andreas-Salome, Lou, 47, 51
Andreev, Leonid, 9, 37, 39, 44, 65, 184, 200, 226; and future anxiety, 11; "The Story of Sergei Petrovich," 44, 84–96, 109
Andreevich (Evgeny Andreevich Solovyov), 10, 38, 40, 200, 201–209, 214; in Nietzsche's critical reception, 54, 61, 63; and Gorky, see Gorky and Andreevich. Works: *A Book on Maksim Gorky and A. P. Chekhov*, 177, 201; *An Essay in the Philosophy of Russian Literature*, 201, 208, 214
Androgyny, 145, 222
Anichkov, Evgeny, 64, 108
Anti-Semitism, attributed to Nietzsche, 106–107, 186–187

Antonovsky, Iuly, 48
Apollonian principle, 130, 210; historicism, 123; naive sensibility, 124; visual aspect of, 124–126, 148, 186
Artist, 43
Artsybashev, Mikhail, 9, 65; and future anxiety, 11; *Sanin*, 98–100, 102–103, 106, 112, 226
Asceticism, 27–28; in Russian literature, 33, 244 n.1
Astafev, Petr, 54, 59

Bakhtin, Mikhail, 129
Bakunin, Mikhail, 58
Balmont, Konstantin, 40, 46, 64, 83, 87, 175
Balmuth, Daniel, 45
Batiushkov, F., 178
Baudelaire, Charles, 117
Bazarov, V. A., 202
Belinsky, Vissarion, 30, 217
Belyi, Andrei (Boris N. Bugaev), 9, 36, 39, 40, 62, 116, 131, 152–172, 227, 229; and Blok, 142, 151, 160–161; Christian myth in, 155–158, 166–168; discovery of Nietzsche, 152–154; and future anxiety, 11, 154; and Ivanov, 141, 156–158, 161–164;

Belyi, Andrei (continued)
and Merezhkovsky, 65, 131, 134, 155–156; in Nietzsche's critical reception, 46, 54; against Nietzscheanism, 116; and populism, 161, 163–164; and Solovyov, 152–153, 158, 166. Works: *On the Border of Two Centuries*, 153; "Friedrich Nietzsche," 154; *Kotik Letaev*, 171, 228; *Petersburg*, 152, 157, 164–170, 228; *Reminiscences on Blok*, 156–157; *The Silver Dove*, 152, 157, 160–164, 165; "Symphonies," 65, 158–160
Berdiaev, Nikolai, 1, 54, 132
Berg, Leo, 62
Blok, Aleksandr, 9, 36, 40, 116, 141–152, 170–171, 227; and Merezhkovsky, 134; Christian motifs in, 146–149; rejects conventional Christianity, 142, 146–147; and Solovyov, 142. Works: "The Creative Work of Viacheslav Ivanov," 143; "Hyperborean Dionysus," 144; "The Present Condition of Russian Symbolism," 151–152; "The Puppet Show," 151; "Snow Mask," 142, 145–150
Blond beast: as moral archetype, 20–21; as social archetype, 60
Bloom, Harold, 2, 10, 11
Boborykin, Petr D., 7, 38, 65, 66, 80, 225, 226; as influence on popular literature, 83, 97, 106–107; as vulgarizer of Nietzsche, 70–78. Works: *The Cruel Ones*, 73, 76–77, 83; *The Pass*, 70–73, 83, 106–107; *The Scum*, 73–76
Bogdanov, A. A. (A. A. Malinovsky), 202, 220
Botticelli, 146

Brandes, Georg, 43, 45, 47, 62
Briusov, V. Ia., 40, 46
Bugaev, Boris N. *See* Belyi, Andrei
Bulgakov, F. I., 38
Bulgakov, Mikhail, 168
Bulgakov, Sergei, 135
Bunin, Ivan, 200
Burkhardt, Jakob, 39, 117

Carlyle, Thomas, 117
Censorship, Russian, 6, 44–52, 240–241 n.19
Chekhov, Anton, 39, 69, 175, 180, 192, 203
Christian archetypes in Russian literature, 33–34, 36–37, 118–119. *See also* separate authors
Chuiko, V. V., 55
Chukovsky, Kornei, 104
Chulkov, Georgy, 141, 151
Compassion, 34, 163, 188, 205. *See also* Pity
Comte, Auguste, 117
Culture: esoteric, 9, 225; middlebrow, 9, 95–96, 225, 226, 244 n.9; popular, 6–7, 9, 95, 96–113, 225, 226, 245 n.15; as translation, 208

Dal, Vladimir, 110
Darwin, Charles, 31, 59, 60–61, 73, 105
Darwinism, social, 106
Dionysian principle: as metaphysical rebellion, 127; as principle of cyclic rebirth, 133, 208–209, 212; as social rebellion, 186, 210–211; as sublimated sexuality, 127–130, 139–140. *See also* Myth, of Dionysus
Dostoevsky, Fedor, 4, 92–95,

115, 155, 226; as mediator for Nietzsche, 15, 37, 54, 59–60, 61; Merezhkovsky's interpretation of, 126–130, 133; and nihilism, 6, 95; as precursor to Nietzsche, 18, 20, 238 n.9. Works: *The Brothers Karamazov*, 32, 33, 36, 93, 166; *Crime and Punishment*, 33, 36, 142; *The Devils*, 33–34, 93–94; *Notes from the Underground*, 20, 22, 32; "The Peasant Marei," 35

Egotism, 55, 56–57, 59, 80, 228–229; aestheticist, 64; anarchistic, 30; collective egotism, 206, 207; proletarian individualism, 206, 209; in symbolist literature, 131, 137, 148–150, 162–165; vulgarized, 71–72, 74–75. See also *Lichnost'* (selfhood, personality)
Eliade, Mircea, 12
Essays in the Philosophy of Collectivism, 203
Eternal return, 25–26, 36, 129–130

Feuerbach, Ludwig, 44, 214
Förster-Nietzsche, Elisabeth, 8, 62, 177
Foster, John Burt, 11, 178
Frank, S. L., 46
Free spirit: as moral archetype, 20, 32, 77

Garshin, V., 192
Gast, Peter, 62
Gershenzon, M. O., 46
Gippius, Zinaida, 40, 85, 117, 132, 141, 143, 151
God-building, 113, 200–223; and populism, 203, 205, 214–215, 218–219
Godseeking, 9, 113, 137–141
Goethe, Johann Wolfgang von, 25, 211–212
Gogol, Nikolai, 89, 155, 164, 171
Gorky, Maksim (Aleksei M. Peshkov), 10, 38, 39, 40, 175–223, 225, 228, 229; and Andreevich, 201–202, 205; attacks Nietzsche, 177–178, 179, 181; and Bolshevism, 198, 199, 201–203, 222–223; early interest in Nietzsche, 176–179; and future anxiety, 11, 12, 217; and Lunacharsky, 179, 201, 205; Merezhkovsky's interpretation of, 133; as popularizer of Nietzsche, 7, 54, 64–65, 83, 84–85, 201; and populism, 175, 188, 190, 195, 199. Works: "Chelkash," 65, 177, 182; *Childhood*, 221–222; *Confession*, 203, 212–213, 222; "Conversations about My Trade," 178; "On Cynicism," 216; "The Destruction of Personality," 203, 210, 216; *Foma Gordeev*, 184, 186–188; "Kain and Artem," 182–184, 188, 189–190; "Konovalov," 64; "Malva," 182; "Man," 190, 195–198, 199; "The Mistake," 177, 188–189, 190–192; "More on Karamazovism," 220; *Mother*, 199; *My Universities*, 177; "Notes on Philistinism," 177; "The Old Woman Izergil," 195; "The Reader," 177, 179, 190; "Song of the Falcon," 177, 184–186, 199; *Summerfolk*, 207, 216; "Varenka Olesova," 65
Grigorev, Apollon, 217

Grot, Nikolai Ia., 38, 54–55, 80
Gurevich, Liubov Ia., 47, 53

Hegel, Georg Wilhelm Friedrich, 47, 72
Heine, Heinrich, 25
Herzen, Aleksandr, 15, 58
Hesychasm, 170

Individualism. *See* Egotism
Influence, 1–13, 29–30, 105, 229–230; as creative adversity, 10; as future anxiety, 11–12, 205, 227; as imitation, 10, 96; Nietzsche's social, 101–113. *See also* separate authors
Ivanov, Evgeny, 142
Ivanov, Viacheslav, 9, 36, 46, 54, 116, 117, 170–172, 227; and Christian-Dionysian literary cult, 136; Christian-Dionysian view, 135–142; concept of ecstasy, 138; discovery of Nietzsche, 47; and Solovyov, 137, 141. Works: "Athena's Spear," 140; "On the Hellenic Religion of the Suffering God," 136, 137–138, 156; "Nietzsche and Dionysus," 140; *Pole Stars*, 141; "The Symbology of Aesthetic Origins," 138–139, 145; *Transparency*, 141
Izraztsov, V., 48

Jauss, Hans Robert, 3, 5

Kamensky, Anatoly, 9; *People*, 99–102, 109, 111–112
Kant, Immanuel, 16, 25, 55, 62, 192
Kelly, Alfred, 6
Kline, George L., 214, 216
Korolenko, Vladimir, 35, 195, 198, 199

Kotliarevsky, Nestor, 62, 78–79
Kuprin, Aleksandr, 9, 37, 65, 200, 226; *The Duel*, 84–96

Lenin, V. I. (V. I. Ulianov), 110, 179, 199, 202, 204, 219–221
Lermontov, Mikhail: Merezhkovsky's interpretation of, 126–128, 133. Works: *Hero of Our Time*, 5, 32, 33; "Mtsyri," 128
Lichnost' (selfhood, personality), 61, 80, 110–111, 221; and cult of personality, 212. *See also* Egotism
Lichtenberger, Henri, 62
Literary Decline, 200
Lopatin, L., 54
Love, 26, 87, 102; Ivanov's revaluation, 136, 140; Merezhkovsky's concept, 130; self-love, 26; Solovyov's idea, 139
Love of neighbor. *See* Pity; Compassion
Lunacharsky, Anatoly, 10, 38, 143, 200, 201–210; concept of enthusiasm, 210, 213; and future anxiety, 11, 217; and Gorky. *See* Gorky and Lunacharsky. Works: "Dialogue on Art," 206, 216; "The Realm of the Unclear," 210; *Religion and Socialism*, 203, 207, 210, 216, 220; "The Russian Faust," 214; "The Tasks of Social Democratic Art," 203, 204
Lvov-Rogachevsky, V., 1

Malinovsky, A. A. *See* Bogdanov, A. A.
Marx, Karl, 39, 67, 109, 214
Marxism, 52, 61, 110, 198, 200, 203, 209, 217
Master: as moral archetype, 20–

21, 25–26; as racial type, 51; as social type, 183
Mercure de France, 207
Merezhkovsky, Dmitry, 9, 37, 39, 40, 46, 115–134, 176, 225, 228; critique of Christianity, 120–121; discovery of Nietzsche, 47, 117–118; and future anxiety, 11, 120, 123; neo-Christianity, 130–134; against Nietzscheanism, 116, 119, 133; as popularizer of Nietzsche, 7, 54, 65, 85; and populism, 117–118, 127, 129, 131, 133; and younger symbolists, 141, 143. *See also* specific names. Works: "Julian the Apostate," 120, 125; "M. Ia. Lermontov," 126, "Not Peace But the Sword," 120, 121; *Peter and Aleksei*, 123, 125, 126–127; "On the Reasons for the Decline," 118; "Revolution and Religion," 119, 122; "The Romance of Leonardo," 121, 125–126; *Tolstoi and Dostoevsky*, 124, 126–130
Mikhailovsky, Nikolai, 15, 44, 46, 117, 176; as cultural critic, 80, 92, 110; as popularizer of Nietzsche, 48, 52, 58–61
Minsky, Nikolai, 67, 73, 110
Mir Iskusstva, 78, 132
Mochulsky, Konstantin, 144
Moral archetypes. *See* Blond beast; Free spirit; Master; Moral rebel, in Russian novel; Philosopher; Priest; Slave; Superfluous man; Superman
Moral consciousness, 4; and aesthetic values, 41, 57, 58, 150–151, 163–164, 229; and culture, 23–24; of mass reader, 5, 245 n.22; and power, 21–23; and psychology, 18–20, 24; and sexuality, 27, 76, 99–104, 121–122, 135–136, 138, 151; and violent acts, 102–104, 209, 242–243 n.58
Morality, Christian, 7, 120–122, 130; and creativity, 144–145
Moral rebel, in Russian novel, 29–38
Morozov, S. T., 199
Mystical anarchism, 141, 151, 157, 163
Myth: of Dionysus, 25, 35, 119; in God-building, 200–223; and morality, 12–13, 35–36, 152, 194–195; in mystical symbolist literature, 115–172; national, 211–212; Nietzsche's Dionysian, 25–26; in nineteenth-century Russian literature, 35–36; in popular Nietzschean fiction, 81, 83–113; underlying Christianity, 17–18; underlying philosophical idealism, 17–18

Nadson, Semyon, 117
Napoleon: in Russian literature, 33, 61
Nevedomsky, M., 109, 176
Nietzsche, Friedrich: attack on Christianity, 16–17, 115; attack on idealism, 15–17; on culture, 22–25, 115, 216; and future anxiety, 24–25; on moral consciousness and morality, 15–29, 134; and nihilism, 17, 19, 23, 26; popular culture of (*see* Nietzscheanism); religious aspects of his thought, 28, 34, 37; seen as social thinker, 5, 55, 60–61, 73, 105–111, 214–216; style, 18–20. Works: *Beyond Good*

Nietzsche, Friedrich (continued) and Evil, 16, 26, 189; The Birth of Tragedy, 16, 46, 136, 143, 153, 156, 216; Gorky and, 185, 186; Merezhkovsky and, 124; The Case of Wagner, 43, 46; The Gay Science, 16, 48; The Genealogy of Morals, 20–21, 27–28, 106, 137; Human-All-Too Human, 16, 46; Thoughts Out of Season, 46; Thus Spoke Zarathustra, 18, 26, 45, 46, 78, 107–108, 213, 216; censorship of, 48–51; and Gorky, 176, 178, 185–186, 190–197; in popular literature, 86, 92; in symbolist literature, 129–130, 139, 149–150, 158–159; The Will to Power, 46
Nietzscheanism, 4, 56, 78–80, 226; as middle-class ideology, 70–71, 74–76, 108–109, 214–215
Nietzsche archives, 177
Nihilism, Russian, 31–35, 112, 168–169, 238–239 n.12
Nikolai I, Tsar, 30
Nikolai II, Tsar, 45
Nordau, Max, 7, 51–52, 59, 106, 183
Novel of Ideas, 29, 225
Novosti, 53
Novy put', 46, 132, 136

Pascal, Blaise, 115
Pasternak, Boris L., 144
Pertsov, Petr P., 46, 181
Peshkov, A. M. See Gorky, Maksim
Peter the Great, 39, 165, 167, 228
Philosopher: as moral archetype, 20, 27–28, 180
Piatnitsky, K. P., 201
Pisarev, Dmitry, 31

Pity, 26, 56, 72, 90–91, 101–102, 188–192, 219. See also Compassion; Love
Plekhanov, Georgy, 203, 204, 223
Pobedonostsev, Konstantin, 45
Poe, Edgar Allan, 117
Polilov, N. N., 186
Populism, 2, 38, 39, 41, 53, 67, 70, 228. See also specific authors
Posse, Vladimir, 46, 176, 198, 201
Preobrazhensky, Vasily P., 48, 53, 54, 55–58, 61, 71, 78–79; impact on Gorky, 181, 188–189
Priest: as character-type in Russian literature, 164, 212; as creative mentality, 169–170, 180, 197; as moral archetype, 20, 22–23, 24, 27–28, 164, 180, 197
Primitivism, 227–228
Pushkin, Aleksandr S., 167, 228; Merezhkovsky's interpretation of, 131, 133

Reader, 2; expectations of, 3; female, 97; mass, 6, 45–46, 63–64, 104–105
Realism, 40; mystical, 132
Reception
 critical, 4, 46, 53, 55–65
 mediated, 6–8, 46; popularization, 6–7, 55–61, 63–66; vulgarization, 7–8, 52–55, 63, 105–108
 popular, 6–7, 55–61, 63–66
 translation, 45–46, 51, 54, 66
Reingoldt, A., 43, 45, 53
Religious-Philosophical Meetings, 132, 135, 155
Renan, Ernest, 44
Repin, Ilya, 179
Revaluation of values, 1, 25

Revolutionary romanticism, 201, 237 n.18
Romanticism, 40
Ropshin, V. (Viktor Savinkov), 9, 65, 226, 227; The Pale Horse, 65, 84-96
Russkaia mysl', 52
Russkii vestnik, 52
Russkoe bogatstvo, 52

Savinkov, V. See Ropshin, Viktor
Schelling, Friedrich, 44, 47
Scherrer, Jutta, 169
Schmidt, Johann Kaspar. See Stirner, Max
Schopenhauer, Arthur, 25, 27, 40, 44, 55, 117, 187; as precursor to Nietzsche, 18
Schutte, Ophelia, 211
Sesterhenn, Raimund, 202, 215
Severnyi vestnik, 40, 47, 53, 74, 132, 200
Sexuality. See Moral consciousness, and sexuality
Shestov, Lev (L. Shvartsman), 47, 54, 63
Shvartsman, L. See Shestov, Lev
Simmel, Georg, 62
Slave: as moral archetype, 20-21, 25-26; as social type, 88
Social utilitarianism, 1, 52, 180-181
Sologub, F. K. (Teternikov, F. K.), 39
Solovyov, Evgeny Andreevich. See Andreevich
Solovyov, Vladimir, 36, 39, 62, 65, 67, 69-70, 80, 115-116. See also Ivanov, Belyi, Blok. Works: "The Idea of the Superman," 67; The Justification of the Good, 67, 73; On the Meaning of Love, 135, 137; "The Story of the Antichrist,"
69-70, 153, 158; Three Conversations, 69-70, 153, 158
Solovyov Society, 135
Sophia, 143, 151, 158-160, 169
Sorsky, Nil, 170
Spencer, Herbert, 62, 105, 117
Sreda literary circle, 84, 200
Stalinism, 212, 223, 252-253 n.57
Stein, Ludwig, 62
Stendahl: as precursor to Nietzsche, 18
Stepun, Fedor, 137, 139
Stirner, Max (Johann Kaspar Schmidt), 30, 40, 58-59, 238 n.11
Strauss, David, 44
Superfluous man, 30-31, 37, 95
Superman, 26, 28, 60-61, 70, 77, 94; and man-god, 34, 94-95, 129; as social type, 109
Symbolism, 9, 40, 53; crisis in, 151-152, 157; and popular culture, 9

Tait, A. L., 220
Tarle, Evgeny, 63
Tenisheva, Princess Anna Dmitrievna, 43, 45
Teternikov, F. K. See Sologub, F. K.
Thatcher, David S., 6
Tolstoi, Lev, 39, 65, 66, 80, 115-116, 155, 171, 228; attack on Nietzsche, 67-70; Merezhkovsky's interpretation of, 115-116, 126-127, 133. Works: "Death of Ivan Ilich," 35; War and Peace, 32, 33, 36
Tolstoianism, 99, 169
Translation. See Reception
Trilling, Lionel, 2
Trubetskoi, Evgeny, 135
Tumanov, Nikolai, 176
Turgenev, Ivan Sergeyevich, 5,

276 Index

160, 161, 196, 209; as mediator for Nietzsche, 15, 54–55, 72, 80; and nihilism, 6; and superfluous man, 30–31. Works: *Fathers and Sons*, 32, 33; *Sportsman's Sketches*, 5, 35
Tynianov, Iury, 7, 10

Upsensky, Gleb, 117, 204

Vengerov, S., 1
Verbitskaia, Anastasia, 7, 8, 9, 227; and future anxiety, 11; *Keys of Happiness*, 8, 98–102, 103–105, 107, 109, 111, 226
Vestnik evropy, 52
Vestnik inostrannoi literatury, 53, 55
Vesy, 151
Violence. See Moral consciousness, and violent acts

Volokhova, Natalia, 145
Volynsky, Akim L. (Flekser, A. L.), 47, 53, 74
Voprosy filosofii i pikhologii, 53, 70, 78
Voprosy zhizni, 132
Vrubel, Mikhail, 142

Wagner, Richard, 39
Wilde, Oscar, 74
Will to power, 25; as sexual aggression, 103–104

Zamiatin, E., 252 n.56
Zelinsky, K. L., 143
Zhirmunsky, Viktor, 3, 4, 10
Zhizn', 201, 203
Zinoveva-Gannibal, Lidia, 141, 142, 143
Znanie Publishing Cooperative, 201

www.ingramcontent.com/pod-product-compliance
Lightning Source LLC
Chambersburg PA
CBHW030103170426
43198CB00009B/480